POSER® 6 REVEALED:
THE OFFICIAL GUIDE

Kelly L. Murdock

THOMSON

™

COURSE TECHNOLOGY

Publisher and General Manager of PTR:
Stacy L. Hiquet

Associate Director of Marketing:
Sarah O'Donnell

Marketing Manager:
Heather Hurley

Manager of Editorial Services:
Heather Talbot

Associate Acquisitions Editor:
Megan Belanger

Senior Editor:
Mark Garvey

Marketing Coordinator:
Jordan Casey

Development Editor:
Jane Hosie-Bounar

Project and Copy Editor:
Kezia Endsley

Technical Reviewer:
John Freitas

PTR Editorial Services Coordinator:
Elizabeth Furbish

Interior Layout Tech:
Sue Honeywell

Cover Designer:
Steve Deschene

Front Cover Image:
Catharina Harders, Mec4D.com

Indexer:
Kelly Talbot

Proofreader:
Kate Welsh

THOMSON

★

COURSE TECHNOLOGY

25 Thomson Place
Boston, MA 02210
www.course.com

Poser® 6 is a registered trademark of Curious Labs, Inc.

All other trademarks are the property of their respective owners.

Important: Thomson Course Technology cannot provide software support. Please contact the appropriate software manufacturer's technical support line or Web site for assistance.

Thomson Course Technology and the author have attempted throughout this book to distinguish proprietary trademarks from descriptive terms by following the capitalization style used by the manufacturer.

Information contained in this book has been obtained by Thomson Course Technology from sources believed to be reliable. However, because of the possibility of human or mechanical error by our sources, Thomson Course Technology , or others, the Publisher does not guarantee the accuracy, adequacy, or completeness of any information and is not responsible for any errors or omissions or the results obtained from use of such information. Readers should be particularly aware of the fact that the Internet is an ever-changing entity. Some facts may have changed since this book went to press.

Educational facilities, companies, and organizations interested in multiple copies or licensing of this book should contact the publisher for quantity discount information. Training manuals, CD-ROMs, and portions of this book are also available individually or can be tailored for specific needs.

ISBN: 1-59200-523-3

Library of Congress Catalog Card Number: 2004109492

Printed in Canada

05 06 07 08 09 WC 10 9 8 7 6 5 4 3 2

I don't need to win the game every time I play,

I don't need to be quoted for everything I say.

But, I need to be kind and polite everyday.

I don't need to be the best at all I do,

I don't need to have the greatest brand of shoe.

But, I need to learn patience and I need to be true.

I don't need to earn awards for every little deal,

I don't need to always escape everything that's real.

But, I need to accept how other people feel.

I don't need to have a pocket full of money,

I don't need the weather to always be sunny.

But, I need to help others and it doesn't hurt to be funny.

I don't need to always get my way,

I don't need to have all my troubles fly away,

But, I need to be humble and I need to pray.

I don't need to be perfect on every exam,

I don't need help to get out of a jam,

But, I need to accept the person that I am.

To Cami for being a confidant, a support, and a sister, 2005

Acknowledgments

While I was busily writing another book, I received a rather timid cry for help. The sender was Megan Belanger who needed help with a book on Poser that she was trying to launch. She seemed so nice and I thought it would be a scenic detour worth taking, so I offered to help. A few emails later and I received word that Megan was dancing on her desk at my willingness to take on another project. That was a few short months ago.

Since then, the project has grown into an important book that is being offered as the official guide to a popular well-loved piece of software used by thousands of artists across the world and now at the release of this book, I'd like to thank Megan for her initial timid little cry for help followed by all the tense concerns over the book's progress. Your enthusiasm has inspired me through all the tough times. It's enjoyable to write for someone that is excited to have me on their team. Let me know if you ever need help again.

I'd also like to thank Kezia Endsley who has done an incredible job in editing chapters and getting them back to me overnight, so we could make our deadlines and for her willingness to allow me to make just one more change, and then one more, and finally one more.

Thanks also to John Freitas for his timely technical editing. As the deadlines got tight, I found that I could trust John's comments on errors to be correct and he found a boatload of errors. Someday, I should really learn the difference between my right and left hands.

Working with beta software is always a chore, but the Poser 6 beta team had great support with Tori Porter, Ulrich Klumpp, and Steve Rathmann. Thanks for all your help and for all the behind-the-scenes developers for working so hard to hunt down and finish off the annoying bugs. Each beta just got better and better and when I needed the software to work, it always came through.

As always, I'd like to thank my family, without whose support I'd never get to the end of a book. To Angela, for making me watch episodes of *Law and Order* to unwind; to Eric, for entertaining himself with cheats to *Age of Empires* instead of accessing the Internet through my computer since it's the only one with sound enabled, and to Thomas, for the nice brown paper buffalo craft that hangs over my desk. It must be some kind of good luck. Okay, guys. This book's done. Time for a nice long game of *Risk* and then some rock climbing. I hope I haven't missed the entire ski season.

About the Author

KELLY L. MURDOCK has a background in engineering, specializing in computer graphics. This experience has led him to many interesting experiences, including using high-end CAD workstations for product design and analysis, working on several large-scale visualization projects, creating 3D models for several blockbuster movies, working as a freelance 3D artist and designer, 3D programming, and a chance to write several high-profile computer graphics books.

Kelly's book credits include five editions of the *3ds max Bible, Maya 6 Revealed, LightWave 3D 8 Revealed,* two editions of the *Illustrator Bible, Adobe Creative Suite Bible, Adobe Atmosphere Bible, gmax Bible, 3D Graphics and VRML 2.0, Master Visually HTML and XHTML,* and *JavaScript Visual Blueprints.*

In his spare time, Kelly enjoys rock climbing, mountain biking, skiing, and running. He works with his brother at his co-founded design company, Logical Paradox Design.

ABOUT THE AUTHOR

C O N T E N T S   A T   A   G L A N C E

CONTENTS

Revealed Series Vision

The *Revealed* series is your guide to today's hottest multimedia applications. These comprehensive books teach the skills behind the application, showing you how to apply smart design principles to multimedia products such as dynamic graphics, animation, Web sites, software authoring tools, and digital video. A team of design professionals including multimedia instructors, students, authors, and editors worked together to create this series. We recognized the unique needs of the multimedia market and created a series that gives you comprehensive step-by-step instructions and offers an in-depth explanation of the "why" behind a skill, all in a clear, visually-based layout. It was our goal to create books that speak directly to the multimedia and design community—one of the most rapidly growing computer fields today. We feel that the *Revealed* series does just that—in a comprehensive yet aesthetically pleasing format.

—The *Revealed* Series

Author Vision

When I was approached to write a book on Poser, I thought, "Okay, I'm a Poser user." It's a great program to use to enhance my other 3D projects if I ever need a figure in some unique pose. But, now after having spent most of my waking hours looking at every control and fiddling with every option over the past several months, I've happily discovered that there is a whole lotta Poser that I never even knew existed. Cloth simulation, dynamic hair styles, ethnic faces, morphed expressions, a bones system that's easy to use, and a elegantly simple set of animation tools. Wow! This stuff is great.

The more I researched and discovered, the more amazed I became. I can see now why this unique piece of software has been so popular for so long. It does one incredibly hard task, that of posing characters, very well, but it has so much more to offer than just positioning figures.

The Poser interface is one of the "love 'em" or "hate 'em" designs with no middle ground. By dividing the entire interface into separate rooms, you can quickly focus your efforts on the task at hand without having to wade through all the tools that you don't need. The ability to rearrange entire sets of controls on-the-fly is also very handy when you need just a little more room to see the right side of the rendered image.

If you're new to Poser, don't be put off by the simplicity of the program. Beneath the slick uncluttered interface is a powerful piece of software that can be used to create, render, and animate entire scenes and projects. A good example of this power can be found with Poser's animation tools. Basic animation tasks are handled using the Animation Controls, a sidebar shelf of controls that rise from the bottom of the interface to take up only a narrow band of desktop space, yet from this basic set of graphical icons, you can create key frame animations. For more functionality, one click opens a grid of cells known as the Animation Palette that lets you manipulate key frames for all scene items. One more click opens editable animation graphs for the selected key. And that's it. No hidden panels with endless knobs and switches or command written in code. Just the features you need when you need them.

Now that I've gushed over the software in a way that would make any Marketing Director proud, let me explain the most logical approach to learning Poser. I've organized each chapter to cover a logical set of features starting with an overview of the Poser interface found in Chapter 1.

From this interface tour, I jump right into a couple of chapters on posing and working with figures. This is the main purpose of Poser and represents some of the most important chapters in the book.

SERIES & AUTHOR VISION

The next several chapters march through the available rooms of features including coverage of the features for working with materials, props, lights, cameras, face, hair, cloth, and bones.

The book concludes with chapters covering animation, rendering, and using Python scripts.

Throughout the book, several special icons are used to highlight special comments including Notes, Cautions, and Tips. These comments provide a way to present special information to you the reader. Be sure to watch for them.

Along with every discussed task are several step-by-step objectives that show you a simplified example of the discussed topic. Each of these examples was created to be extremely simple to keep the number of steps to a minimum. I've tried to add some variety here and there, but none of these examples should be overwhelming (or will win a prize at the county fair). The real creative work is up to you, but these simplified examples will be enough to show you how to use a feature and give you some practice.

Each objective example begins from the default setting that appears when the program is first loaded, but you don't need to close and reopen the software to begin each example; just select the File, New menu command, and you'll be ready to go. For some of the more complex examples, the steps instruct you to open an example file. You can download these files from the Course Technology Web site (www.course. com/poser6), or you can use your own files as a beginning point. Included with the downloadable files at the Course Technology Web site are the final saved files from each example. These are available for you to compare with your own work to learn where you might have made a mistake.

Poser is an amazing piece of software, but it isn't overwhelming. Most every feature is covered, providing you with a reference that you can use whenever you get stuck or to give you some creative inspiration.

—Kelly L. Murdock

POSER® 6 REVEALED:
THE OFFICIAL GUIDE

1

LEARNING THE
Poser Interface

1. Explore the interface controls.

2. Use the Pose Room controls.

3. Use the Document Window.

4. Explore the other rooms.

5. Work with files.

6. Configure the interface.

7. Get help.

chapter 1 LEARNING THE
Poser Interface

The Poser **interface** is one of the most unique and interesting interfaces found in any software. Yes, it has the traditional menus and windows, but you can move and place each control precisely where you want it. Even the main view window is portable.

Each set of specific features is divided into what Poser calls *rooms,* with each room accessed using tabs that run along the top of the interface. The available Poser rooms include Pose, Material, Face, Hair, Cloth, Setup, and Content.

The main default room is the Pose Room. In this room, you can work with the **Document Window** and several other controls to view the exact part of the figure you want to see. The Light Controls lets you set how light strikes the figure, the Camera Controls lets you focus the view on specific body parts, and the Display Styles conrol lets you change how the figure is rendered.

The Document Window also includes controls that you can use to change the number of views, and several other display options such as shadows and background colors.

The menus include commands for loading, saving, importing, and exporting files and access to preferences that you can use to configure the interface. Finally, the menus include a Help option for accessing the PDF-based documentation.

Tools You'll Use

Room tabs

Document Window

Menus

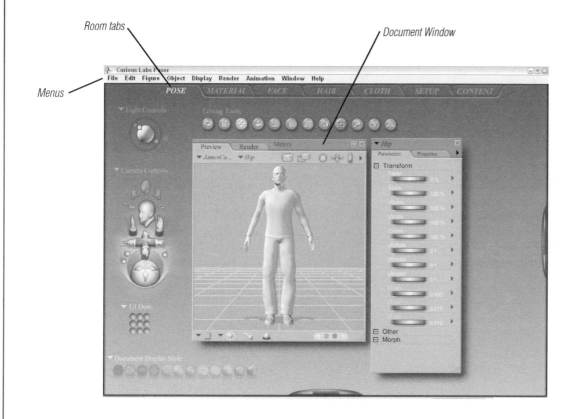

EXPLORE THE
INTERFACE CONTROLS

What You'll Do

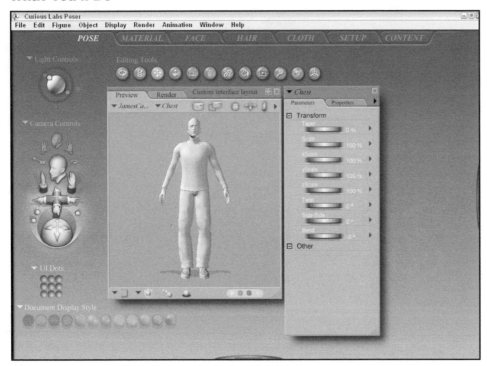

In this lesson, you learn how to work with the various interface controls.

The Poser interface includes several interface controls, but you can place each control exactly where you want it in a fluid interface. You can drag each control using its title and position it. You can even move the background graphic if you want to.

TIP

Clicking the faint interface background image with the Alt key held down cycles through the available background images.

You start Poser by clicking its icon or selecting it from a menu of applications just like other software. When Poser first opens, a default figure is displayed, letting you get right to work.

NOTE

The default figure in Poser 6 is named James, and you can find hairstyles and clothes that fit him in the Library.

Using Menus

The one interface element that is in common with other software are the menus, shown in Figure 1-1, located at the top of the interface.

These menus work by clicking and dragging to select the specific menu command that you want to execute. You also can access menu commands by using keyboard shortcuts, which are listed to right of the menu command. Arrow icons to the right of a menu command indicate that a submenu of additional options is available, and menu commands that are followed by an

ellipsis (three small dots) open a dialog box. If a menu command is unavailable, the command is light gray and cannot be selected.

Using the Room Tabs

Directly below the menus are seven **room tabs** with the current room highlighted. The Room tabs include Pose, Material, Face, Hair, Cloth, Setup, and Content, as shown in Figure 1-2. Clicking these tabs opens a separate interface with specialized features. For example, the Material Room includes all the controls for creating materials that you can apply to the figure and the Hair Room includes controls for creating and editing

hairstyles. The Pose Room opens by default when Poser first starts.

NOTE

Not all menu commands are available for every room. For example, the File, Save menu command is available only in the Face and Content Rooms.

Using Floating Controls

Located about the interface are several floating sets of controls. These controls have a transparent background and you can move them around the interface by clicking

FIGURE 1-1

Sample menu

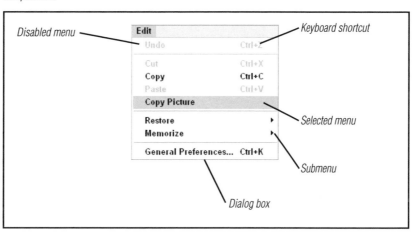

FIGURE 1-2

Room tabs

and dragging their titles. For the Pose Room, the **floating controls** include the Light Controls, Camera Controls, Display Styles control, Memory Dots control, and the Editing Tools. Other sets of floating controls are available in the other rooms. The floating control's title changes as you move the mouse over the various buttons and icons in the set revealing the name of the icon that the cursor is over. Some of the floating controls include a small down-arrow icon, which opens a pop-up menu of options.

TIP

Double-clicking a floating control's title bar or a window title bar will roll up the controls so that only the title is visible. This is a great way to hide a set of controls until you need them.

Moving the Document Window

The figure you are working on is displayed in the Document Window. You can reposition this window by dragging its title bar and resize it by dragging on its lower-right corner. The Document Window is divided

into two panels—Preview and Render. The Preview panel is covered later in this chapter and the Render panel is covered in Chapter 12, "Rendering Scenes." Click the tabs at the top of the window to access each panel. In the upper-right corner are two icons you can use to maximize, minimize, and close the Document Window. Figure 1-3 shows the Document Window maximized.

NOTE

Closing the Document Window closes the current file. You will be prompted to save the file if you have made any changes to it.

FIGURE 1-3
Maximized Document Window

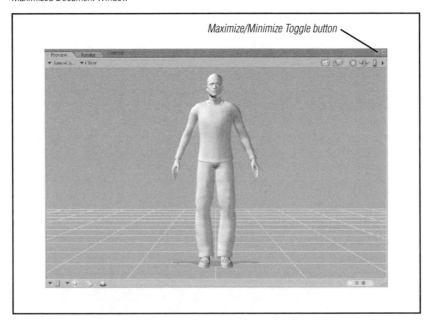

Maximize/Minimize Toggle button

Using the Parameters/Properties Palette

Another useful floating control is the Parameters/Properties Palette. This palette, shown in Figure 1-4, includes tabs for accessing parameters and properties. Within the palette are parameter dials that you can drag to the right or left to change a parameter's value. The parameters define the selected element such as its position and orientation. You can also click each numeric value on the right side of the palette and change its value by entering numbers on the keyboard. To the right of the numeric value is an arrow icon that opens a pop-up menu of options.

Accessing the Side Window Controls

If you look closely along the right and bottom edges of the interface, you'll notice two **side window controls**. If you click these controls, a panel of controls appears in the interface area. The side window control to

FIGURE 1-4

Parameters/Properties Palette

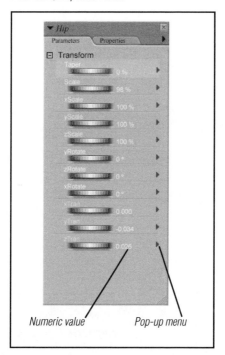

Numeric value   Pop-up menu

the right opens the Library and the side window control to the bottom opens the Animation Controls, as shown in Figure 1-5. You close the side window control panels by clicking again on the side window control that has now moved out into the interface. You can also close the Library by clicking the Close button in the upper-right corner of the panel.

QUICKTIP

If you open both the Library and the Animation Controls at the same time, the Library will obscure part of the Animation Controls.

Showing and Hiding Interface Elements

The Window menu includes commands for displaying and hiding all the various interface elements. When a listed interface element is visible, a check mark appears to the left of its menu command. You can also use the Window, Show All Tools (Ctrl+\) and the Window, Hide All Tools (Ctrl+0) commands to show or hide all interface elements except for the Document Window.

When tools are hidden, only their title is visible if the Window, Tool Titles menu is enabled. Disabling the Window, Tool Titles menu command hides all the interface titles.

FIGURE 1-5
Side window controls

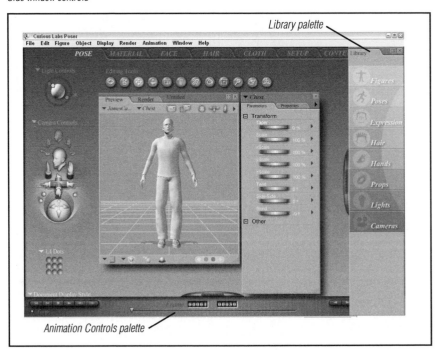

FIGURE 1-6
Interface elements in custom positions

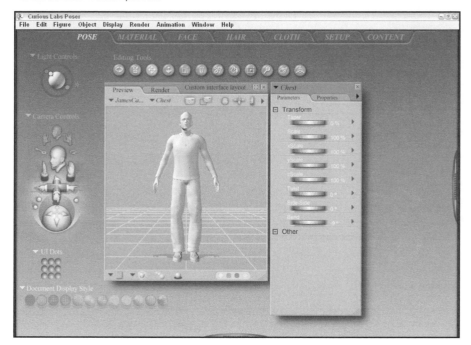

1. Click the Start button on the taskbar, point to All Programs, click Curious Labs, click Poser 6, and then click Poser (Win) or double-click the hard drive icon, navigate to and double-click the Poser folder, the double-click the Poser icon 🦶 (Mac).

   The Poser interface loads using the default settings. The Pose Room displays the default figure, a man in street clothes.

2. Click Window on the menu bar, and then click Show All Tools.

   All of the tools are visible in the interface.

3. Click and drag the Light and Camera Controls and the Memory Dots to the left of the interface, drag the Document Window to the center of the interface, and then position the Parameter/Properties palette to the right of the Document Window.

4. Drag the Editing Tools above the Document Window and drag the Document Display Styles underneath and to the left of the Document Window.

   As you position the interface elements, leave enough room at the bottom and right of the interface for the Library and Animation Controls to appear, as shown in Figure 1-6.

5. Click File on the menu bar, click Save As, type **Custom interface layout.pz3** in the File name text box, and then click Save.

Maximize the Document Window

1. Click the Maximize/Minimize button 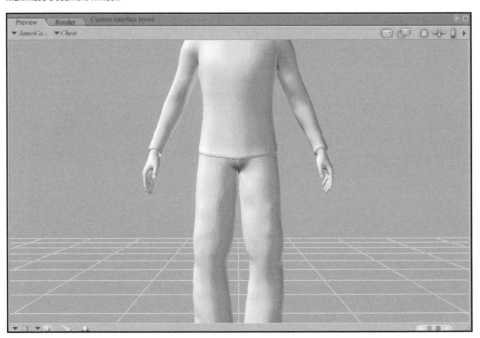 in the upper-right corner of the Document Window.

2. Click the Close button ⊠ in the upper-right corner of the Parameters/Properties palette to close it.

   The Document Window is maximized, as shown in Figure 1-7.

FIGURE 1-7

Maximized Document Window

USE THE
POSE ROOM CONTROLS

What You'll Do

In this lesson, you learn how to use the interface controls found in the Pose Room.

The Pose Room is the default room that opens when Poser is first started. It is the main interface for posing figures and will be the room where you'll probably spend the most time. Posing and editing figures is covered in Chapter 3, "Editing and Posing Figures," but this lesson covers the various controls that change how the figure is displayed in the Window. The controls covered in this lesson include the Light, Camera, and Document Display Styles controls.

QUICKTIP

This lesson only covers the basics of using the Light and Camera Controls. Lights and cameras are covered in detail in Chapter 6, "Establishing a Scene."

Using the Light Controls

The Light Controls directly affect the figure in the Document Window. By surrounding a figure with lights, you'll be better able to see its details. Enabling shadows can give you a sense of depth, but too many bright lights can wash out the figure.

The Light Controls, shown in Figure 1-8, are used to set the lighting effects for the figure in the Document Window. The large sphere in the center of the Light Controls is a sample that shows the current lighting settings. Surrounding this large sphere are three smaller circles connected to the larger one. These smaller circles are the individual lights. You can change their location by dragging them about the larger sphere. When you select a circle representing a light, controls for changing its intensity, color, and properties appear. There are also buttons for removing the selected light and creating new lights.

Using the Camera Controls

The Camera Controls are also a critical set of controls that you can use to zoom in and rotate around a specific body part for a close-up view. These controls, shown in Figure 1-9, have a direct and immediate impact on the figure displayed in the Document Window. By using these controls, you can control precisely which part of the figure is displayed. The top three icons focus the view on the right hand, the left hand, and the face. The key icon toggles animating on

and off. The key icon is colored red when animating is enabled. Animating is covered in Chapter 11, "Animating Figures." The Flyaround button spins the camera about the figure's center and you can use it to get a quick look at all sides of your character.

Using Camera Presets

The centered head icon lets you switch between preset camera views including the Main, Auxiliary, Left, Right, Front, Back, Top, Bottom, Face, Posing, Right Hand, and Left Hand cameras. Each of these cameras has its own icon, which you can access by clicking repeatedly on the icon to cycle through the available cameras or by clicking and dragging to the left or right. You

FIGURE 1-8

Light Controls

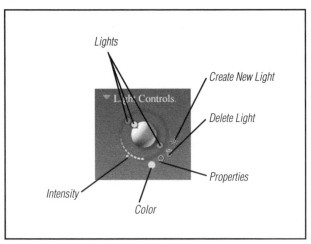

Lights

Create New Light

Delete Light

Properties

Intensity

Color

FIGURE 1-9

Camera Controls

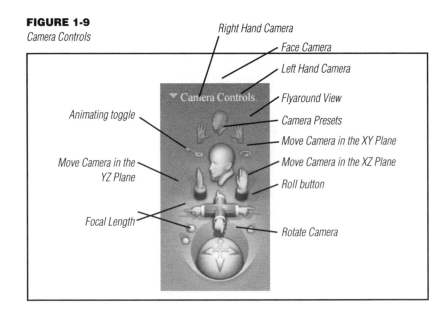

Right Hand Camera

Face Camera

Left Hand Camera

Flyaround View

Camera Presets

Move Camera in the XY Plane

Move Camera in the XZ Plane

Roll button

Rotate Camera

Animating toggle

Move Camera in the YZ Plane

Focal Length

can also select each of the preset cameras from the Camera Control pop-up menu and from the Display, Camera View menu.

TIP

The Display, Show Camera Name menu command displays the name of the current camera in the upper left corner of the Document Window.

Moving a Camera

The hand icons are used to move the camera view within the YZ plane, the XY plane, or XZ plane. To use these icons, just click them and drag in the direction that you want to move the camera. The figure in the Document Window is updated as you drag. For example, dragging down on the XY plane pans the camera in the Document Window upward, causing the figure's view to sink downward.

Rotating a Camera

The sphere with arrows on it at the bottom of the Camera Controls is used to rotate the camera. It is used like the move icons, by clicking and dragging in the direction you want to rotate the camera. The Roll button spins the figure within the Document Window about its center.

TIP

Small move and rotate camera icons also exist in the top-right corner of the Document Window. These small controls work just like their large counterparts in the Camera Controls.

Changing a Camera's Scale and Focal Length

The final two buttons to the left of the Rotate Camera control are for adjusting the camera's scale and focal length. Dragging on the Scale button changes the size of the figure within the viewpane and dragging with the Focal Length button changes the center focus point for the camera, which affects how close or far the figure appears from the camera.

NOTE

The Camera Scale button doesn't work when one of the face or hand cameras is selected.

Changing Display Styles

The more details that are displayed with a figure, the longer it takes to be updated when a change is made. For example, a figure with lots of details and textures could take quite a while to be redrawn in the Document Window every time a change is made. By changing between the various styles in the Display Style control, shown in Figure 1-10, you can control how much detail and what kind of detail is displayed in

FIGURE 1-10
Document Display Style controls

the Document Window. For example, complex scenes might work best when a simple Wireframe style is used, but for looking at a close-up of the face, you might want to switch to the Texture Shaded style.

You can apply display styles to the entire scene, to a single figure, or to a single element or body part. You select the application level from the pop-up menu or from the Display menu.

TIP

You can make the Display Style controls (along with the Editing Tools controls) vertical by holding down the Alt key while clicking one of its buttons.

The styles available in the Display Style control include the following. Some of these styles have shortcut keys, indicated in parentheses:

- **Silhouette (Ctrl+1):** Displays the entire figure as if cut out and displayed against the gray background. This style is good for isolating edges.
- **Outline (Ctrl+2):** Displays just the figure lines that outline the various body parts.
- **Wireframe (Ctrl+3):** Displays all the mesh lines that make up the entire figure.
- **Hidden Line (Ctrl+4):** Displays only those lines that are facing the camera. Lines on the backside of the figure aren't shown.

- **Lit Wireframe (Ctrl+5):** A wireframe view that is colored based on the scene lights.
- **Flat Shaded (Ctrl+6):** Displays the figure using the correct material colors for each mesh face without any smoothing.
- **Flat Lined:** Displays flat shading with lines.
- **Cartoon:** Displays the figure in a hand-drawn cartoon rendering style.

- **Cartoon with Line (Ctrl+7):** Same as the Cartoon style, but with distinct black outlines.
- **Smooth Shaded (Ctrl+8):** Displays the figure using the correct material colors.
- **Smooth Lined:** Same as Smooth Shaded style, but with visible lines.
- **Texture Shaded (Ctrl+9):** Displays the figure using full textures as if it were rendered.

NOTE

If you select one of the Cartoon styles, you can set the number of tones used for the style by right-clicking the Document Window and selecting the Toon Tones menu. The options include One Tone, Two Tones, Three Tones, Three Tones + Hilite, and Smooth Toned.

Figure 1-11 shows how each of these styles looks up close on a face.

FIGURE 1-11
Display Styles

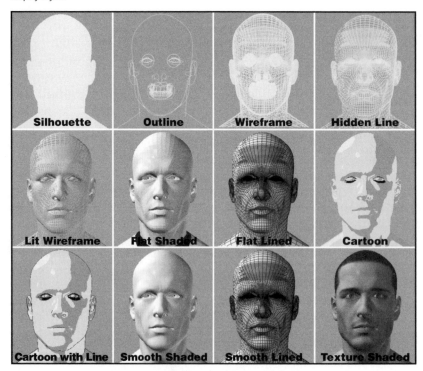

FIGURE 1-12
Modified lights

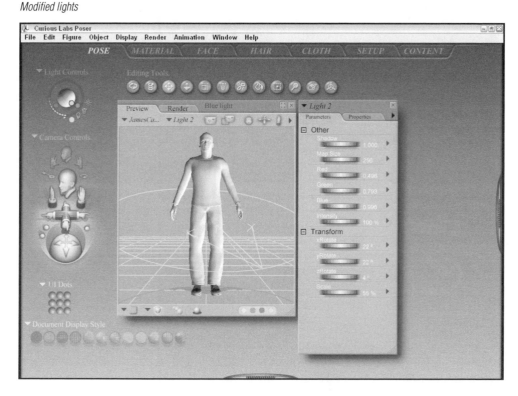

Control lights

1. With the default figure loaded, click the light circle icon in the upper-left of the Light Controls and drag to the lower-left.

   The light's position changes and the updated light is displayed in the Document Window.

2. Click and drag the center light circle in the Light Controls to the lower-right side of the centered larger sphere.

3. With the center light selected, click the Light Color icon and select a blue color.

   The center light changes position and color, as shown in Figure 1-12.

4. Select File, Save As and save the file as **Blue light.pz3**.

Control cameras

1. Click the Camera Presets icon in the Camera Controls until the Main Camera view is displayed in the Document Window.

2. Click the Move Camera in XZ Plane icon and drag down until the center of the figure is visible around the hips.

3. Click the Move Camera in YZ Plane icon and drag down until the figure is visible from the chest up.

4. Drag the Rotate Sphere control to the left to rotate the figure about its center.

   After you rotate the camera, the view in the Document Window is updated to show a diagonal view of the figure, as shown in Figure 1-13.

5. Select File, Save As and save the file as **Diagonal view.pz3**.

Change the display style

1. Open Poser with the default figure visible.

2. Click Window on the menu bar, and then click Preview Styles to make the Display Styles options visible if they aren't already.

3. Drag the mouse over the various styles.

   Each style icon sphere is highlighted as the mouse is rolled over it.

4. Click the Cartoon with Lines style icon sphere.

   The view of the figure is updated with the Cartoon with Lines style, as shown in Figure 1-14.

5. Choose File, Save As and save the file as **Cartoon figure.pz3**.

FIGURE 1-13
Diagonal view

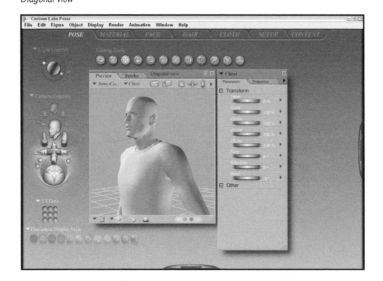

FIGURE 1-14
Cartoon with Lines style

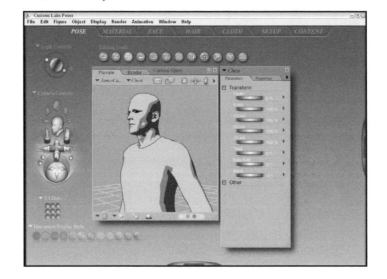

USE THE DOCUMENT WINDOW

What You'll Do

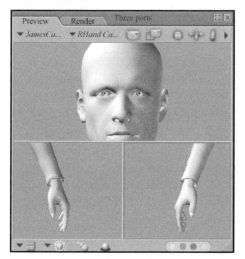

In this lesson, you learn how to use the interface controls found within the Document Window.

The Document Window, shown in Figure 1-15, displays the current figure using the light and camera settings in the selected display style. The title bar displays the name of the saved file along with buttons to maximize and close the window. Directly below the title bar are two tabs that let you switch between the Preview

FIGURE 1-15
Document Window controls

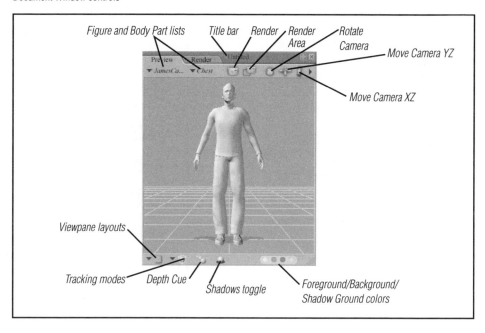

and Render panels. The Preview panel displays a figure as a rough approximation that can be easily manipulated and posed. The Render panel lets you render the figure using textures, materials, and effects, but this process can take some time depending on the complexity of the figure and the render settings. The rendering process and all of the available render settings are covered in Chapter 12, "Rendering Scenes."

Beneath the panel tabs are two drop-down lists called the Figure List and the Actor List, where you can select the figure to work on and the specific body part or element you want to work on. To the right of these lists are the icon buttons Render and Render an Area, which render the entire scene, or just a selected area, respectively. There are also buttons to rotate and move the camera view. The rotate and move camera icons work just like the controls found in the Camera Controls.

Displaying Additional Ports

At the bottom of the Document Window are several controls for changing the display settings for the Document Window. The Viewpane Layout list in the lower-left corner, includes several options for configuring the ports that fill the Document Window. The options include Full Port, Four Ports, Three Ports – Big Top, Three Ports – Big Bottom, Three Ports – Big Right, Three Ports – Big Left and Two Ports. Each separate port can have its own selected camera, but only one port can be active at a time. A red border identifies the active port. The Camera Controls affect the camera view in the active viewpane only. You can quickly change the camera view for any port by right-clicking within the port and selecting a view from the Camera View menu. You can manually resize each port by dragging its interior border. Figure 1-16 shows the Four Ports layout.

QUICKTIP

Pressing the F key will cycle through the available viewpane layout options and pressing the D key switches between a single port and the last selected multiple port layout.

FIGURE 1-16
Four Ports viewpane option

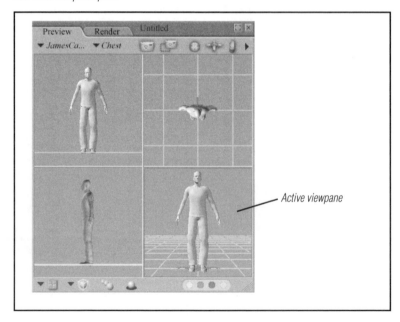

Active viewpane

Setting Tracking Modes

To the right of the Viewpane Layout options is a drop-down list of three **tracking modes**. These modes are Box, Fast, and Full. By changing these modes, you can affect how quickly the figure in the Document Window is updated as changes are made. The Box tracking mode displays all body parts as simple rectangular boxes, as shown in Figure 1-17. It is the quickest update mode. The Fast tracking mode displays the figure in its high-resolution form when the figure is static and displays the figure as boxes when the figure or its camera is moving. The Full tracking mode displays the high-resolution figure at all times.

Enabling Depth Cueing and Shadows

The Depth Cue toggle, to the right of the Tracking modes, turns depth cueing on and off in the Document Window. When on, objects farther back in the scene get fainter and objects closer to the camera are shown in greater detail, as shown in Figure 1-18. Note how the hand farthest from the camera isn't as clear as the hand closest to the camera. Depth cueing has no effect when the scene is rendered.

When the Shadows toggle is enabled, a simple shadow for the figure and any scene props is shown on the ground plane in the Document Window. Document Window shadows, like depth cueing, are also not rendered. Repositioning the lights in the Light Controls also has no effect on these

FIGURE 1-17
Box tracking mode

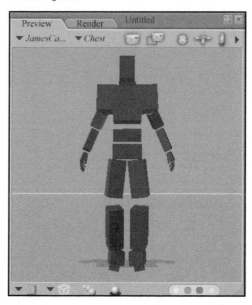

FIGURE 1-18
Depth cueing enabled

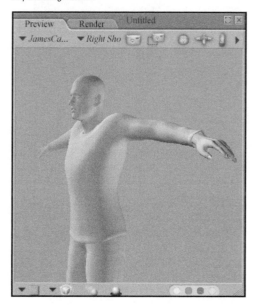

shadows. Rendered shadows can be enabled for scene lights. Figure 1-19 shows the figure with Document Window shadows enabled.

Changing the Document Window Colors

In the lower-right corner of the Document Window are four radio buttons. Moving the mouse over these buttons changes the cursor to a small eyedropper. If you click any of these buttons, a pop-up color selector palette appears, as shown in Figure 1-20.

The four radio buttons correspond to the following scene elements:

- **Foreground:** Changes the color of the grid lines for the ground plane and the figure's line color in the Silhouette, Outline, Wireframe, and Lit Wireframe display styles.

- **Background:** Changes the color of the background.
- **Shadow:** Changes the shadow color if the shadow is enabled.
- **Ground:** Changes the ground color.

FIGURE 1-19
Shadows enabled

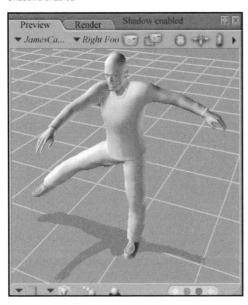

FIGURE 1-20
Pop-up color palette

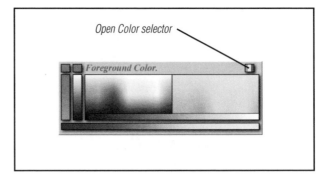

Figure 1-21 shows the Document Window with several custom colors.

Changing the Document Window Size

You can change the size of the Document Window by dragging on the lower-right corner of the window, but you can also size the Document Window to precise dimensions using the Window, Document Window Size menu command. This command opens the Preview Dimensions dialog box,

FIGURE 1-21
Document Window with custom colors

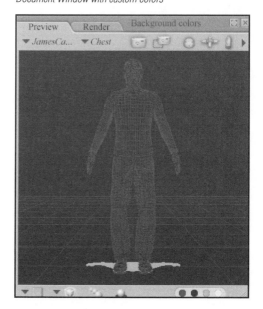

shown in Figure 1-22, where you can enter the desired size of the Document Window. The size of the Document Window is the default size used for rendered images and animations unless the dimensions are changed.

TIP

Double-clicking the lower-right corner of the Document Window opens the Preview Dimensions dialog box.

FIGURE 1-22
Preview Dimensions dialog box

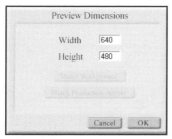

Enabling Hardware Acceleration

Another way to speed up the update rate of the Document Window is to enable hardware acceleration using **OpenGL**. Many modern video cards include capabilities that let them compute redrawing the Document Window using the video card hardware instead of the computer's central processing unit (CPU). This leaves the CPU, which is the main brain of the computer, free to handle other tasks such as dealing with the interface. The language that makes this hardware acceleration possible is OpenGL and it is automatically detected and enabled if your system includes the capabilities to use it. You can also manually select it by right-clicking the Document Window and selecting the OpenGL option. The **SreeD** option is a software option.

NOTE

Using hardware acceleration can cause display problems under certain circumstances. If you notice any trouble with your display, switch the display to the SreeD option.

Change viewpane layout and tracking mode

1. Click the lower-left corner icon 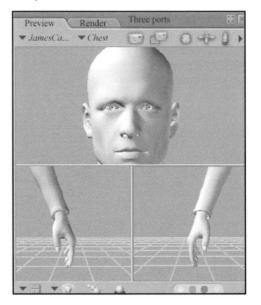 in the Document Window and select the Three Ports – Big Top option.

   The Document Window is split into three panes with the largest pane being on top.

2. Click the icon next to the viewpane layout and select the Full option as the tracking mode.

   The figures in the viewpanes are displayed in high resolution, as shown in Figure 1-23.

3. Select File, Save As and save the file as **Three ports.pz3**.

Change Document Window display options

1. Click the Depth Cue icon button at the bottom of the Document Window, and then drag the Rotate Camera control in the Camera Controls to turn the figure sideways.

   The arm that is farther from the camera starts to fade with the Depth Cue option enabled.

2. Click the Shadow toggle icon to enable a shadow in the Document Window (if necessary).

FIGURE 1-23

Three ports

FIGURE 1-24

Modified Document Window

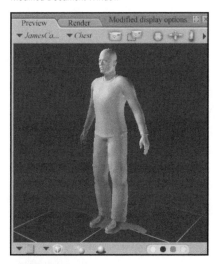

FIGURE 1-25

Resized Document Window

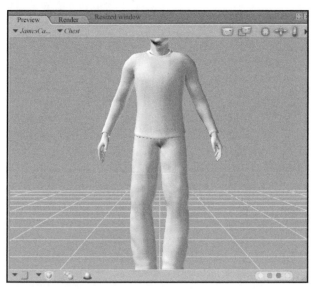

3. Click the Background color button, select a black background color, click the Shadow color, and then change it to light gray.

   The display of the Document Window changes, as shown in Figure 1-24.

4. Select File, Save As and save the file as **Modified display options.pz3**.

Change the Document Window's size

1. Choose Window, Document Window Size.

2. In the Preview Window dialog box, enter **640** as the Width value and **480** as the Height value, and then click OK.

   The size of the Document Window changes, as shown in Figure 1-25.

3. Select File, Save As and save the file as **Resized window.pz3**.

EXPLORE THE
OTHER ROOMS

What You'll Do

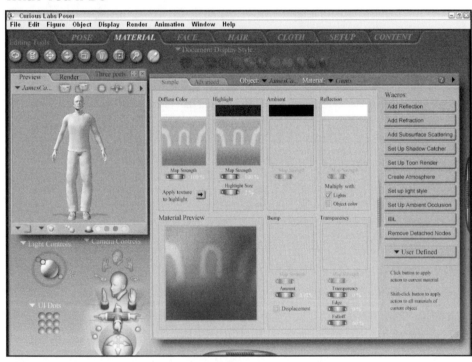

Although the Pose Room is the default room, Poser includes several other rooms, each with its own set of features. Each of these rooms is covered in a separate chapter, but this lesson introduces each room and shows some features that are common among them all. To switch between the various rooms, you simply need to click the room tabs located at the top of the interface.

 In this lesson, you learn how to access the other Poser rooms using the room tabs.

Using the Material Room

The Material Room, shown in Figure 1-26, includes an interface used to apply materials to the various body parts. You apply these materials using an interface dialog box for Diffuse Color, Highlight, Ambient, Reflection, Bump, and Transparency. The resulting material is shown in the Material Preview panel. In addition to these simple material properties, the Advanced panel includes many additional material properties. The Material Room also includes all the interface controls found in the Pose Room including the Document Window.

Using the Face Room

The Face Room interface, shown in Figure 1-27, includes controls for specifying the details included in the figure's face. It includes support for loading front and side view photos of the face you want to use along with tools to map the images onto the figure's face. The Face Room interface also includes the Face Shaping Tool dialog box, which lets you change the various attributes of the current face including the position of the various facial features, and its gender, age, and ethnicity. The Face Sculpting pane lets you see a preview of the current face settings.

FIGURE 1-26

Material Room interface

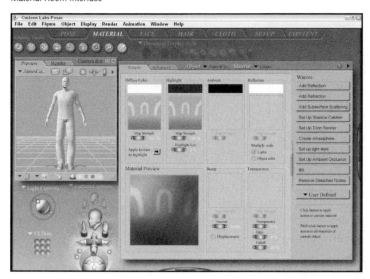

FIGURE 1-27

Face Room interface

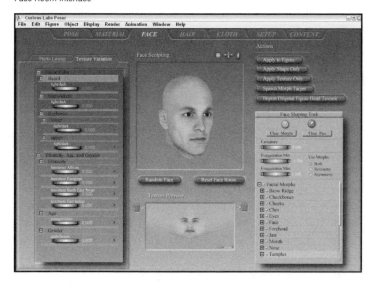

Using the Hair Room

The Hair Room, shown in Figure 1-28, includes all the controls needed to grow and style hair for the figure. You can grow hair for any body part and view the hair using the Texture Shaded style in the Document Window. The Hair Room also includes the standard Pose Room interface controls.

Using the Cloth Room

You use the Cloth Room, shown in Figure 1-29, to clothe the current figure and to define the dynamics of those clothes. These controls can make clothes that are smooth and flowing or clothes that fit tightly. You can use dynamic objects to add forces such as wind and gravity for animation

sequences. The resulting clothes are viewed in the Document Window.

FIGURE 1-28

Hair Room interface

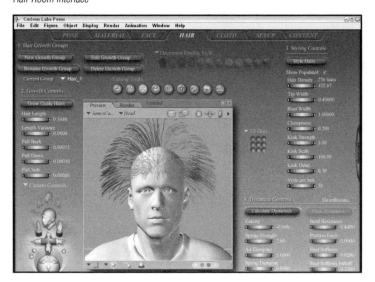

FIGURE 1-29

Cloth Room interface

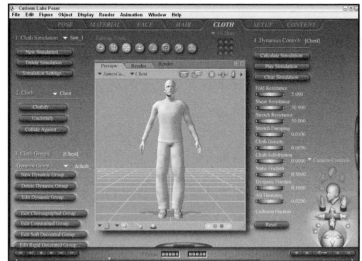

Using the Setup Room

The Setup Room, shown in Figure 1-30, overlays the figure in the Document Window with a set of bones that are positioned about the figure's joints. Using this room, you can add new custom bones to the figure as needed. These new bones are used to animate the custom imported objects.

Using the Content Room

The Content Room, shown in Figure 1-31, provides a convenient way to add new figures, materials, and props to the Library. It also provides access to Content Paradise, an online repository of available content.

FIGURE 1-30

Setup Room interface

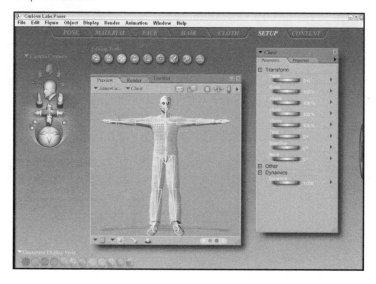

FIGURE 1-31

Content Room interface

Switch between rooms

1. Click the Poser icon to start the Poser interface.

   The Pose Room is the default room that appears when Poser is first loaded.

2. Click the Material tab at the top of the interface.

   The Material Room interface, shown in Figure 1-32, is displayed.

3. Click the appropriate room tabs to access the various rooms.

FIGURE 1-32
The Material Room interface

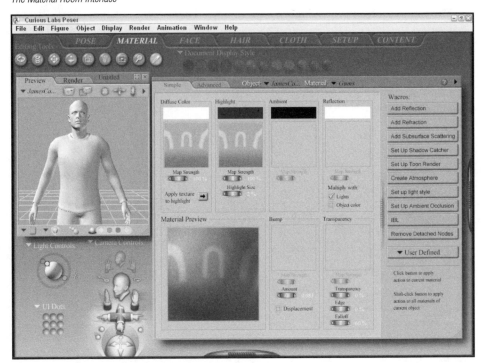

WORK WITH FILES

What You'll Do

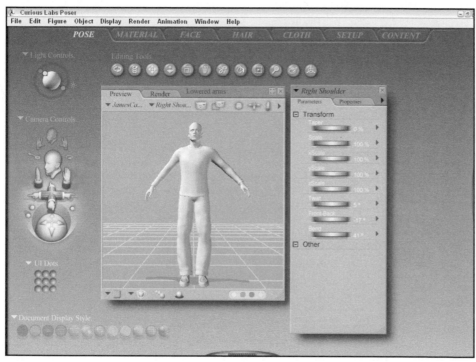

In this lesson, you learn how to load, save, import, and export files.

The File menu on the menu bar includes several commands for working with the various Poser file formats. In addition to loading and saving files, the File menu includes commands that let you **import** and **export** several specific file formats.

Creating a New File

The File, New menu command creates a new scene with the default figure. If the current scene includes any changes, a confirmation dialog box appears asking you if you want to save the current changes.

Loading Saved Files

You load saved files into Poser using the File, Open command. This command opens the Open Poser Scene dialog box, as shown in Figure 1-33. This dialog box can load several different file types including:

- **All Poser Scene Files:** Includes all Poser file types.
- **Poser Scene Files:** Saves with the .pz3 file extension.
- **Compressed Poser Scene Files:** Saved with the .pzz file extension. Compressed files are smaller than regular files.
- **Poser 1 Scene Files:** Saved with the .poz file extension.
- **Poser 2 Scene Files:** Saved with the .pzr file extension.

The Open as Read Only option opens a file for viewing, but does not allow changes. The File, Revert menu command throws away any current changes and reverts to the last saved state of the file.

QUICKTIP

The File, Close button closes all interface elements and presents an empty interface with only the menus visible.

Saving Files

The File, Save menu command saves the current scene file using the same file name. The File, Save As command lets you rename the current scene file. Files saved in Poser 6 are saved by default using the Poser 3 file format with the .pz3 extension. You can also save them as compressed scene files with the .pzz file extension.

QUICKTIP

You can select to compress all saved files using the General Preferences dialog box.

FIGURE 1-33

The Open Poser Scene dialog box

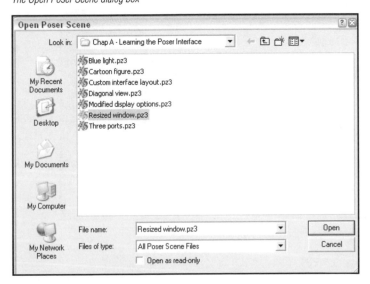

Importing Files

Imported files can include everything from movies and sound files to object files and background images. The files that you can import into Poser include the following:

- **Movies:** These including the AVI file format for Windows and QuickTime files for Macintosh systems. The imported movie appears in the background of the Poser figures.
- **Background Picture:** Image file formats that you can import include SGI, 8BP, BMP, DIP, Flash Pix, GIF, JPEG, MAC, PICT, PIC, PNG, PNTG, PSD, TGA and TPIC files. These images also appear in the background behind the figures.
- **Poser Document/Prop:** Imports the selected scene or prop file into the current scene file. This command is useful for combining figures and props into a single scene file.
- **Poser 1.0 Library:** Imports a Poser 1.0 Library that has a unique format.
- **Sound:** Loads WAV sound files for use in an animation sequence.
- **BVH Motion:** Loads a Biovision motion-capture file, which is a format that describes how the figure should move between poses.

- **QuickDraw 3DMF:** Imports geometry objects using the QuickDraw 3DMF file format.
- **3D Studio:** Imports geometry objects using the .3ds file format from 3D studio max.
- **DXF:** Imports geometry objects using the .dxf file format.
- **Lightwave 5:** Imports geometry objects using the .lwo file format.
- **Wavefront OBJ:** Imports geometry objects using the .obj file format.
- **Detailer Text:** Imports geometry objects using the .vxt file format.

Exporting Files

Poser can also export files using the File, Export menu command. The file formats that you can export include the following:

- **Image:** Exporting an image saves the current Document Window using the designated style using one of the following formats BMP, Flash Pix, JPEG, PICT, PNG, PSD, or TIF.
- **Viewpoint Experience Technology:** Exports to the Viewpoint Media Player format.
- **RIB:** Exports to the Renderman .RIB file format.

- **BVH Motion:** Exports to a Biovision motion-capture file.
- **Painter Script:** Exports to the Painter Script file format from Poser's Sketch Designer interface.
- **QuickDraw 3DMF:** Exports to the QuickDraw 3DMF file format.
- **3D Studio:** Exports geometry objects to 3D studio max using the .3ds file format.
- **DXF:** Exports geometry objects using the .dxf file format.
- **HAnim:** Exports geometry objects using the .hanim file format.
- **Lightwave 5:** Exports geometry objects using the .lwo file format.
- **Wavefront OBJ:** Exports geometry objects using the .obj file format.
- **Detailer Text:** Exports geometry objects using the .vxt file format.
- **VRML:** Exports geometry objects using the .wrl file format.

When exporting geometry, an Export Range dialog box, shown in Figure 1-34, appears where you can select to export the entire animation or only a single frame. After this, a Hierarchy Selection dialog box, shown in Figure 1-35, appears where you can select exactly which objects are exported from your scene.

NOTE

Poser 3 enabled figures to be created using text-based hierarchy files. The File, Convert Hier File menu command opens a file dialog box where you can select and covert these hierarchy files to a figure. In Poser 6, new figures can be defined using the Setup Room instead of hierarchy files, but this command is included for backwards compatibility.

FIGURE 1-35
Hierarchy Selection dialog box

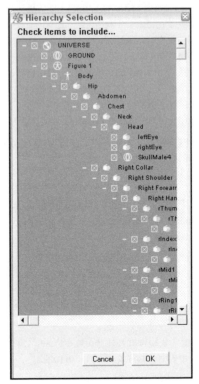

FIGURE 1-34
Export Range dialog box

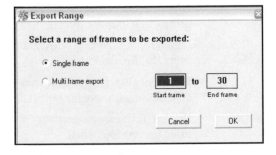

FIGURE 1-36
Saved scene file

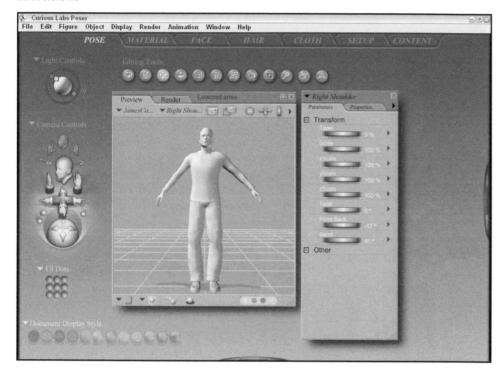

Load and save a scene file

1. Click File on the menu bar, click Open, navigate to the drive and folder where your data files are stored, click Raised arms.pz3, and then click Open.

   A scene file containing the default figure with raised arms is loaded.

2. Select and lower the figure's arms.

3. Save the file as **Lowered arms.pz3**.

   The modified scene file is saved using the new name, as shown in Figure 1-36.

Export and import a scene file

1. Click File, Open and select and open the Raised arms.pz3 file.

2. Click File, Export, Wavefront OBJ. In the Export Range dialog box, select the Single Frame option and click OK.

   A Hierarchy Selection dialog box appears where you can select exactly which objects are exported.

3. Click OK in the Hierarchy Selection dialog box.

   The Export as Wavefront OBJ dialog box appears.

4. Give the file a name and click Save.

A list of export options appears, as shown in Figure 1-37. Click OK to use the default export options. The exported file is saved.

5. Click File, Import, Wavefront OBJ. Select the Raised arms.obj file and click Open.

A Prop Import Options dialog box appears, shown in Figure 1-38, where you can select the size and position of the imported object. Click OK to accept the default options.

FIGURE 1-37

Export options dialog box

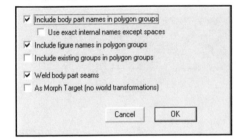

FIGURE 1-38

Prop Import Options dialog box

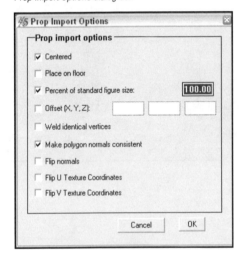

CONFIGURE THE
INTERFACE

What You'll Do

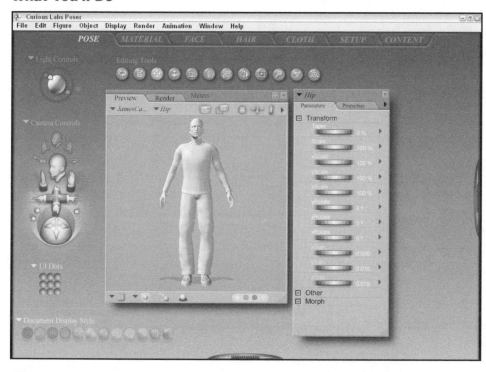

Saving a scene file also saves the position of the interface elements. This is convenient because Poser remembers exactly how you configured the interface and retains your preferences.

Using the UI Dots

If you like to use several different interface configurations, you can save them using the **UI Dots** options in the Memory Dots control. To use a memory dot, simply click a dot to save the current UI layout. Clicking again on the dot recalls the saved layout. Holding down the Alt key while clicking a dot clears it.

TIP

You can use memory dots also to save poses and camera settings.

In this lesson, you learn how to configure the interface by changing preference settings.

Using Preferences

Poser lets you set general preferences with the Edit, General Preferences (Ctrl+K) command. This General Preferences dialog box includes four separate panels—Document, Interface, Library, and Misc. The Document panel of the General Preferences dialog box, shown in Figure 1-39, includes options for launching Poser using its factory state or a preferred state. The preferred state option remembers the interface's previous location and size when it is reloaded, and the factory state option loads Poser using the default size and position.

The Smoothing Default crease angle determines the angle between adjacent faces that is required before the edge they share forms a crease. The Render option determines the maximum number of cached renders that are retained before being deleted.

Setting the Interface Preferences

The Interface panel of the General Preferences dialog box, shown in Figure 1-40, includes options for loading the last saved layout of interface elements or restoring the factory state of the interface layout. If you want Poser to remember how you've positioned the various interface controls, then enable the Launch to Previous State option.

This panel also includes a Display Units setting. The available options include Poser native units, Inches, Feet, Millimeters, Centimeters, and Meters.

FIGURE 1-39

Document panel of the General Preferences dialog box

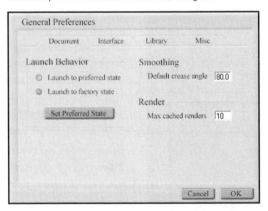

FIGURE 1-40

Interface panel of the General Preferences dialog box

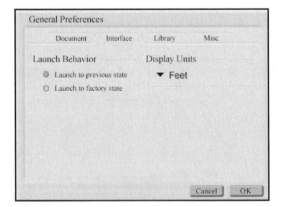

Setting Library Preferences

The Library panel of the General Preferences dialog box, shown in Figure 1-41, includes options for defining the action of double-clicking Library objects. The options include Add to Scene or Replace Existing Object. You can also select to never collapse thumbnails (which requires more memory) or to display text-only when the number of items in the folder exceeds a designated value. The value of thumbnails is that they show what the item looks like, but with many items in a Library folder, showing all thumbnails can slow down the system.

Setting Miscellaneous Preferences

The Misc panel of the General Preferences dialog box, shown in Figure 1-42, includes options for causing all files to be saved as a compressed file. You can also enable the Use External Binary Morph Targets option, which saves morph targets as separate files to be shared by other figures. Finally, you can select the editor to use to edit Python scripts and check the Curious Labs Web site for Poser updates.

FIGURE 1-41

Library panel of the General Preferences dialog box

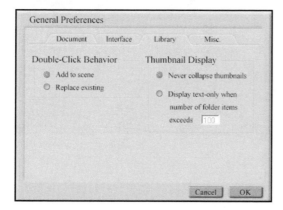

FIGURE 1-42

Misc panel of the General Preferences dialog box

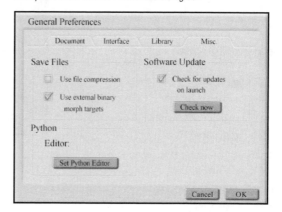

Configure the interface

1. Drag the titles of the various interface elements to your liking.

2. Choose Edit, General Preferences (or press Ctrl+K).

   The General Preferences dialog box opens with the Document panel selected.

3. In the Document panel, enable the Launch to Preferred State option.

4. Select the Interface panel, enable the Launch to Previous State option, and click OK.

5. Close and relaunch Poser.

   The layout configuration is retained from the previous session.

Change display units

1. Choose Edit, General Preferences (Ctrl+K) and click the Interface panel tab.

   The Interface panel of the General Preferences dialog box opens.

2. Select Meters as the Display Units option and click OK.

3. Select the hip object and open the Parameters/Properties panel.

   The translation values are listed in meter values, as shown in Figure 1-43.

4. Choose File, Save As and save the file as **Meters.pz3**.

FIGURE 1-43

Meters display units

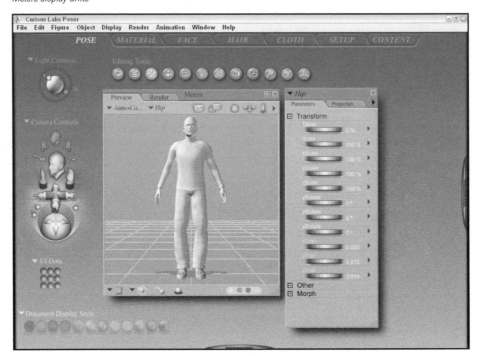

LESSON 7

GET HELP

What You'll Do

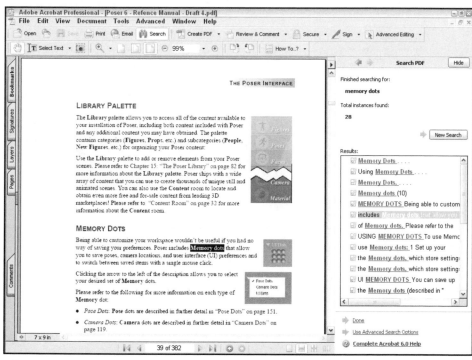

If you're looking for more help, Poser includes a detailed PDF-based set of help files that have all the answers.

 In this lesson, you learn how to access the Poser Help documentation.

Using Poser Documentation

To access the Poser documentation, select the Help, Poser 6 Help menu command. This command opens the Web files in Acrobat Reader, as shown in Figure 1-44. The Acrobat Reader interface lets you open specific topics using the pane on the left or search for specific words with its search feature.

FIGURE 1-44
Poser 6 Help

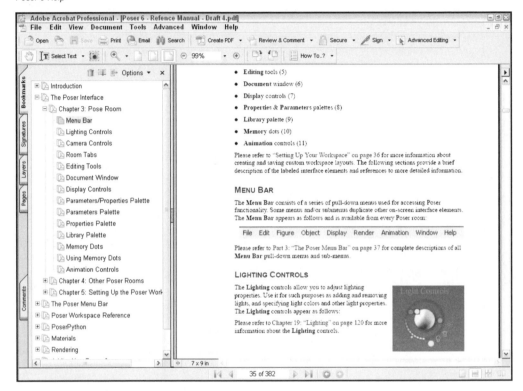

Enabling Room Help

If you need help with a particular room, you can enable Room Help with the Window, Room Help menu command. When enabled, a pop-up help window appears, as shown in Figure 1-45, with help specific to the open room.

Accessing Python Help

If you need help scripting using the Python Scripting language, the Help menu includes a separate PDF containing on the scripting commands. Choose the Poser Help, PoserPython Help command to open Python help.

Accessing Tutorials

Many people learn better by seeing how a certain task is accomplished. You can learn from the Poser Tutorials using the Help, Tutorials menu command.

FIGURE 1-45

Room Help window

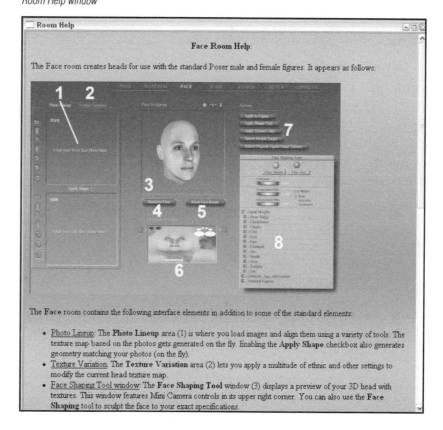

Access Poser help

1. Choose Help, Poser 6 Help.

   The Poser 6 Help PDF file is opened within Acrobat Reader.

2. Click the Search button in the Acrobat Reader toolbar and type **Memory Dots** in the Search field.

   After Poser searches the PDF file, it displays the available links, as shown in Figure 1-46.

3. Click a link to see the information on a topic.

FIGURE 1-46

Searching Poser Help

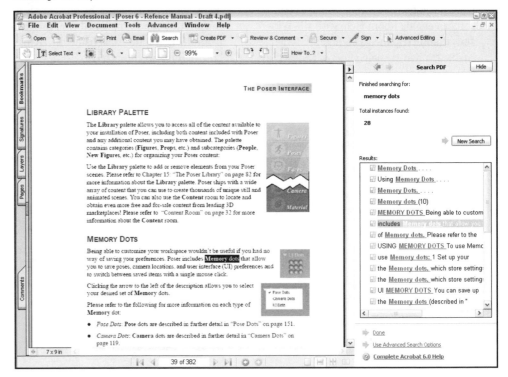

CHAPTER SUMMARY

This chapter introduced the Poser interface, including the various floating controls and the Document Window. It also introduced the different rooms that are available. By reading about the various menus, you learned about the commands for working with files, including opening, saving, importing, and exporting files. You read about methods for configuring the interface along with the general preferences. The final lesson explained how to get help.

What You Have Learned

In this chapter, you

- Learned to work with the various interface controls, including menus, floating controls, and the Document Window.
- Used the Camera and Light Controls and changed the Display Styles.
- Changed the number of views displayed in the Document Window.
- Altered the Document Window display options, including the tracking method, depth cueing, shadows, and colors.
- Explored the remaining rooms using the interface tabs.

- Learned how to work with files including loading, saving, importing and exporting them.
- Configured the interface using the UI dots and preference settings.
- Accessed the Poser help files as a way to get additional help.

Key Terms from This Chapter

Interface. A set of controls used to interact with the software features.

Room tabs. A set a tabs located at the top of the Poser interface that allow access to various feature interfaces.

Floating control. A interface object that isn't attached to the interface window and can be placed anywhere within the interface window.

Document Window. The main window interface where the posed figure is displayed.

Side window control. A simple control positioned on the side of the interface used to open another set of controls.

Display styles. Render options for the Document Window.

Display ports. Additional sections of the Document Window that can display a different view of the scene.

Tracking mode. Modes that define the detail of the objects displayed in the Document Window.

Importing. The process of loading externally created files into Poser.

Exporting. The process of saving Poser files to a format to be used by an external program.

UI Dots. Interface controls used to remember and recall a specific interface configuration.

OpenGL. An option used to enable hardware acceleration for fast Document Window updates.

SreeD. An option used to enable software rendering to be used if the OpenGL option causes display problems.

Preferences. An interface for setting defaults and for configuring the interface.

chapter

2

WORKING WITH
Figures

1. Load Library figures.

2. Position figures within the scene.

3. Set figure properties.

4. Alter a figure.

5. Select elements.

6. Work with hierarchies.

chapter 2 WORKING WITH
Figures

When you first launch Poser, it loads a default figure, but there are several additional figures available and you can even import your own custom figures. The easiest way to load new figures is using the Library. The Poser Library comes pre-populated with content—including figures, poses, expressions, hair, props, and more—spread across several different categories. Accessing these categories and their content is easy and you can also add new content to the Library as needed.

After loading a custom figure, you can select and move it into position within the scene before starting to pose the figure. Moving a figure moves the entire figure as one unit and lets you separate multiple figures within a single scene.

Several commands are available for working with figures, including changing its height, locking a figure in place, and hiding a figure to speed the update within the Document Window.

Before moving on to the process of posing, which you do in the Pose Room, this chapter concludes by looking at several ways to select the various **body parts** or elements and looking at the Hierarchy Editor, which is an interface listing all the elements in the entire scene.

Tools You'll Use

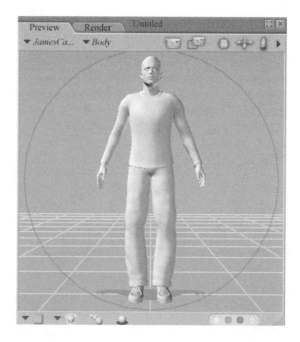

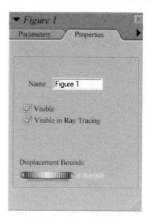

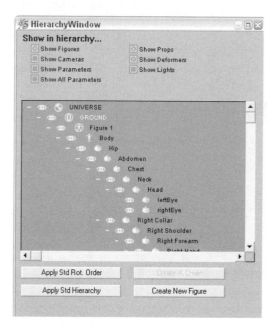

LOAD LIBRARY
FIGURES

What You'll Do

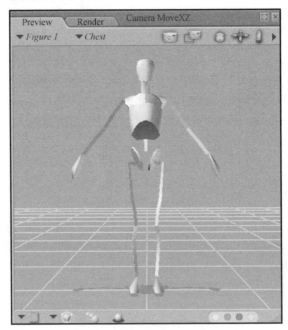

In this lesson, you learn how to load new figures from the Library.

The first place to look if you want to work with a new **figure** is the **Library palette** located on the right side of the interface. This palette includes a repository of content organized by category including Figures, Poses, Expressions, Hair, Hands, Props, Lights, and Cameras. To open the Library palette, click the side window tab on the right side of the interface. The Library palette will extend from the edge of the palette displaying all default categories, as shown in Figure

2-1. You can also open the Library palette with the Window, Libraries menu command.

FIGURE 2-1
Library palette

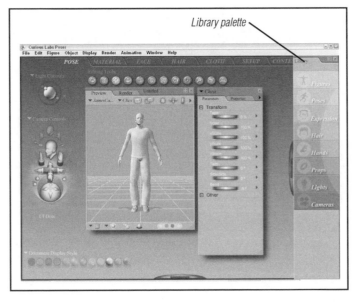

In addition to Library figures, you can use models created in other 3D packages by importing them using the File, Import command. Keep in mind that a bone structure needs to be attached to imported models before you can pose them. All default Library figures already have bones attached. Building a bone structure is covered in Chapter 10, "Working with Bones."

Viewing the Library Figures

You can select and load new figures from the Library palette. To do this, click the Figures category. Several folder images of the available Library figures are displayed. Double-clicking a folder will open it to reveal its contents. Within the folders are thumbnails of the various available figures, as shown in Figure 2-2. When a figure thumbnail is selected, four buttons appear at the bottom of the palette. These buttons are Change Figure, Create New Figure, Add to Library, and Remove from Library.

Undocking the Library Palette

If you click the Dock/Undock button in the upper-right corner of the Library palette, the palette becomes a floating window that you can move by dragging its title bar and resize by dragging its lower-right corner. The undocked palette also shows both thumbnails and the categories at the same time.

Accessing Custom Libraries

At the top of each category folder is a folder with an up arrow on it. Double-clicking this folder thumbnail opens the previously selected folder. If you keep clicking up the **hierarchy** of folders, you'll eventually reach two folders labeled *Poser 6* (with a red dot by it) and *Downloads*. The Poser 6 folder is the default folder that includes all the content that was installed with Poser 6 and the Downloads folder includes all the content that is downloaded and installed using the Content Room. Clicking the Add Library button at the bottom of the palette opens a dialog box where you can browse to a folder on your hard disk that includes content. The selected folder then appears in the Library palette.

FIGURE 2-2
Figure thumbnails

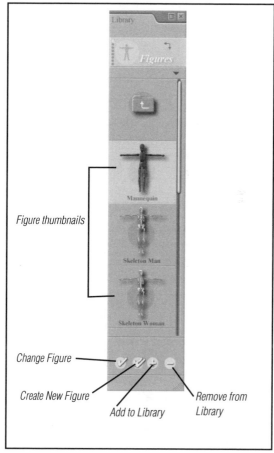

Figure thumbnails

Change Figure

Create New Figure

Add to Library

Remove from Library

Accessing Other Library Categories

From the figure thumbnails, you can access the Library categories again by clicking the Category button located at the top of the Library palette, as shown in Figure 2-3. You can also access the various categories directly using the small circle category buttons to the left of the current category title or from a list using the pop-up menu.

Replacing the Current Figure

Selecting a figure thumbnail and clicking the Change Figure button replaces the current Poser figure with the selected thumbnail figure. When you click the Change Figure button, the Keep Customized Geometry dialog box, shown in Figure 2-4, appears. Using the options in this dialog box, you can maintain any modified geometries, and keep any props or deformers attached to the figure. There is also a button to cancel the figure change. Following the Keep Customized Geometry dialog box, the Keep Scales dialog box, shown in Figure 2-5; appears, there you can select to maintain the current figure proportions. Figure 2-6 shows the Mannequin figure that has replaced the default figure.

FIGURE 2-3

Library palette navigation controls

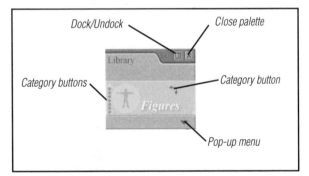

FIGURE 2-4

Keep Customized Geometry dialog box

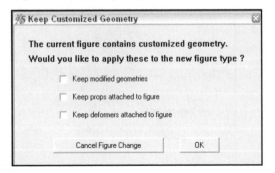

FIGURE 2-5

Keep Scales dialog box

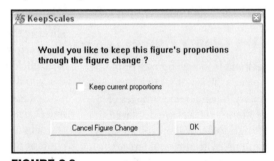

FIGURE 2-6

Replaced figure

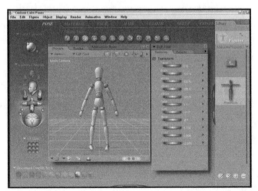

If you spent some time posing and moving a figure, you can keep the work even though you're loading a new figure by selecting the options in the Keep Customized Geometry and Keep Scales dialog boxes.

Adding a Figure to the Current Scene

Clicking the Add New Item button in the Library palette adds the selected figure to the scene without removing the existing figure. Using this button, you can add multiple figures to a single scene. Figure 2-7 shows the default man sharing the scene with a mannequin figure loaded from the Library.

Adding and Removing Figures from the Library

You use the right two buttons at the bottom of the Library palette to add the current scene figure to the Library and remove the selected thumbnail from the Library. When the Add to Library button is clicked, a simple dialog box appears where you can name the new figure. Figure 2-8 shows the default and skeleton figures added to the Library as a new set. When you click the Remove from Library button, a warning dialog box appears asking if you want to permanently delete the selected item. Click the Yes button to complete the deletion.

CAUTION

Removing items from the Library removes them from your computer's hard drive also.

FIGURE 2-7
Multiple figures

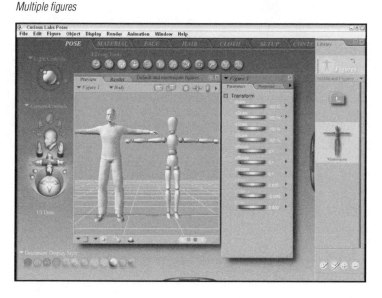

FIGURE 2-8
New figure thumbnail

Replace the current figure with a new figure

1. Open the Poser interface.

2. Click the side interface control to open the Library palette.

   The Library palette is displayed with seven category icons.

3. Click the Figures category icon.

   Several figure thumbnails are displayed within the Library palette.

4. Scroll downward in the Library palette and select the Stick Man thumbnail.

5. Click the Change Figure button 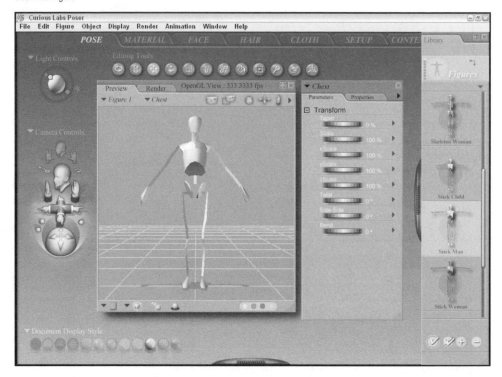 at the bottom of the Library palette.

6. Click OK in the Keep Customized Geometry and the Keep Scale dialog boxes that appear.

   The new figure replaces the default figure in the Document Window, as shown in Figure 2-9.

7. Select File, Save As and save the file as **Stick man figure.pz3**.

FIGURE 2-9

Stick man figure

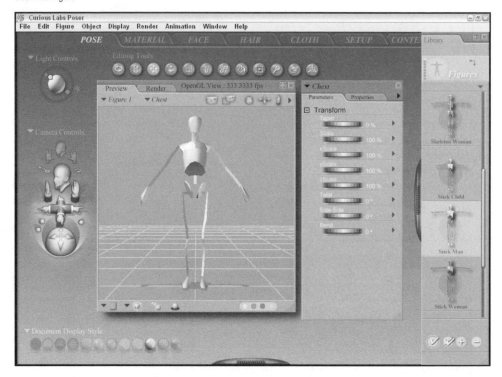

FIGURE 2-10

Two figures in the same scene

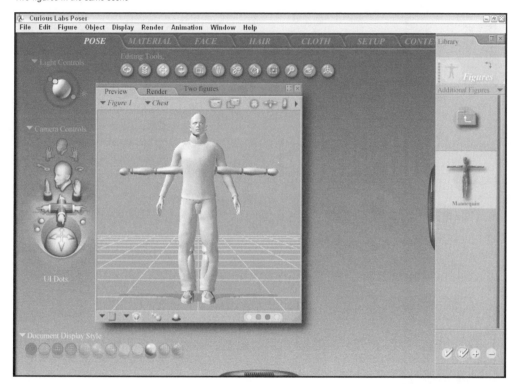

1. Open a new Poser file with the default man visible.

2. Click the side interface control to open the Library palette or select the Window, Libraries menu command (if necessary).

3. Click the Figures category icon and double-click the Additional Figures folder to open it.

4. Select the Mannequin thumbnail.

5. Click the Add New Item button at the bottom of the Library palette.

   The new figure is added to the scene in the same location, as shown in Figure 2-10.

6. Select File, Save As and save the file as **Two figures.pz3**.

Add scene figures to the Library

1. Click the side interface control to open the Library palette or select the Window, Libraries menu command (if necessary).

2. Click the Figures category icon and double-click the Additional Figures folder to open it.

3. Select the Mannequin thumbnail.

4. Click the Add to Library button ⊕ at the bottom of the Library palette.

   The Set Name dialog box appears.

5. Type the name, **Default Man**, in the Set Name dialog box and click OK.

   The default figure is added to the Library with its thumbnail listed in alphabetical order, as shown in Figure 2-11.

FIGURE 2-11
Default man added to the Library

POSITION FIGURES
WITHIN THE SCENE

What You'll Do

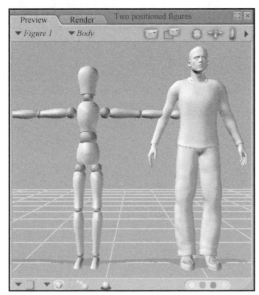

In this lesson, you learn how to position objects within the scene.

Loaded figures appear in the center of the Document Window, but you can move them as needed using the Document Window controls.

Selecting Figures

If the scene includes multiple figures, you can select an individual figure using the Figure Selection list located in the upper-left corner of the Document Window. Each figure is given a name when first loaded from the Library. The default names are "Figure" and a number such as Figure 1, Figure 2, and so on, but you can change a figure's name using the Properties palette.

Using the Figure Circle Control

Dragging over a figure in the Document Window highlights the various body parts, but if you move the mouse cursor towards the edges of the Document Window, a large circle appears that surrounds the figure, as shown in Figure 2-12. This circle

is the **Figure Circle control**. Clicking and dragging on this control lets you edit the entire figure using the various Editing tools, including translating, rotating, and scaling the entire figure. A complete description of the various Editing tools

FIGURE 2-12
Figure Circle control

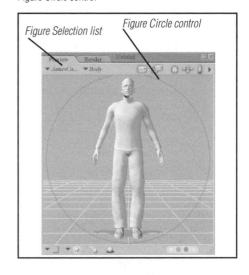

Figure Selection list   Figure Circle control

appears in Chapter 3, "Editing and Posing Figures."

Changing Figure Parameters

In addition to the Figure Circle control and the Editing tools, you can also change a figure's position and orientation using the Parameter values found in the Parameters palette. You change these parameter values by dragging on the dial controls or by entering a new value. Doing so updates the figure in the Document Window.

Dropping a Figure to the Floor

As objects are moved, you can position them above the ground plane, which can make it look like they are walking on air. The figure shadow is a good indication if the figure is above the ground plane, but there is a feature that can return the figure to the ground plane. The Figure, Drop to Floor (Ctrl+D) menu command moves the selected figure downward until it contacts the ground plane. The Drop to Floor command also works if part of the figure is positioned below the ground plane.

Locking Figures

Once you have a figure positioned exactly where you want it, you can lock it so it won't be moved by accident. To lock the selected figure, select Figure, Lock Figure. Body parts of a locked figure also cannot be moved. A check mark appears in the Figure menu next to the Lock Figure command when it is enabled. To unlock a figure, simply select Figure, Lock Figure again.

NOTE

The Figure menu also includes a command to Lock Hands Parts. Locking the hands is helpful. Because the hands include so many different parts, it is easy to select the wrong part accidentally.

Restoring a Figure

If you make a mistake while positioning a figure, you can use Edit, Undo to undo the last move or you can restore the figure to its last saved, loaded, or memorized position using the Edit, Restore, Figure menu command. To memorize a figure's current position so you can restore it, use Edit, Memorize, Figure.

TIP

In addition to figures, you can also use the Memorize and Restore commands on elements, lights, cameras, and all items.

FIGURE 2-13

Two positioned figures

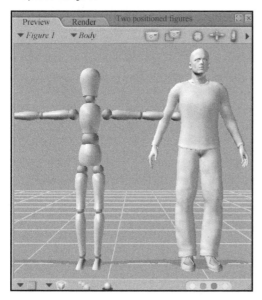

Position a figure within a scene

1. Select File, Open and open the Two figures.pz3 file.

   This file includes three separate figures all positioned in the same place.

2. From the Figure Selection drop-down list at the upper-left of the Document Window, select the Figure 1 option.

3. In the Document Window, click and drag the circle surrounding the figure and move the figure to the right.

4. Select the figure that was moved and choose Figure, Drop to Floor or press the Ctrl+D keys.

   The figures are now positioned apart from one another and aligned with the ground plane, as shown in Figure 2-13.

5. Select File, Save As and save the file as **Two positioned figures.pz3**.

Memorize and restore figure positions

1. Select File, Open and open the Default and skeleton figures.pz3 file.

   This file includes two separate figures positioned side by side.

2. From the Figure Selection drop-down list at the upper-left of the Document Window, select the Figure 1 option.

3. Select Edit, Memorize, Figure.

4. In the Document Window, click and drag on the circle surrounding the figure and move the figure to the right. Then select and drag one of the figure's arms.

5. Select Edit, Restore, Figure.

   The default figure is returned to its memorized position.

SET FIGURE PROPERTIES

What You'll Do

(►) In this lesson, you learn how to set figure properties.

When a figure is selected, you can use the Properties panel of the Parameters/Properties palette, shown in Figure 2-14, to change several properties that are unique to the selected figure, such as its name and whether it is visible.

Naming Figures

The default names of Figure 1 and Figure 2 can get confusing if you have several figures in the scene. Accessing the Properties palette lets you type a new name for the selected figure. Once a figure has a new name, this name will appear in the Figure Selection list.

FIGURE 2-14
Figure Properties palette

Hiding Figures

With several figures in a scene, the redraw time can slow down, but you can speed up the redraw time by hiding the figures that you aren't working with. To hide the selected figure, simply disable the Visible option in the Properties palette. This won't delete the figure, but only hides it from view. Enabling the Visible option will make the figure visible in the Document Window again. You can also hide the current figure using Figure, Hide Figure (Ctrl+H). The Figure, Show All Figures menu command makes all hidden figures visible.

Setting Other Properties

The Visible in Ray Tracing option causes the figure's reflection to be cast to objects in the scene when raytracing is enabled during the rendering phase. Raytracing is covered in Chapter 12, "Rendering Scenes."

The Displacement Bounds value is used to set the maximum depth that a displacement map can indent an object. Displacement maps are discussed in more detail in Chapter 4, "Adding Materials."

Deleting Figures

You can delete selected figures from the scene using Figure, Delete Figure or by pressing the Delete key. When you select this command, a warning dialog box appears asking if you want to delete the figure. Clicking Yes permanently deletes the figure from the scene.

FIGURE 2-15

Named figure

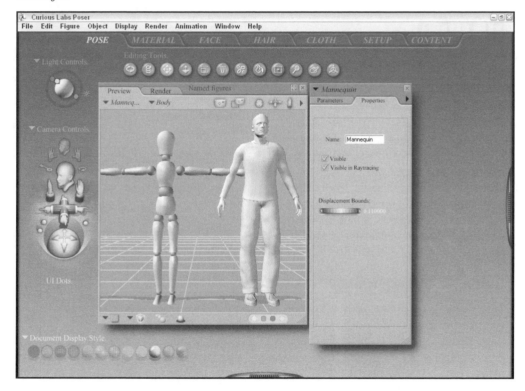

1. Select File, Open and open the Two positioned figures.pz3 file.

2. From the Figure Selection drop-down list at the upper-left of the Document Window, select the Figure 1 option.

3. Select Window, Parameter Dials to open the Parameters/Properties palette if it isn't already open.

4. Click the Properties tab in the Parameters/Properties palette.

5. In Name field, type the name, **Mannequin**.

   Each of the figures now has a unique name, as shown in Figure 2-15.

6. Select File, Save As and save the file as **Named figures.pz3**.

Hide figures

1. Select File, Open and open the Named figures.pz3 file (if necessary).

2. From the Figure Selection drop-down list at the upper-left of the Document Window, select the Default Man figure.

3. Select Figure, Hide Figure or press the Ctrl+H keys.

   The default man figure is hidden.

4. Select File, Save As and save the file as **Hidden figure.pz3**.

ALTER A FIGURE

What You'll Do

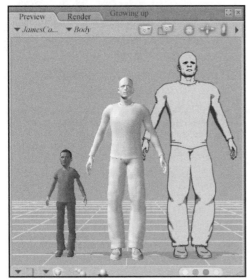

In this lesson, you learn how to change a figure's height, details, and style.

In addition to positioning and setting figure properties, the Figure menu includes several commands that you can use to alter figures, such as changing the figure's height and making **genitalia** visible. As you begin to change a figure's height, several display guides are available for checking the relative height of different figures.

Setting a Figure's Height

The default figure appears using a standard adult height, but you can change the selected figure's height using the Figure, Figure Height menu command. The height of each option is measured relative to the size of the head. The height options include Baby, Toddler, Child, Juvenile, Adolescent, Ideal Adult, Fashion Model, and Heroic Model.

Figure 2-16 shows each of the various figure heights. Notice how the body's proportion is changed along with its height.

FIGURE 2-16
Various figure heights

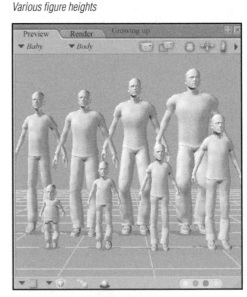

Adding Genitalia

Most Poser models without clothes are anatomically correct, but you can enable and disable whether the genitalia is visible. Enabling this option enables it for all models in the scene, as shown in Figure 2-17.

Not all figures include genitalia. Enabling this option for figures that don't have modeled genitalia will have no effect. It also has no effect for figures that are covered with clothes like the default figure.

Setting Figure Style

The Display Style control sets the display style for all items in the scene, but you can also set the display style for just the selected figure using Display, Figure Style or by clicking the Display Style pop-up menu. The default option is Use Document Style or you can select one of the 12 display styles. Figure 2-18 shows three figure display styles applied to the same figure.

Using Display Guides

The Display, Guides menu command includes several useful display guides that can help to keep the relative size of the different figures consistent. The Display, Guides, Head Lengths guide divides the figure into seven evenly sized head lengths shown as simple rectangular boxes, as shown in Figure 2-19. Because all humans are about seven head lengths in size, you can use these guides to determine if the figure's size has the correct proportions.

Another useful display guide is the Hip-Shoulder Relationship guide. This guide shows the width of the hip and the shoulders as two boxes. You can access it from the Display, Guides menu command.

FIGURE 2-17
Anatomically correct figures

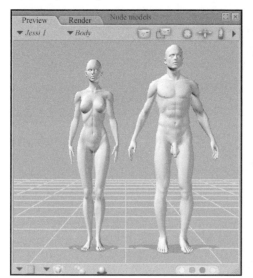

FIGURE 2-18
Figure display styles

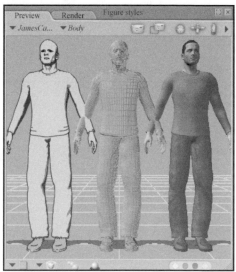

FIGURE 2-19
Head lengths guide

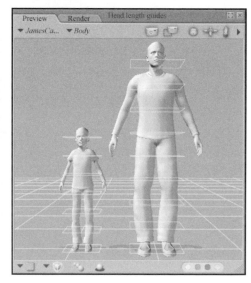

Change a figure's height and style

1. Choose File, Open and select and open the Three default men.pz3 file.

2. From the Figure Selection drop-down list at the upper-left of the Document Window, select the JamesCasual 1 option.

3. Select Figure, Figure Height, Heroic Model.

4. Select Display, Figure Style, Cartoon with Lines.

5. From the Figure Selection drop-down list at the upper-left of the Document Window, select the JamesCasual 2 option.

6. Select Figure, Figure Height, Child.

7. Select Display, Figure Style, Texture Shaded.

   Each of the figures is displayed in three different heights, as shown in Figure 2-20.

8. Select File, Save As and save the file as **Growing up.pz3**.

FIGURE 2-20
Cartoon style figures of different heights

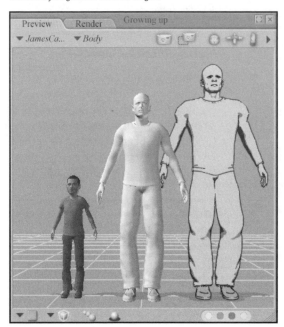

SELECT ELEMENTS

What You'll Do

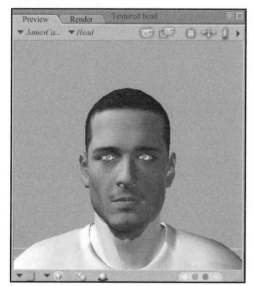

▶ In this lesson, you learn how to select various figure elements.

Each figure is made up of several distinct body parts that you can select independently. Any object that can be selected from the Actor List is an **element** consisting of body parts, props, lights, and cameras. Selecting specific elements is the key to being able to pose a figure.

Selecting from the Document Window

When you drag over an element in the Document Window, it becomes highlighted, as shown for the Chest element in Figure 2-21. If you click the element when it is highlighted, the element is selected and its name appears in the Actor List at the top of the Document Window and in the title bar of the Parameters/Properties palette.

FIGURE 2-21
Selected element

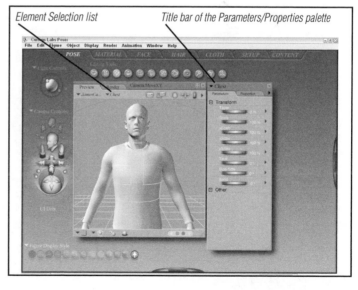

Element Selection list   Title bar of the Parameters/Properties palette

Selecting from a List

Another way to select figure body parts is by selecting them from the Actor List at the top of the Document Window and in the title bar of the Parameters palette. Both of these lists are identical and include menu options for selecting body parts, body, props, cameras, and lights. Selecting the Body Parts menu presents a long list of body parts. Only one figure element can be selected at a time.

NOTE

Selecting the Body option from the Actor List selects the entire figure.

Naming Elements

The default names in the Actor List match the various body parts such as Chest, Right Hand, and Left Forearm, but you can use the Name field in the Properties palette, shown in Figure 2-22, to change the name of any selected element. Once an element has a new name, this name will appear in

the Actor List, but Poser also maintains an internal name that it uses to coordinate the body part with its adjacent body parts.

Hiding Elements

You can hide elements by disabling the Visible option in the Properties palette. This won't delete the element, but only hide it from view. Figure 2-23 shows a figure with its chest, left collar, and right collar elements hidden. To make a hidden element visible again, you'll need to select the element from the Actor List and enable the Visible option again.

FIGURE 2-22

Element properties

FIGURE 2-23

Hidden elements

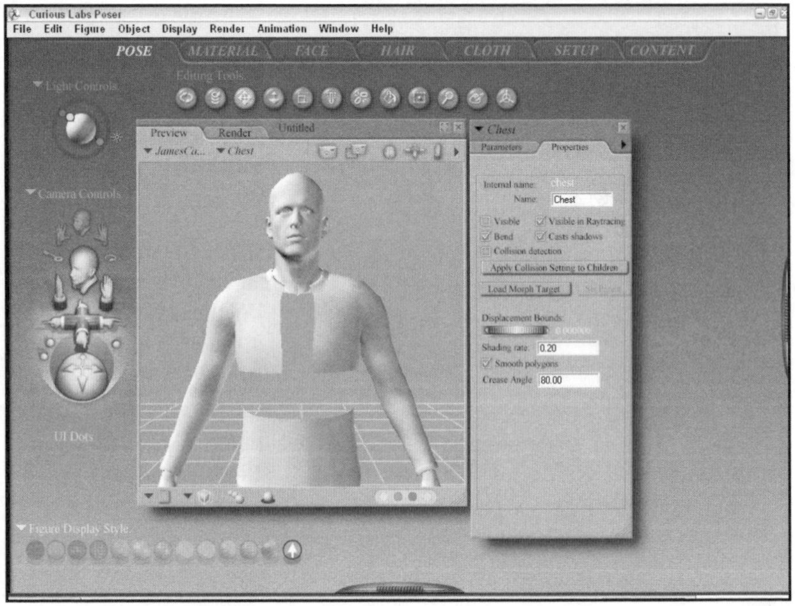

Setting Other Element Properties

The Visible in Ray Tracing option causes the element's reflection to be cast to objects in the scene when raytracing is enabled during the rendering phase. Raytracing is covered in Chapter 12, "Rendering Scenes."

The Bend option lets you specify whether the selected element bends to stay connected to its adjacent parts when moved. Disabling this option can cause gaps to appear in the figure. The Casts Shadows option causes the element to display a shadow in the Document Window.

Setting Element Styles

Just like setting a specific figure style is possible, you can also set the display style for a specific element using the Display, Element Style menu command. The default option is Use Figure Style or you can select one of the 12 display styles. Figure 2-24 shows a figure that uses several element display styles.

FIGURE 2-24

Different element styles

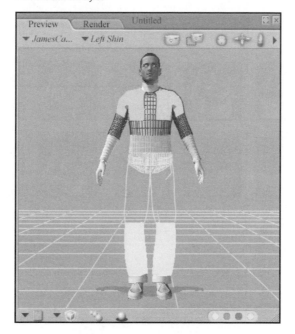

Select and hide elements

1. Open Poser with the default man figure visible.

2. Click the Left Thigh element in the Document Window to select it.

   The element is highlighted and its name appears in the Actor List at the top of the Document Window.

3. Select Window, Parameter Dials to open the Parameters/Properties palette, if it isn't already open, and click the Properties tab.

4. Disable the Visible option.

5. Repeat steps 2 and 4 for the Right Thigh, Left Shin, and Right Shin elements.

   With several elements hidden, the figure appears as shown in Figure 2-25.

6. Select File, Save As and save the file as **Hidden elements.pz3**.

Change an element's style

1. Open Poser with the default man figure visible.

2. Click the Head element in the Document Window to select it.

3. Click the Face Camera icon in the Camera Controls.

4. Select Display, Element Style, Texture Shaded.

   The Head element is displayed using the Texture Shaded style, as shown in Figure 2-26.

5. Select File, Save As and save the file as **Textured head.pz3**.

FIGURE 2-25

Default figure with hidden elements

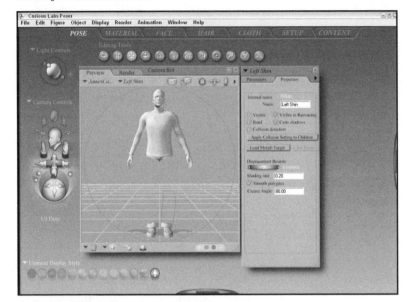

FIGURE 2-26

Textured Shaded head style

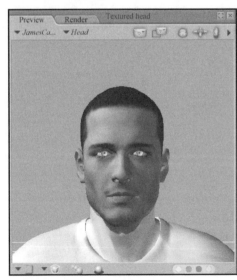

WORK WITH HIERARCHIES

What You'll Do

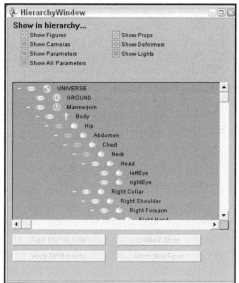

In this lesson, you learn how to work with the Hierarchy Editor.

A *hierarchy* is a list of elements ordered in such a way that the **parent-child relationships** between the elements are evident. These relationships are established by linking (or parenting) child objects to parent objects. When the parent object is moved, the child object follows along, thus helping to maintain the hierarchy. To see a complete hierarchy of the selected figure, you can open the Hierarchy Editor.

Opening the Hierarchy Editor

You can open the Hierarchy Editor, shown in Figure 2-27, using the Window, Hierarchy Editor menu command. It includes a list of all the items that are included in the current scene indented to show the parent-child relationships of the scene items.

Selecting View Options

The options at the top of the editor window let you select which types of items to make visible, including Figures, Cameras, Parameters, All Parameters, Props, Deformers, and Lights.

To the left of each item name are three icons. The first icon is a plus or minus sign. By clicking this icon, you can expand or collapse the children listed underneath

FIGURE 2-27

Hierarchy Editor

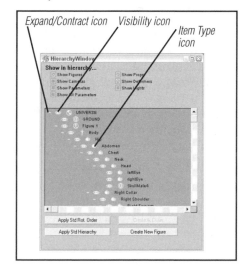

the current item. For example, the Forearm is a child of the Shoulder element and clicking the collapse icon hides the Forearm element and all its children and changes the icon to a plus sign.

Hiding Items

The second icon is the Visibility icon. Clicking this icon hides the selected item in the Document Window, but not any of its children. The third icon identifies the item. For example, all body parts are identified with a hand icon, all props have a ball icon, the entire scene (called the *Universe*) has a world icon, the Body object has a stick figure, lights have a light bulb icon, cameras have a camera icon, deformers have a small magnet, IK chains have a chain link icon, and parameters have a wheel icon.

Selecting Items

Selecting an item in the Hierarchy Editor automatically highlights the item name in white and selects the same item in the Document Window. Double-clicking a parameter in the Hierarchy Editor opens the Parameters palette where you can edit the selected parameter.

Renaming Items

Double-clicking an item title in the Hierarchy Editor selects the item name in a text field where you can type a new name for

the selected item. You can also delete certain items, including props and figures.

Setting a Figure's Parent

By default all figures in the scene are children to the Universe item, which is the top (or root) item in the scene, but you can change the figure's parent using the Figure, Set Figure Parent menu command. This command causes the Figure Parent dialog box, shown in Figure 2-28, to open. From within this dialog box, you can select a new parent for the figure. For example, you might want to parent a figure to a bicycle or an elevator prop.

NOTE

You can parent figures only to the items listed in the Figure Parent dialog box, including lights, cameras, and props.

A new figure parent can also be assigned using the Hierarchy Editor. To do this, simply select and drag the figure title to the item that you want to be its parent and the hierarchy will be reordered to show the change.

Setting an Item's Parent

Figures aren't the only items that can be assigned a new parent. Most items, including elements, cameras, and props, can be

FIGURE 2-28

Figure Parent dialog box

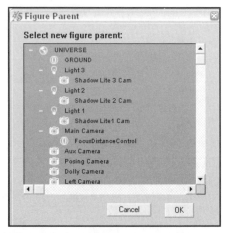

made children objects. To assign a new item to be the selected item's parent, select the Object, Change Parent menu command. This opens the Choose Parent dialog box, which is similar to the Figure Parent dialog box shown previously, where you can choose the item to be the parent.

You can also drag the item's title in the Hierarchy Editor and drop it on the item that you want to be its parent. A third way to choose an item's parent is to click the Set Parent button in the Properties palette for the selected item. This opens the Change Parent dialog box.

FIGURE 2-29

Elements hidden using the Hierarchy Editor

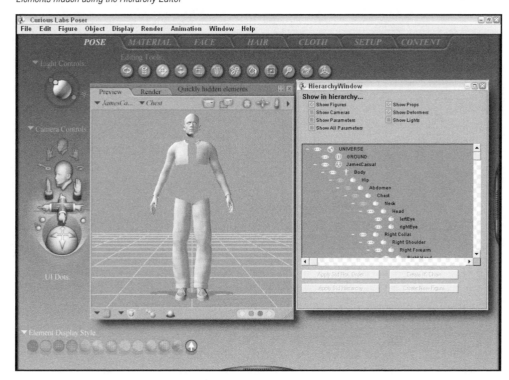

1. Open Poser with the default man figure visible.

2. Select Window, Hierarchy Editor.

   The Hierarchy Editor opens.

3. Click the Visibility icon to the left of the Hip, Abdomen, Chest, and Neck items.

   The selected elements are hidden, as shown in Figure 2-29.

4. Select File, Save As and save the file as **Quickly hidden elements.pz3**.

Set a figure's parent

1. Open Poser with the default man figure visible.

2. From the Figure Selection drop-down list at the upper-left of the Document Window, select the James Casual option.

3. Select Figure, Set Figure Parent.

    The Figure Parent dialog box appears, as shown in Figure 2-30.

4. In the Figure Parent dialog box, select the Ground object and click OK.

    The default figure becomes a child of the ground item.

5. Select File, Save As and save the file as **New figure parent.pz3**.

FIGURE 2-30

The Figure Parent dialog box

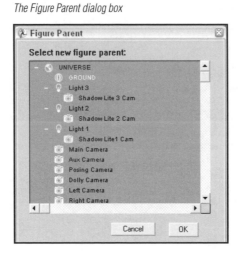

CHAPTER SUMMARY

This chapter explained how to work with figures in the Pose Room including loading figures from the Library, moving figures within the scene, and changing figure parameters and properties. You can use several menu commands in the Figure menu to alter a figure's height and style. You also learned how to select body parts in the Document Window and in the Hierarchy Editor.

What You Have Learned

In this chapter, you
- Loaded figures from the Library and saved the altered figures back to the Library.
- Moved figures about the scene and aligned the current figure to the floor.
- Changed a figure's properties, including its name and visibility.
- Altered the figure's height and style using menu commands.
- Selected various body parts using the Actor List in the Document Window.
- Used the Hierarchy Editor to select, hide, rename, and re-parent scene elements.

Key Terms from This Chapter

Figure. A character loaded into Poser that can be posed using the various interface controls.

Library. A collection of data that can be loaded into the scene.

Figure Circle control. A circle that surrounds the figure and enables the entire figure to be moved as one unit.

Genitalia. Male and female sex organs that can be visible or hidden.

Body part. The defined pieces that make up a figure.

Element. Any scene object that can be selected, including body parts, props, cameras, and lights.

Hierarchy. A linked chain of objects connected from parent to child.

Parent. The controlling object in a hierarchy chain. Child objects also move along with the parent object.

Child. The following object in a hierarchy chain. Child objects can move independently of the parent object.

chapter

3

EDITING AND POSING
Figures

1. Load and save poses.

2. Use the basic editing tools.

3. Use the parameter dials.

4. Use symmetry, limits, and balance.

5. Use inverse kinematics.

6. Use deformers.

7. Create morph targets.

chapter 3 EDITING AND POSING
Figures

I've covered enough background material, so in this chapter you'll finally get to posing, the task that Poser was made for. Posing figures is surprisingly easy, just grab a body part and move it into position. All attached body parts will move along with the selected part in the same way they move in real life. In other words, if you raise the upper arm of a model, the lower arm, wrist, and hand will move with it.

To help with the task of positioning figure body parts, you can use the **Editing tools**. Within the Editing tools are tools to **translate**, rotate, twist, **scale**, **taper**, and even color the various elements. Another way to position elements is to alter their parameters using the Parameter Dials that appear in the Parameters/Properties palette. By dragging these dials, you can alter the parameter values.

Poser includes several menu options that you can use to help you as you pose figures in the scene. The **Symmetry** menu includes options for copying the element

poses on the left side of the object to the right side and vice versa. You can also copy arm and leg poses between opposite sides, swap poses on either side and straighten the torso. The Use Limits option restricts the movement of elements to be within designated values, and the Auto Balance option automatically moves figure elements to maintain its center of gravity.

The **Inverse Kinematics** options enable you to move all the elements in a pre-set chain by positioning the last (or goal) element in the chain. This is particularly convenient for positioning hands and feet and having the arms and legs follow naturally. Poser also lets you create your own Inverse Kinematic chains.

To deform the surface of an object, you can use the magnet and wave deformers to actually pull vertices away from a body part. You can turn these deformations into **morph targets** that appear in the Parameters palette.

Tools You'll Use

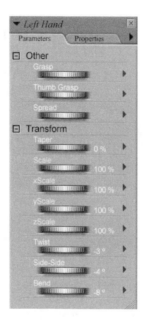

LOAD LIBRARY
FIGURES

What You'll Do

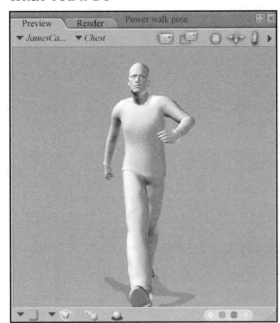

In this lesson, you learn how to work with the Library to load and save poses.

LOAD AND SAVE POSES

If you don't know where to start to create a figure pose, you can once again look to the Library to find some predefined poses that you can load on the current figure. You can also easily save poses in a number of ways including saving them to the Library or using the memory dots.

Loading Poses from the Library

To access the available poses from the Library, click the Poses category and navigate the folders to the folder containing the types of poses you want to apply to the current figure. Within each folder are thumbnails of

FIGURE 3-1

Loaded Library pose

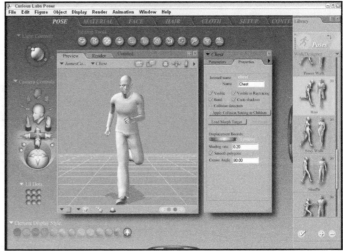

the various poses. With a pose thumbnail selected, click the Change Pose button at the bottom of the Library palette. The selected pose is then applied to the current figure. Figure 3-1 shows several pose thumbnails contained in the Action folder with one applied to the default figure.

Saving Poses to the Library

You can also save poses to the Library using the Add to Library button located at the bottom of the Library palette. This button opens a simple dialog box where you can name the current pose. The thumbnail for the current pose is added to the top of the open Library folder.

Removing Poses from the Library

The Remove from Library button in the Library palette permanently deletes the selected thumbnail pose.

CAUTION

Removing a thumbnail from the Library palette permanently removes the item from the hard drive.

Using the Pose Dots

If you want to temporarily remember a specific pose for use during the current session, you can use the memory dots to place the current figure's pose. To remember poses, select the **Pose Dots** option from the pop-up menu at the top of the Memory Dots control. Clicking a dot once adds the current pose to the selected dot where it can be recalled at any time by clicking again on the dot that holds the pose. Holding down the Alt key while clicking a pose dot clears the dot. For example, if you pose the right arm raised up high and you like its position, you can click one of the pose dots to remember the position of the figure. Then if you make a mistake, you can recall this saved pose by simply clicking the Set Pose Dot. You can accomplish the same task using the Edit, Memorize and Edit, Restore menu commands.

Load a pose from the Library

1. Open Poser with the default man visible.

2. Click the side control to the right of the interface to open the Library palette or select Window, Libraries.

3. Click the Poses category at the top of the Library palette and navigate to the Walk Designer folder.

4. Select the Power Walk thumbnail and click the Replace Pose button at the bottom of the Library palette.

   The selected pose is applied to the default figure, as shown in Figure 3-2.

5. Select File, Save As and save the file as **Power walk pose.pz3**.

Save a pose to the Library

1. Open Poser with the default man visible.

2. Click the side control to the right of the interface to open the Library palette or select Window, Libraries.

3. Click the Poses category at the top of the Library palette and navigate to the Other Actions folder.

4. Click and drag the right upper arm upward to raise the figure's arm.

FIGURE 3-2

Power walk pose from the Library

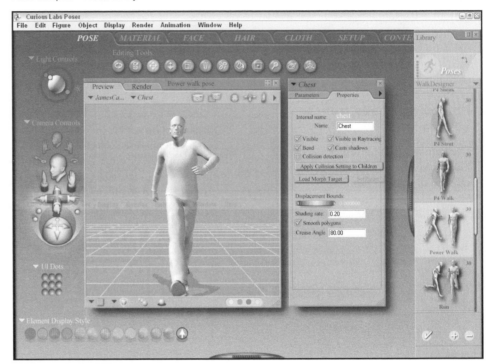

FIGURE 3-3

New pose added to the Library

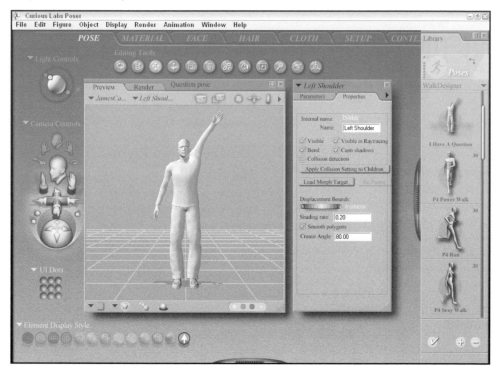

5. Select the Jumping 02 thumbnail and click the Add to Library button ⊕ at the bottom of the Library palette.

   The Set Name dialog box appears.

6. Enter **I have a question** as the name of this pose and click OK.

   Another dialog box appears asking if you want to save the morph channels.

7. Click Yes. The Save Frames dialog box then appears where you can save multiple animation frames with the pose. Select the Single Frame option and click OK.

8. Select File, Save As and save the file as **Question pose.pz3**.

   The new pose appears with the open folder of thumbnails, as shown in Figure 3-3.

USE THE BASIC
EDITING TOOLS

What You'll Do

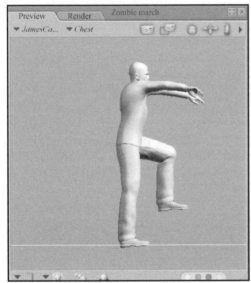

In this lesson, you learn how to pose figure elements using the basic editing tools.

In order to pose figures, you need to learn how to move, rotate, twist, and scale the different figure elements. The Editing tools in Figure 3-4 can help you accomplish these tasks. You can open this set of tools using Window, Editing Tools. You can select only one editing tool at a time, with the current tool being highlighted in yellow.

QUICKTIP

You can use all the Editing tools also on figures and props in addition to body parts.

Moving Figure Elements

One of the first places to start when posing a figure is to move the various elements. A good example of this is dragging the upper arm to raise or lower the entire arm. There are a couple of Editing tools you can use to move figure elements, including the Translate/Pull tool and the Translate In/Out tool.

FIGURE 3-4

Editing tools

Rotate tool
Twist tool
Translate/Pull tool
Translate In/Out tool
Scale tool
Taper tool
Chain Break tool
Color tool
Grouping tool
View Magnifier tool
Morphing tool
Direct Manipulation tool

Editing Tools

The Translate/Pull tool (T) is the one tool that is selected when Poser is first started. It allows you to move figure elements within the XY plane. The Translate In/Out tool (Z) moves the selected element in and out of the Z plane, which is towards or away from the current camera view. Figure 3-5 shows a simple pose accomplished by translating the upper arms using these two tools.

Rotating and Twisting Elements

You use the Rotate tool (R) to rotate elements about their joints. For example, if you drag on the selected forearm object with the Rotate tool, it will rotate about the elbow joint. Dragging an element with the Twist tool (W) causes it to rotate about its joint axis. For example, dragging the abdomen element with the Twist tool makes a figure twist about its waist. Figure 3-6 shows a figure whose forearms have been rotated with the Rotate tool and whose waist has been twisted with the Twist tool.

Scaling and Tapering Elements

The Scale tool (S) changes the size of the element along a single axis, but you can

FIGURE 3-5
Translated arms

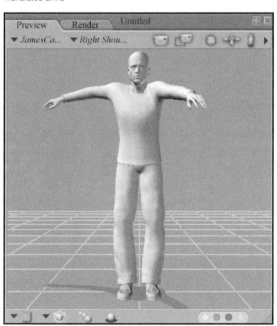

FIGURE 3-6
Rotated forearms and twisted waist

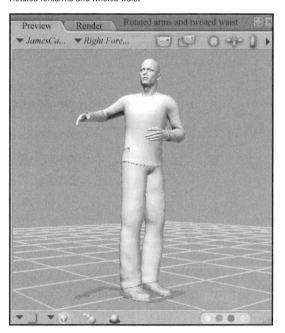

cause the element to be uniformly scaled along all axes at the same time by holding down the Shift key while dragging. The Taper tool (P) is similar to the Scale tool, except it scales only one end of an element, leaving the other unchanged. The result of a tapered element is to make the object long and thin or short and fat. Figure 3-7 shows a figure whose chest and collarbones have been scaled.

Coloring Elements

Although the real place to apply colors and textures to a figure element is in the Material Room, which is covered in Chapter 4, "Adding Materials," you can place basic flat colors to elements using the Color tool (C). Clicking with this tool on an element causes a pop-up color palette, shown in Figure 3-8, to appear. You can select a color from this pop-up color palette by dragging over the color that you want to select.

Clicking a color in the palette closes the pop-up color palette. Figure 3-9 shows a figure with several colors.

NOTE

The Color tool adds colors to material groups such as Shirt, Pants, Skin Color, and so on, instead of to elements. More on material groups is covered in Chapter 4, "Adding Materials."

FIGURE 3-7
Scaled chest

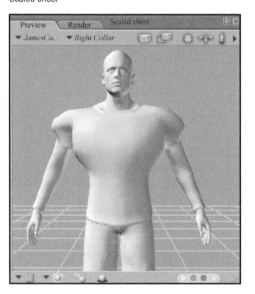

FIGURE 3-8
Pop-up color palette

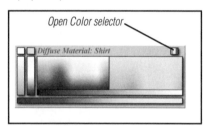

FIGURE 3-9
Figure with colors

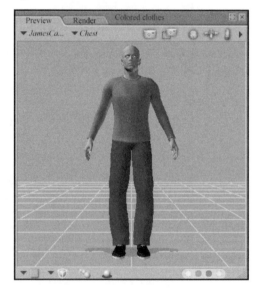

Using the View Magnifier Tool

The View Magnifier tool allows you to zoom in on an area without changing the parameters of the current camera. To use it, simply click the area that you want to zoom in on. Each successive click zooms further in on an area. Clicking with the Ctrl key held down zooms out. You can also zoom in on a region by dragging over the zoom area with the View Magnifier tool. Figure 3-10 shows a zoomed figure that used the View Magnifier tool.

Using the Direct Manipulation Tool

The Direct Manipulation tool surrounds the selected element with icons that can be used to move, rotate, and scale the selected element, as shown in Figure 3-11. By dragging these controls, you can change the element's position, **rotation**, and scale in the X, Y, and Z axes. These controls have the same effect as dragging the corresponding parameter dial.

FIGURE 3-10
Zoomed figure

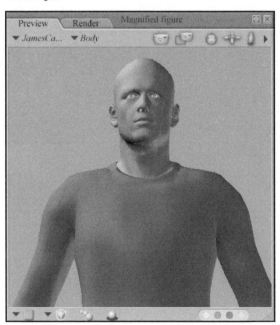

FIGURE 3-11
Direct Manipulation Tool controls

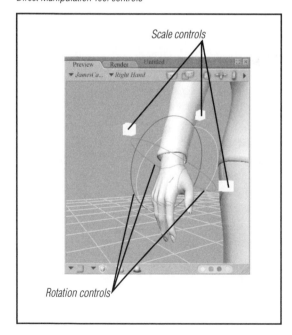

Lesson 2   Use the Basic Editing Tools

Use the Editing tools

1. Open Poser with the default man visible.

2. Select Window, Editing Tools to make the Editing Tools buttons visible if they aren't already visible.

3. Click the Translate/Pull tool 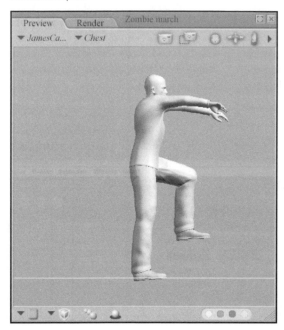 (or press the T key) and drag on the left shoulder to raise it to be horizontal with the ground. Repeat for the right shoulder so both arms are outstretched.

4. Click the Translate In/Out tool (or press the Z key) and drag the left shoulder until it is stretched in front of the figure. Repeat for the right shoulder so both arms are stretched out in front of the figure.

   The chest of the figure will lean forward as you pull the arms forward.

5. Select From Left from the Camera Controls pop-up menu.

6. Click the Rotate tool (or press the R key) and drag the abdomen until the figure's torso is vertical again.

7. Click the Translate/Pull tool (or press the T key), select and drag the left foot, and pull it out and up from the figure as if the figure were taking a step.

   The side view of the figure shows the figure with both arms outstretched taking a step forward, as shown in Figure 3-12.

8. Select File, Save As and save the file as **Zombie march.pz3**.

FIGURE 3-12

Zombie march pose

FIGURE 3-13

Figure with green shirt and black pants

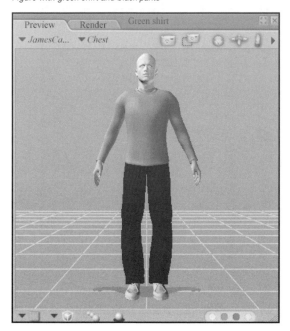

1. Open Poser with the default man visible.

2. Select Window, Editing Tools to make the Editing Tools buttons visible, if necessary.

3. Click the Color tool ⊙ (or press the C key) and click the figure's chest.

   A pop-up color palette appears with the title Diffuse Material: Shirt.

4. Select a green color.

   The shirt area of the figure is colored green and the pop-up color palette is closed.

5. Apply a black color to the figure's pants and a light red color to the figure's hand.

   Notice that changing the skin color doesn't change the figure's head color or the figure's fingernails, as shown in Figure 3-13.

6. Select File, Save As and save the file as **Green shirt.pz3**.

Use the Direct Manipulation tool

1. Open Poser with the default figure visible.

2. Select Window, Editing Tools to make the Editing Tools buttons visible (if necessary).

3. Select the hip object in the Document Window and drag the Move Camera in XZ Plane control in the Camera Controls to zoom in on the hip region.

4. Select the Direct Manipulation tool from the Editing tools.

   Manipulation controls surround the hip element.

5. Drag the right scale control icon to the right in the Document Window.

6. Drag the red rotation control to rotate the figure slightly forward.

   The figure now has a larger belly section, as shown in Figure 3-14.

7. Select File, Save As and save the file as **Direct manipulation tool.pz3**.

FIGURE 3-14
Scaled and rotated element

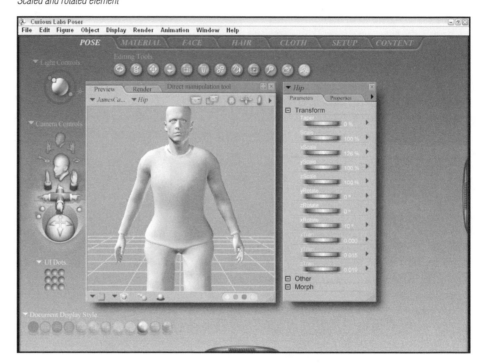

USE THE PARAMETER
DIALS

What You'll Do

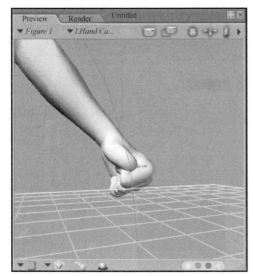

In this lesson, you learn how to pose figure elements using the parameter dials.

For more precise changes to a pose, you can use the parameter dials found in the Parameters/Properties palette, shown in Figure 3-15. You can open this palette by selecting Window, Parameter Dials. The parameter dials affect the selected element that is listed at the top of the palette.

NOTE

The available dials are different depending on the item and figure that is selected.

Changing Dial Values

To the right of each parameter dial is its value. To change this value, click and drag the dial to the right to increase its value or to the left to decrease its value. If you click the value itself, the value is selected within a text field where you can type a new value using the keyboard.

FIGURE 3-15
Parameters/Properties palette

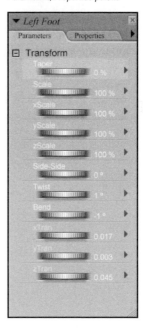

Resetting Dial Values

To the right of each parameter dial is a black arrow icon that opens a pop-up menu of options. If you select the Reset option, the value changes to its last memorized value. You can set the memorized value for a figure, element, light, or camera using the Edit, Memorize menu command.

QUICKTIP

You can also reset a parameter value by clicking the parameter dial with the Alt key held down.

Changing Parameter Settings

Double-clicking the parameter dial or selecting the Settings option from the pop-up menu opens the Edit Parameter Dial dialog box, shown in Figure 3-16. Using this dialog box, you can change the current value, minimum and maximum limit values, the parameter name, and its sensitivity. Lower sensitivity values require a larger mouse drag to change the parameter value.

Understanding Unique Parameters

Most of the parameter dials relate directly to the Editing tools such as Taper, Scale, Twist, and Translate, but several of the dials found in the Parameters palette are unique. These unique parameters are actually morph targets and you can alter them by changing the parameters' values. Some sample morph targets include the following:

- **Side-Side, Bend, Up-Down, Front-Back:** Causes elements to be rotated in a specific direction based on the element. For example, the Side-Side parameter rotates the torso and feet to the side, the Bend parameter rotates the torso forward and backwards and the feet up and down, and the Front-Back parameter moves the arms forwards and backwards.

- **Eye Morphs:** When an eye element is selected, several parameters are available for changing the size of the pupil and iris.

- **Grasp, Thumb Grasp, Spread:** When hand objects are selected, the palette includes parameters for clenching all fingers together and the thumb together and spreading the fingers apart.

TIP

A lesson later in this chapter shows how you can create your own morph targets using **deformers**.

FIGURE 3-16

Edit Parameter Dial dialog box

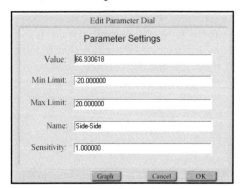

Creating Parameter Groups

Custom figures can have many parameters. For example, many animal figures include custom parameters for controlling the curve of their tails. To handle figures with a large number of parameters, you can create a parameter group using the pop-up menu located at the top of the Parameters/ Properties palette. Selecting the Create New Group option from the pop-up menu opens a simple dialog box where you can name the new parameter group. This group name then appears in the Parameters palette.

To add parameters to the group, simply drag the parameter title and drop it on the new group name. Clicking the plus or minus icon to the left of the group name lets you expand and contract the parameter group. Figure 3-17 shows a new group named *NewGroup* added to the Parameters/Properties palette. You can delete selected groups by selecting the Delete Selected Group option in the pop-up menu.

QUICKTIP

The order of the parameters in the new group follows the order that they were dropped into the group, but parameters can be rearranged by dragging and dropping parameters above or below other parameters.

FIGURE 3-17

Custom parameter group

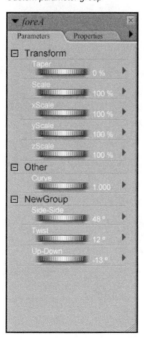

Use the parameter dials

1. Open Poser with the default man visible.

2. Select Window, Parameter Dials to make the Parameters/Properties palette visible, if necessary.

3. Select the abdomen element in the Document Window and drag the Side-Side parameter dial to the right to 45 degrees.

4. Select the left foot element and click the xTran parameter, and then type the value **0.531**.

   The figure's torso bends to the right and its left foot is pointed away from the body, as shown in Figure 3-18.

5. Select File, Save As and save the file as **Pointed toe.pz3**.

FIGURE 3-18

Pointed toe pose

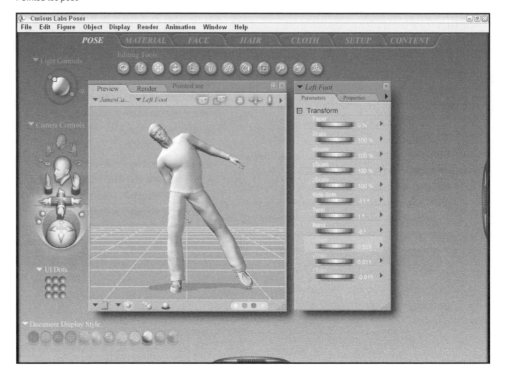

FIGURE 3-19

Clenched fist

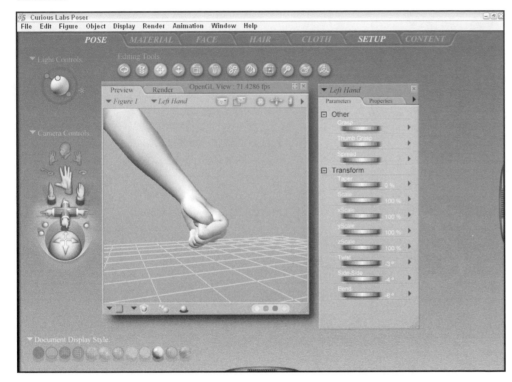

1. Open Poser with the default man visible.

2. Select Window, Parameter Dials to make the Parameters/Properties palette visible, if necessary.

3. Click the right hand camera 🖐 in the Camera Controls.

4. Select the right hand element in the Document Window and drag the Grasp parameter dial and the Thumb Grasp parameter dial all the way to the right.

   Changing the custom Grasp and Thumb Grasp parameters results in a clenched fist, as shown in Figure 3-19.

5. Select File, Save As and save the file as **Clenched fist.pz3**.

Create a parameter group

1. Open Poser with the default man visible.

2. Select Window, Parameter Dials to make the Parameters/Properties palette visible, if necessary.

3. Select the hip element in the Document Window.

4. Select the Create New Group option from the pop-up menu at the top of the Parameters/ Properties palette.

5. In the New Group Name dialog box that opens, name the group **X-axis parameters**.

6. Select and drag the xScale, xRotate, and xTran parameters and drop them on the new group name.

7. Repeat steps 4-6 to create groups for the Y-axis and Z-axis parameters.

   After expanding each of the new groups, the Parameters palette looks like the one shown in Figure 3-20.

8. Select File, Save As and save the file as **Custom parameter groups.pz3**.

FIGURE 3-20

Custom parameter groups

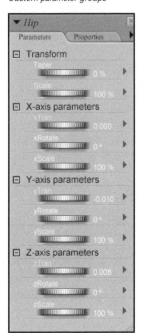

USE SYMMETRY, LIMITS, AND BALANCE

What You'll Do

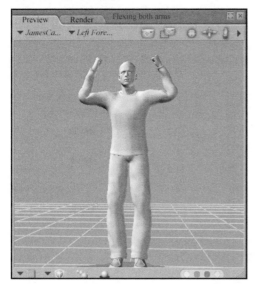

In this lesson, you learn how to control figure poses using the Symmetry, Limits, and Auto Balance options.

Human figures have a wonderful symmetry that you can use to your advantage. If you work to get the right arm in a perfect position, you can use the Figure, Symmetry menu command to copy this pose to the left arm. Two other common properties that you can mimic using commands found in the Figure menu are limiting the movement of the various body parts to be realistic and having Poser compute the center of mass to have the figure maintain its balance.

Copying Between Sides

If the pose you are trying to realize is symmetrical, you can make it perfectly symmetrical by copying all parameter values applied to the left side of the figure to the right side and vice versa. Simply select the Figure, Symmetry, Left to Right or Right to Left menu commands. This causes a dialog box to appear asking if you want to

copy the joint zone's setup also. Figure 3-21 shows a simple figure whose left arm and foot were moved and its poses copied to the opposite side.

FIGURE 3-21
Left and right side symmetry

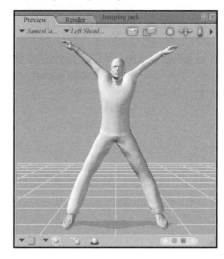

Copying Arm and Leg Poses

To copy the assumed pose of just an arm or a leg to the opposite arm or leg, select Figure, Symmetry. The options include Left Arm to Right Arm, Right Arm to Left Arm, Left Leg to Right Leg, and Right Leg to Left Leg.

Swapping Sides

If you've spent some time posing a figure only to realize that you've got the right side confused with the left side, you can use Figure, Symmetry, Swap Right and Left to fix the problem. This command symmetrically swaps all poses on either side of the figure's midline. There are also options to swap right and left arms and legs.

Straightening the Torso

As you pull on a hand or an arm to position the arm, you'll often find that the torso will follow. To straighten the torso, select Figure, Symmetry, Straighten Torso. This option leaves the arm and leg poses in place, but straightens the torso.

Using Limits

Poser is aware of exactly how far each body part can actually bend in order to maintain a realistic pose, but you can disable this option to allow body parts to move through one another. The Figure, Use Limits option is a toggle that you can enable or disable. When enabled, Poser restricts the movement of the body parts to realistic positions. For example, when dragging a figure's arm straight up with the Use Limits option enabled, Poser prevents the arm from moving farther than the head, as shown in Figure 3-22.

FIGURE 3-22
Using Limits prevents unnatural poses

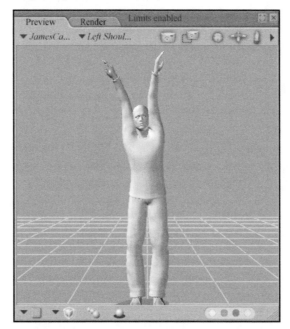

Using Auto Balance

Another helpful setting that can aid you in creating realistic poses is the Figure, Auto Balance option. This option, like Use Limits, is also a toggle button. When enabled, counter body parts are moved in order to maintain the centered weight of the figure. The pose shown in Figure 3-23 was created by moving the right foot with the Auto Balance option enabled. Poser moved the top half of the figure to the right to counter the foot's position.

FIGURE 3-23

Auto Balance center-balances figures

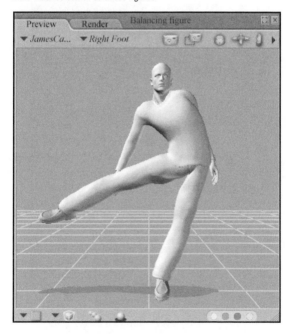

Use symmetry

1. Choose File, Open and select and open the Flexing arm.pz3 file.

   The file includes a figure with its left arm flexed and its fist closed.

2. Select Figure, Symmetry, Left to Right. A dialog box appears asking if you want to copy the joint zone's setup. Click Yes to accept this option.

   The pose for the left arm is then copied to the right arm, as shown in Figure 3-24.

3. Select File, Save As and save the file as **Flexing both arms.pz3**.

Use limits

1. Open Poser with the default man visible.

2. Enable the Figure, Use Limits option.

3. Select and drag the right forearm towards the center of the figure.

   With the Use Limits option enabled, you cannot move the forearm object into the center of the figure, as shown in Figure 3-25.

4. Select File, Save As and save the file as **Limits enabled.pz3**.

FIGURE 3-24
Symmetrical flexing arms

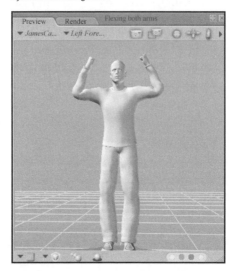

FIGURE 3-25
Figure with limits enabled

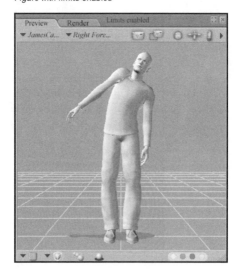

FIGURE 3-26

Figure with Auto Balance enabled

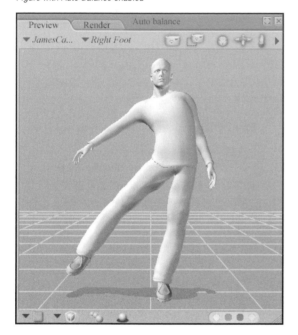

1. Open Poser with the default man visible.

2. Enable the Figure, Auto Balance option.

3. Select and drag the right foot upwards and away from the center of the figure and the right shoulder away from the body.

   With the Auto Balance option enabled, the torso automatically adjusts to the foot movement in order to maintain the object's center, as shown in Figure 3-26.

4. Select File, Save As and save the file as **Auto balance.pz3**.

USE INVERSE KINEMATICS

What You'll Do

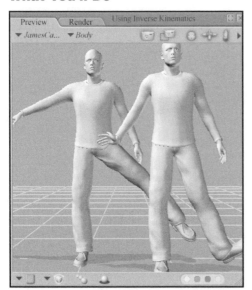

In this lesson, you learn how to use inverse kinematics.

Kinematics is the physics behind the movement of linked objects. Bone structures are a good example of a set of linked objects that can be defined using kinematic solutions. For example, because the shoulder is connected to the arm bones, which are connected to the hand, you can use kinematic equations to determine the position of the hand as the shoulder moves. Inverse kinematics works backwards by solving the shoulder's position as the hand is moved.

The benefit of inverse kinematics is that it is often easier to animate characters by placing their hands and feet than placing their hips and shoulders. For example, imagine a character walking across the floor and reaching for a door handle. To animate this sequence by moving only the upper thigh and upper arm bones would be difficult, but with inverse kinematics enabled, you can position the feet for the steps and the hand for the door handle and the remaining body parts just follow.

Enabling Inverse Kinematics

Inverse kinematics can only be enabled for a set of connected body parts referred to as a *kinematic chain*. For Poser, you can enable inverse kinematics (IK) for four kinematic chains—right and left arms and legs. IK is enabled by default for the legs, but not for the arms. You can enable or disable IK using the Figure, Use Inverse Kinematics menu·command. When enabled, a small check mark appears next to the menu.

Working with Inverse Kinematics

When Poser first loads, select the default figure's Left Thigh object and try to move it with the Translate/Pull tool. The Upper Thigh element might twist a little, but because it is part of the **IK chain**, it won't move out of place unless the end of the IK chain, the foot, is moved.

Now try disabling IK and moving the Upper Thigh element again. This time the upper thigh moves easily and the foot moves along with it. The trick is to learn when to use IK and when to disable it.

QUICKTIP

You should enable and use IK if you need to place the end of an IK chain such as a hand or a foot in a specific location, but for general body movement and poses, you can disable IK.

Viewing IK Chains

All existing IK chains are listed at the bottom of the Hierarchy Editor, as shown in Figure 3-27. Each IK chain lists all the elements included in the chain from root to end element, called the *goal*. To the left of each IK chain is a check box that you can use to enable and disable the selected IK chain.

Creating New IK Chains

You can create new IK chains using the Hierarchy Editor. You can create new IK chains for manually imported characters, for new types of figures such as the tail of an animal, or to add an attached prop to an existing IK chain. To create an IK chain, select Window, Hierarchy Editor to open the Hierarchy Editor. Scroll to the bottom of the Hierarchy Editor dialog box and select the IK Chains title. This makes the

FIGURE 3-27
IK chains in the Hierarchy Editor

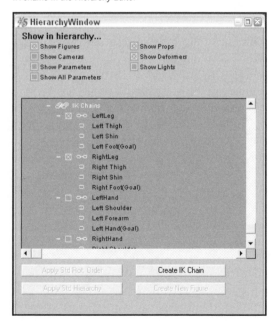

Create IK Chain button active. Clicking the Create IK Chain button opens a dialog box where you can give the new IK chain a name. The newly named IK chain appears at the bottom of the Hierarchy Editor. You can then drag and drop elements of the chain onto the new chain name. The first element under the new IK chain title is the root element and the last one is the goal. The goal element is marked with the word *goal* in parentheses.

NOTE

Newly created IK chains are also listed in the Figure, Use Inverse Kinematics menu command.

Using the Chain Break Tool

IK chains aren't the only elements that have control over other body parts. Actually, almost all body parts are connected and can influence one another. If you drag an arm element far enough, the torso will move along with it, but you can use the **Chain Break tool** (L) to prevent the movement of connected elements.

If you select the Chain Break tool, several chain break icons appear on the figure in Document Window, as shown in Figure 3-28. These icons mark body parts that are prevented from moving with adjacent elements. By default, the head, hip, right and left buttock elements have a chain break icon on them. This means that the head moves independently of the torso and the torso moves independently of the legs.

FIGURE 3-28
Default chain break icons

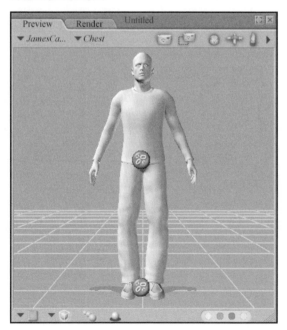

If you click an element with the Chain Break tool, you can place or remove these icons. For example, if you click the right and left collar elements, moving the arms will have no effect on the torso.

CAUTION

The chain break icon for the hip cannot be removed.

FIGURE 3-29

Inverse kinematics poses

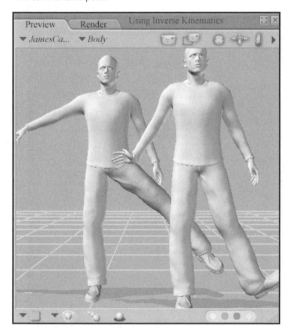

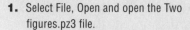

1. Select File, Open and open the Two figures.pz3 file.

   The figure on the left of the Document Window has inverse kinematics enabled for both arms and legs, but the figure on the right has IK disabled.

2. Select and drag the left foot on both figures away from the center of the figure.

3. Select and drag the right hand on both figures away from the center of the figure.

   Notice how the figure with IK enabled allowed the entire arm to move when the IK goal (the hand and the foot) was selected and moved. Also, notice that the figure with IK disabled lets you move independent elements and all children elements move with their parent, but moving a child's elements has little effect on their parent, as shown in Figure 3-29.

4. Select File, Save As and save the file as **Using Inverse Kinematics.pz3**.

Create an IK chain

1. Select File, Open and open the Lion.pz3 file. This file includes a loaded lion figure.

2. Select Window, Hierarchy Editor to open the Hierarchy Editor.

3. Scroll to the bottom of the Hierarchy Editor and select the IK Chains title. Then, click the Create IK Chain button at the bottom of the dialog box.

4. In the Set Name dialog box that appears, type the name, **Tail**, and click OK.

5. Scroll back up in the Hierarchy Editor and select and drag the Tail 1, Tail 2, Tail 3, Tail 4, and Tuft elements and drop them on the newly created Tail IK Chain title.

6. Reorder the tail elements so they appear in order with the Tuft element designated as the goal.

7. Click the square box to the left of the Tail title ☑ ∞ Tail to enable the IK chain. Then, select and move the Tuft element.

   As the Tuft element is moved, the other members of the IK chain are also moved, as shown in Figure 3-30.

8. Select File, Save As and save the file as **New IK chain.pz3**.

FIGURE 3-30

New tail IK chain

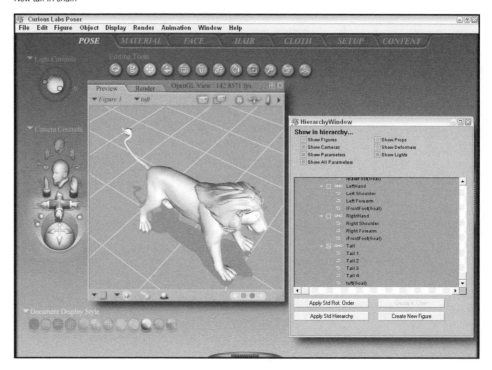

FIGURE 3-31

Chain break applied to right collar

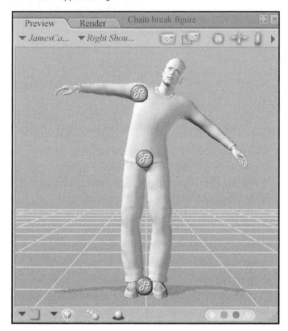

1. Open Poser with the default figure visible.

2. Select Window, Editing Tools to make the Editing Tools buttons visible, if necessary.

3. Select and pull the left shoulder element away from the center of the figure.

   Notice how the torso moves with the shoulder element.

4. Select the Chain Break tool from the Editing tools (or press the L key) and click the right collar element.

   A chain break icon is placed in the center of the element, as shown in Figure 3-31.

5. Select the Translate/Pull tool from the Editing tools (or press the T key) and drag the right shoulder.

   With the chain break icon placed on the right collar element, the torso remains fixed as you move the right upper arm.

6. Select File, Save As and save the file as **Chain break figure.pz3**.

USE DEFORMERS

What You'll Do

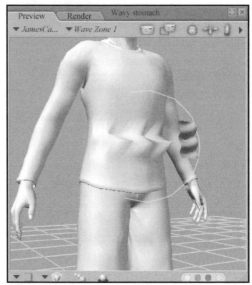

In this lesson, you learn how to use deformers to manipulate the surfaces of objects.

The Editing tools limit the editing that you can do to the individual body parts, but they cannot change the surface of objects to bulge muscles or stretch the body's skin. To deform the skin in this manner, you can use several specialized objects called *deformers*.

There are three deformer objects and they are all available in the Object menu. The three deformers are:

- **Magnet:** Used to pull vertices away from an object.

- **Wave:** Used to deform surface vertices in a wave pattern.

- **Wind Force:** Used to add a wind force to the scene that is used by the hair and cloth simulations. More on the Wind Force deformer is covered in the Chapter 8, "Working with Hair," and Chapter 9, "Working with Cloth."

Creating a Magnet Deformer

You can add the magnet deformer to the scene using the Object, Create Magnet menu command. The magnet deformer can only be applied when the body part that you want to deform is selected. It cannot be used on a figure. The magnet deformer consists of three separate parts—the magnet object, its base, and the magnet zone. You can move, rotate, and scale each of these parts using the standard Editing tools.

Using the Magnet Parts

The magnet base and the magnet object set the amount of pull that's applied to deform the body parts. The farther away these two parts, the stronger the deformation. The magnet zone defines the area that can be deformed by the magnet deformer. Figure 3-32 shows an example of the magnet deformer in action. The magnet base is positioned at the side of the head and the magnet object is positioned away from the head, thus causing all vertices within the magnet zone to be attracted towards the magnet object, but the magnet zone limits only the ear to be deformed.

TIP

You can hide deformers from the scene using the Display, Deformers, Hide All menu command and make them visible again with the Display, Deformers, Show All or the Display, Deformers, Current Selection Only menu commands.

Deforming Additional Elements

Initially, only the part that is selected when the magnet is created is deformed. However, you can add more elements to be deformed by the same magnet object by clicking the Add Element to Deform button in the Properties palette when the magnet object is selected. This button opens a

Choose Actor list that displays all the available scene elements in a hierarchical list. Select the additional element you want to deform and click OK. The additional element will be deformed only if it is within the magnet zone.

FIGURE 3-32
Magnet deformer

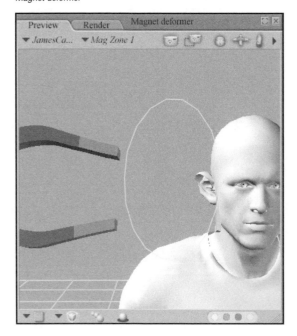

Setting Magnet Zone Falloff

When deforming muscles, you'll want a nice smooth bulge instead a sharp pointy one. You can control the shape of the vertices that are deformed using a Falloff graph. To open the Magnet Zone Falloff curve, select the magnet zone object and click the Edit Falloff Graph button in the Properties palette. The Magnet Zone Falloff curve, shown in Figure 3-33, displays the falloff curve. You can edit this curve by dragging its control points, which are small vertical lines on the curve. To create a new control point, just click the curve where you want the new control point to be.

Creating a Wave Deformer

You can add the wave deformer to the scene using the Object, Create Wave menu command. It deforms objects using wave patterns. The wave deformer consists of two separate parts—the wave object and the wave zone. You can move, rotate, and scale both of these parts using the standard Editing tools. The wave object includes options in the Properties palette for applying the deformation in a Radial direction using concentric circles or a Directional option for creating linear waves. You can also select to deform the vertices in the

FIGURE 3-33

Magnet Zone Falloff curve

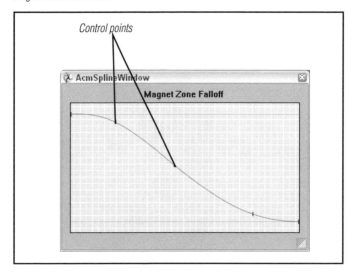

Editing and Posing Figures   Chapter 3

direction of the wave deformer or along the object's normal vectors. Figure 3-34 shows a wave deformer applied to a figure's arm.

Deforming Additional Elements

Initially, only the part that is selected when the wave is created is deformed. However, you can add more elements to be deformed by the same wave object by clicking the Add Element to Deform button in the Properties palette when the wave object is selected. This button opens a Choose Actor list that displays all the available scene elements in a hierarchical list. Select the additional element you want to deform and click OK. The additional element will be deformed only if it is within the wave zone.

Setting Wave Zone Falloff

The wave deformer includes the same Falloff curve that you can select and edit using the Edit Falloff Graph button in the Properties palette.

FIGURE 3-34

Wave deformer

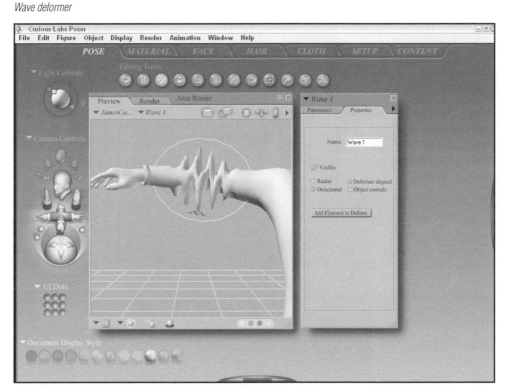

Use the magnet deformer

1. Open Poser with the default figure visible.

2. Select the Face camera 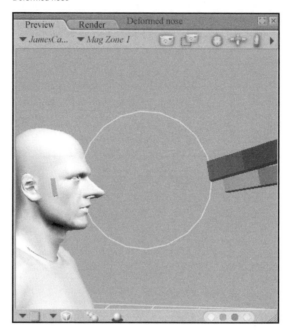 and rotate it with the Rotate sphere so the side of the head is visible.

3. Select the head object in the Document Window and choose Object, Create Magnet.

   The magnet object, the magnet base, and the magnet zone are all added to the scene.

4. Select the Rotate tool from the Editing tools and rotate the magnet base so it is positioned at the base of the figure's nose. Select the Translate/Pull tool and move the magnet zone so only the nose is within it. Then, move the magnet object away from the head.

   The nose is deformed and extended from the face, as shown in Figure 3-35.

5. Select File, Save As and save the file as **Deformed nose.pz3**.

FIGURE 3-35

Deformed nose

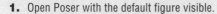
FIGURE 3-36

Wavy stomach

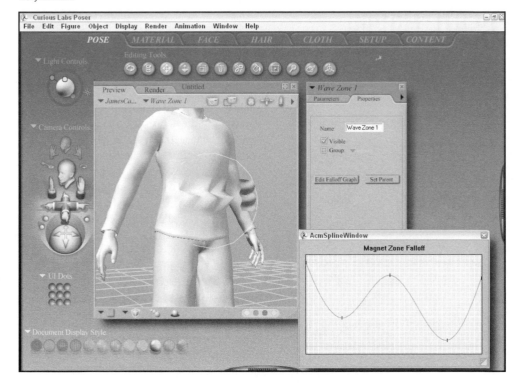

1. Open Poser with the default figure visible.

2. Drag on the Move XZ Plane control in the Camera Controls to zoom in on the stomach region. Rotate the view with the Rotate sphere.

3. Select the abdomen object in the Document Window and choose Object, Create Wave.

   The wave object and the wave zone are added to the scene.

4. Use the Rotate and Translate tools from the Editing tools and move and rotate the wave base so it is vertically positioned in front of the stomach. Select the Translate/Pull tool and move the magnet zone so only the front of the stomach is within the zone.

5. Select the wave zone object and click the Edit Falloff Graph button in the Properties palette to open the Falloff graph. Click at the center of the curve to add a new control point and drag the control points to create a wavy pattern.

   The stomach is deformed with a wave pattern, as shown in Figure 3-36.

6. Select File, Save As and save the file as **Wavy stomach.pz3**.

CREATE MORPH
TARGETS

What You'll Do

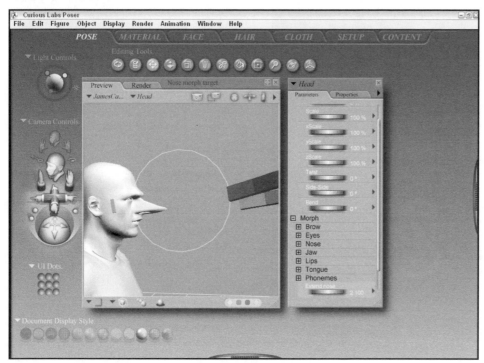

In this lesson, you learn how to create morph targets.

Once the surface of an object is deformed, you can use the deformation to create a new morph target. Morph targets appear within the Parameters palette as a new named parameter. Dragging the parameter dial changes the deformation between the full deformation amount (with a value of 1.0) to an inverted deformation (with a value of -1.0). Morph targets provide an easy way to create subtle surface changes and they can be animated.

Spawning a New Morph Target

With a deformation set to its maximum value, you can create a new morph target using the Object, Spawn Morph Target menu command. This command opens a simple dialog box where you can name the morph target. This name appears in the Parameters palette for the selected object. Figure 3-37 shows a new morph target created for the ear-pulling deformation.

Deleting Morph Targets

To delete a morph target, open the Hierarchy Editor, locate and select the morph target, and press the Delete key. Morph targets will be visible when the Show Parameters option is enabled. The morph target will be located under its object.

Creating Full Body Morphs

If your figure includes several morphs that you want to include all together in a single morph target, such as a figure flexing all his arm muscles, you can create a full body morph targets using the Figure, Create Full Body Morph menu command. This command will make a simple dialog box appear where you can name the morph target. The morph target appears in the Parameters palette when the Body actor is selected.

Using the Morphing Tool

The Morphing tool (also known as the Morph Putty tool) can directly deform an

FIGURE 3-37

Ear-pulling morph target

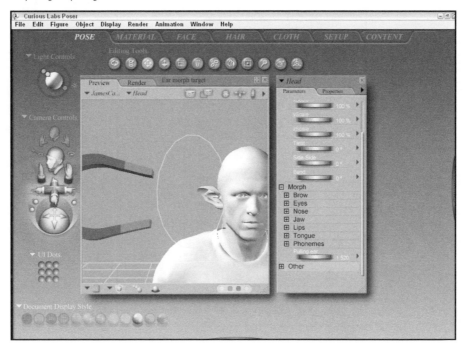

element with a morph target applied to it by moving its vertices. Selecting the Morphing tool opens the Morphing Tool panel for the selected object and displays all the available morph targets that you can work with. Figure 3-38 shows the Morphing Tool panel for the head object, which includes morph targets for deforming the ears, mouth, nose, and so on.

At the top of the Morphing Tool panel are two buttons. The Putty button lets you drag to move vertices for the selected morphs and the Pin button lets you click to set vertices that will not move. The Clear Morphs button removes any morph editing done with the Putty tool and the Clear Pins button removes any placed pins. The Exaggeration Min and Max dials are used to control

the limits of the morph. Clicking the small button to the left of each morph will toggle a lock on the morph. Locked morphs have a small lock icon displayed next to their name.

FIGURE 3-38
Morphing Tool panel

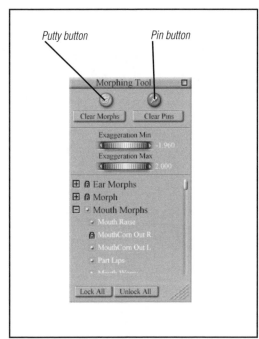

FIGURE 3-39

Extended nose

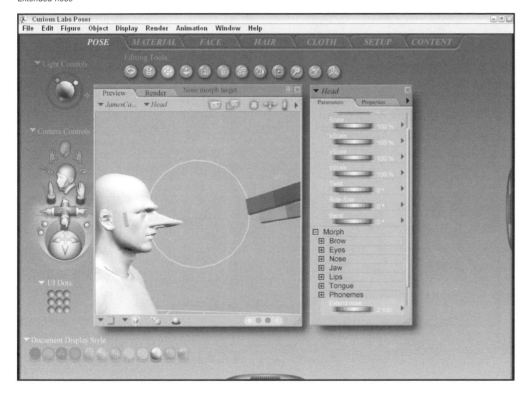

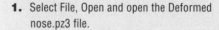

Create a morph target

1. Select File, Open and open the Deformed nose.pz3 file.

2. Select the head object in the Document Window and select Object, Spawn Morph Target.

3. In the Morph Name dialog box, type the name **Extend nose** and click OK.

   A new morph target is added to the bottom of the Parameters palette.

4. Drag the Extend nose parameter to a value over 2.0.

   The nose is extended in the Document Window, as shown in Figure 3-39.

5. Select File, Save As and save the file as **Nose morph target.pz3**.

Use the Morphing tool

1. Open Poser with the default figure visible.

2. Select Window, Editing Tools to make the Editing Tools buttons visible, if necessary.

3. Select the head object in the Document Window and choose the Face camera in the Camera Controls.

4. Select the Morphing tool 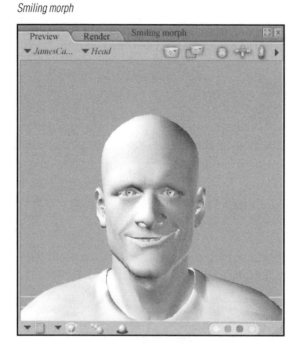 from the Editing tools.

   The Morphing Tool panel opens with all available morphs listed.

5. Click the small button Morph to the left of the Nose and Eyes sections in the Morphing Tool panel to lock them.

6. Click above and to the side of the mouth and drag with the Morphing tool.

   The mouth morphs into a smile, as shown in Figure 3-40.

7. Select File, Save As and save the file as **Smiling morph.pz3**.

FIGURE 3-40
Smiling morph

CHAPTER SUMMARY

This chapter showed how figures can be edited and posed within the Pose Room using the Editing tools, the parameter dials, and several menu commands in the Figure menu, including Symmetry, Set Limits, and Auto Balance. Inverse kinematics was also explained and demonstrated along with the remaining editing tools. The final section discussed using the magnet and wave deformers to create new morph targets.

What You Have Learned

In this chapter, you
- Loaded and saved poses to and from the Library.
- Remembered a specific pose using the pose dots.
- Moved, rotated, twisted, scaled, and tapered figure body parts using the Editing tools.
- Changed body parts colors using the Color tool.
- Used the View Magnifier tool to zoom in on an area in the Document Window.
- Changed a figure's body part using the parameter dials.

- Used the Symmetry, Use Limits, and Auto Balance Figure menu commands to control a figure while being posed.
- Learned how inverse kinematics can be used to position parent objects by moving their children.
- Created a new IK chain for the figure.
- Controlled which objects are moved along with other body parts using the Chain Break tool.
- Used the magnet and wave deformers to deform the element surfaces.
- Created new morph targets for the Parameters palette.

Key Terms from This Chapter

Pose dots. An interface control used to remember and recall a specific figure pose.

Editing tools. A selection of tools used to manipulate and transform scene elements.

Translation. The process of moving an object within the scene.

Rotation. The process of spinning and reorienting an object within the scene.

Scaling. The process of changing the size of an object within the scene.

Tapering. A scaling operation that changes the size of only one end of an object.

Symmetry. A property that occurs when one half of an object is identical to the opposite side.

Kinematics. The branch of physics that is used to calculate the movement of linked objects.

Inverse kinematics. A unique method of calculating the motion of linked objects that enables child objects to control the position and orientation of their parent object.

IK chain. A hierarchy of linked objects that have an inverse kinematics solution applied.

Chain Break tool. A tool used to prevent the movement of one object from moving a connected object from its current position.

Deformer. An object used to deform the surface of body parts by moving vertices.

Morph target. A custom parameter that defines an object deformation that appears as a parameter in the Parameters palette.

4

ADDING
Materials

1. Learn the Material Room interface.

2. Load and save materials.

3. Create simple materials.

4. Use material nodes.

5. Learn the various material nodes.

6. Create a material group.

chapter 4 ADDING Materials

After loading and posing a figure, you can add many details to the scene using materials. *Materials* are coverings used for the various elements in the scene. They can be as simple as a color, or as complex as a full texture with bumps and highlights.

You can load Poser materials, like many other facets of Poser, from the Library palette or create them by hand using the controls found in the Material Room. Within the Material Room is the **Shader Window**, which includes two different interface panels. The Simple panel includes only basic material properties such as **Diffuse Color**, **Highlights**, Ambient, Reflection, Bump, and **Transparency**. The Advanced panel includes an interface for compositing nodes to create multilayer materials.

Advanced materials are created using sets of values called *nodes*, which are combined in such a way that one node controls the value of a connected node. Every node includes a Value Input and a Value Output icon that can be connected, forming a chain of values. You can create several categories of nodes, including a set for performing mathematical functions, a category to control different lighting models, and several 2D and 3D textures that can be manipulated using values.

To apply materials to certain sections of a figure, you can create custom **material groups** using the Grouping tool and the Group Editor panel.

Tools You'll Use

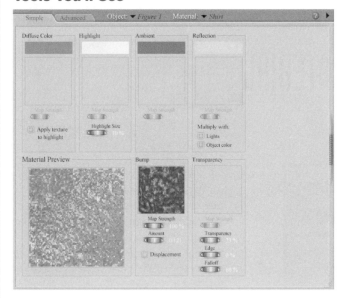

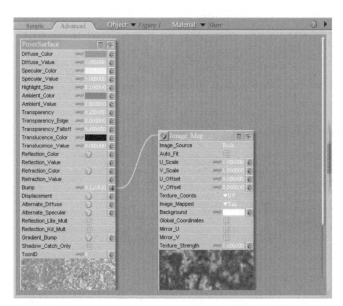

LEARN THE MATERIAL
ROOM INTERFACE

What You'll Do

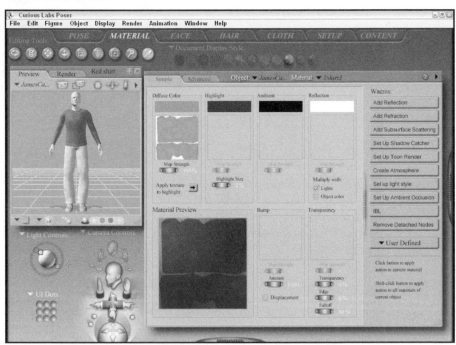

 In this lesson, you learn how to use the Material Room interface.

You open the Material Room by clicking the Material tab at the top of the Poser interface or by selecting the Render, Materials menu command. This opens an interface setup, as shown in Figure 4-1, that is different from the Pose Room, although it includes all of the same controls as the Pose Room, including the Document Window, the Camera and Light Controls, and the Display Styles and Editing Tools button sets. The main interface found in the Material Room is the Shader Window.

Using the Shader Window

The Shader Window, shown in Figure 4-2, is a large interface for creating and editing materials. The material displayed in the Shader Window is applied to the material group listed in the Material List at the top of the Shader Window. The Material List includes all the material groups for the object selected in the Object List. The Object List lets you select from the scene props, lights, the current figure, or the background or atmosphere. The top of the Shader Window also includes a help icon that opens the Room Help and a pop-up menu.

NOTE

The Shader Window's pop-up menu is accessible only in the Advanced Material Panel.

FIGURE 4-1

Material Room interface

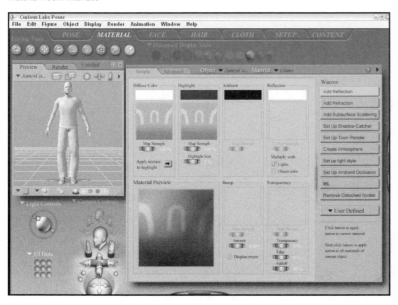

FIGURE 4-2

Shader Window

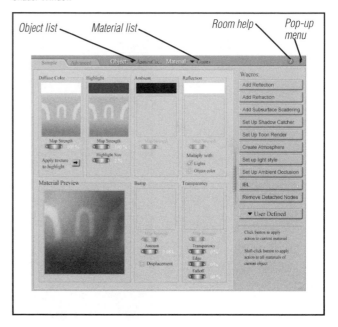

Selecting Material Groups

In addition to the Material List located at the top of the Shader Window, you can also select material groups using the Material Select tool (which looks like an eyedropper) found among the Editing Tools buttons. When you drag this tool over the figure in the Document Window, the cursor looks like an eyedropper. Any material group that is selected automatically appears in the Material List and its material is displayed in the Shader Window.

Using the Simple Material Panel

The Shader Window is divided into two separate panels, each opened with the corresponding tab. The Simple Material Panel, shown in Figure 4-3, includes the most basic materials and offers a quick and easy way to quickly build and apply materials. The materials included on the Simple Material Panel include Diffuse Color, Ambient, Highlight, Reflection, Bump, and Transparency along with all the controls to define and edit these properties. The panel also includes a Material Preview pane which displays a rendered example of the designated material.

FIGURE 4-3
Simple Material panel

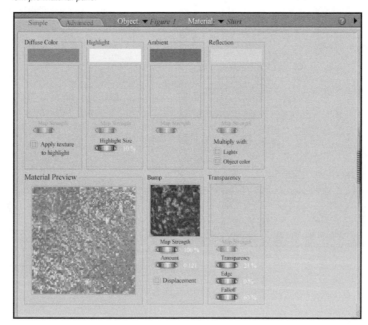

Using the Advanced Material Panel

The Advanced Material Panel, shown in Figure 4-4, includes panels known as *nodes*. Each node has many material properties and you can connect multiple nodes to create unique and diverse material types. In the top-right corner of each node are two icons that you can use to show or hide the material values and the preview pane.

Accessing the Wacros Pane

To the right side of the Shader Window is a side window control bar. Clicking this bar opens the Wacros pane, as shown in Figure 4-5. **Wacros** are scripted actions that you can access to help automating the building of advanced materials such as adding refraction and reflection to the current material and setting up toon rendering. Using the User Defined button, you can access custom created wacros. You create custom wacros by using *PoserPython*, a scripting language available within Poser. More on wacros is covered in Chapter 13, "Using PoserPython Scripts."

FIGURE 4-5

Wacros pane

FIGURE 4-4

Advanced Material panel

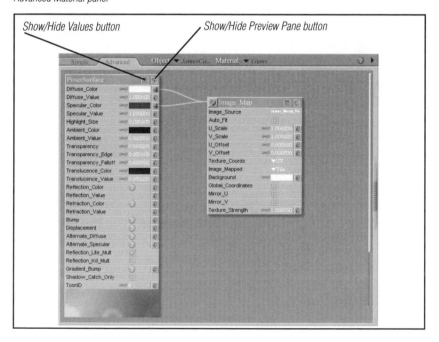

Show/Hide Values button   Show/Hide Preview Pane button

Access the Shader Window

1. Open the Poser interface with the default figure visible.

2. Click the Material tab to access the Material Room.

   A new interface appears including the same controls available in the Pose Room.

3. Select James Casual from the Object List at the top of the Shader Window.

4. Click the chest element in the Document Window.

   The TShirt3 material group is automatically selected in the Material List at the top of the Shader Window.

5. Click the color swatch beneath the Diffuse Color title in the Simple panel of the Shader Window and select a red color from the pop-up color palette.

   The default figure shown in the Document Window is displayed with a red-colored shirt, as shown in Figure 4-6.

6. Select File, Save As and save the file as **Red shirt.pz3**.

FIGURE 4-6

Simple red shirt

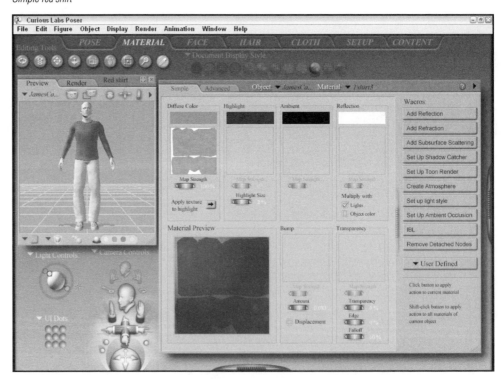

LOAD AND SAVE
MATERIALS

What You'll Do

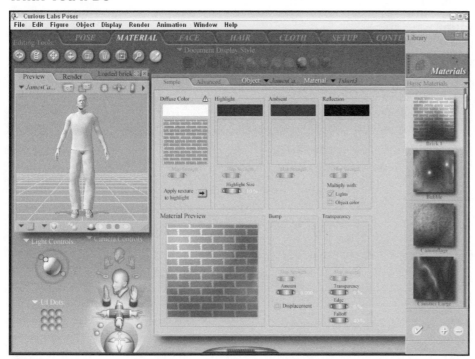

In this lesson, you learn how to work with the Library to load and save materials.

In addition to figures and poses, the Library palette also includes many preset materials that you can apply directly to material groups or that you can load in the Material Room for editing to create something new. You can also easily save new materials into the Library.

CAUTION

The Materials category in the Library can be accessed only from within the Material Room.

Loading Materials from the Library

To access the available materials from the Library, click the Materials category and navigate to the folder containing the types of materials you want to apply to the current figure. Several unique sets of material folders are available in the default installation. Within each folder are thumbnails of the various materials. With a material thumbnail selected, click the Apply Library Presets button at the bottom of the Library palette and the selected material is loaded into the Shader Window and applied to the selected material group. Figure 4-7 shows several material thumbnails contained in the Basic Materials folder with the Fireball material loaded.

NOTE

For some loaded materials viewed in the Simple panel, a small exclamation point icon is visible in the upper-right corner of the various properties, as shown in Figure 4-7. This icon indicates that some additional parameter values are available for this property that can only be accessed from within the Advanced panel.

Saving Materials to the Library

The current material can also be saved to the Library using the Add to Library button located at the bottom of the Library palette. This button opens a simple dialog box where you can name the current material and the thumbnail for the current material is added to the top of the open Library folder. The dialog box also includes options to save a single material or a material collection. If the Material Collection option is selected, you can click the Select Materials button to open a separate dialog box where you can select which materials to include in the collection.

Removing Materials from the Library

The Remove from Library button in the Library palette permanently deletes the selected thumbnail material.

FIGURE 4-7
Loaded Library material

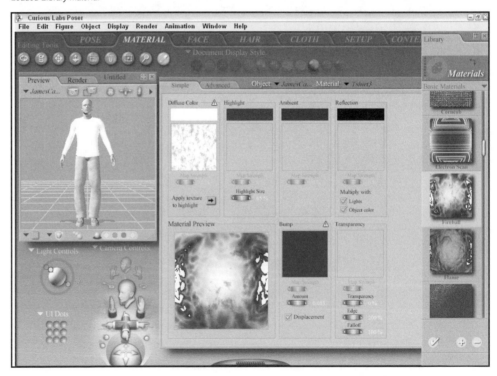

FIGURE 4-8

Brick material from the Library

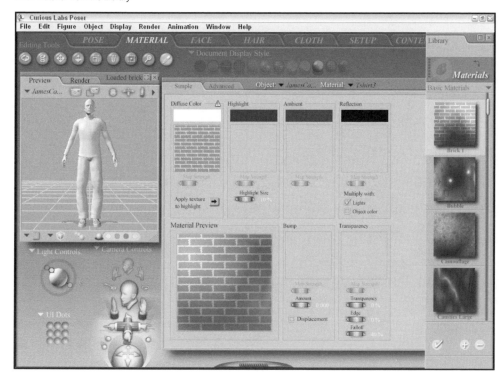

1. Open Poser with the default man visible.

2. Click the Material tab to access the Material Room.

3. Click the side control to the right of the interface to open the Library palette or select the Window, Libraries menu command.

4. Click the Materials category at the top of the Library palette and navigate to the Basic Materials folder.

5. Select the Brick 1 thumbnail and click the Replace Material button at the bottom of the Library palette.

   The selected material is loaded into the Shader Window, as shown in Figure 4-8.

6. Select File, Save As and save the file as **Loaded brick material.pz3**.

Save a material to the Library

1. Open Poser with the default man visible.

2. Click the Material tab to access the Material Room.

3. Click the side control to the right of the interface to open the Library palette or select the Window, Libraries menu command.

4. Click the Materials category at the top of the Library palette and navigate to the Basic Materials folder.

5. Click the color swatch beneath the Diffuse Color title in the Simple panel of the Shader Window and select a purple color from the pop-up color palette.

6. Select the Brick 1 thumbnail and click the Add to Library button ⊕ at the bottom of the Library palette.

   The New Material Set dialog box appears.

7. Enter **Purple** as the name of this material, select the Single Material option, and click OK.

   The new material appears in the folder thumbnails, as shown in Figure 4-9.

FIGURE 4-9

New material added to the Library

Remove from Library

Change Material

Add to Library

CREATE SIMPLE
MATERIALS

What You'll Do

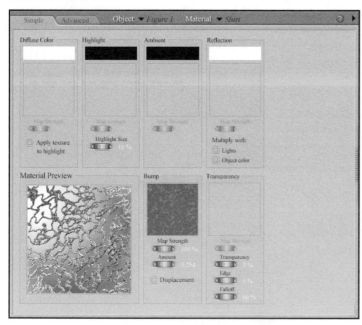

In this lesson, you learn how to create simple materials.

The Simple Material Panel of the Shader Window only includes six simple material properties, but you can create an amazing variety of materials from these simple properties.

Changing Color

Directly underneath the Diffuse Color, Highlight, Ambient, and Reflection material properties in the Simple Material Panel is a color swatch that sets the color for the respective property.

You can change the current color by clicking this color swatch and selecting a new color from the pop-up color palette, shown in Figure 4-10. To open the standard color selector dialog box, click the icon in the upper-right corner of the pop-up color palette.

Adding Texture Maps

The open space underneath the color swatches is to hold a **texture map** that is loaded from the hard disk. To load a texture map, simply click the open space and

FIGURE 4-10
Pop-up color palette

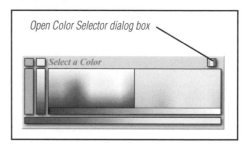

Open Color Selector dialog box

Select a Color

the Texture Manager dialog box, shown in Figure 4-11, opens. This dialog box includes a preview of the selected image, a drop-down list containing recently loaded images, and a Browse button where you can locate new images to load. Once a texture map is loaded, you can change its brightness using the Map Strength dial. Each property that can use a texture map has a Map Strength parameter dial. This value sets how strong the texture map is. For example, a Map Strength value of 100 will cause the full texture map to be used and a Map Strength value of 0 will turn off the texture map.

Adding Highlights

Highlights are surface areas where the reflected light is most intense. The color brightness determines the intensity of the highlights and you can also set the size of the highlights using the Highlight Size dial. Smooth shiny surfaces will have smaller, brighter highlights and rougher surfaces will have larger, fuzzier highlights because the reflected light is scattered more. If the Apply Texture to Highlight option is enabled for the Diffuse Color property, the texture map for the Diffuse Color property is copied to the Highlight property and only the bright areas of the

texture image receive the highlights. Figure 4-12 shows a material with a highlight.

TIP

For realistic scenes, make sure the highlight color is the same as the main light color.

Using Diffuse and Ambient Colors

The Diffuse Color property sets the surface color of the material and the Ambient property sets the color of the indirect light in the scene. These two colors are combined when used together. For example, a mate-

FIGURE 4-11
Texture Manager dialog box

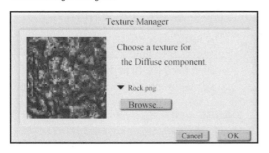

FIGURE 4-12
Material with highlights

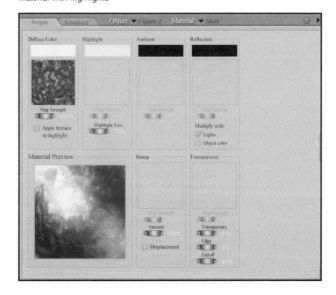

rial with a red Diffuse Color and a blue **Ambient color** would appear purple.

TIP

The diffuse color will tint any texture map that is applied to the Diffuse Color property. To avoid tinting the texture map, set the Diffuse Color property to white.

Enabling Reflections

You can use reflections to reflect an environment image off the current surface. When you click the texture map area, a selection dialog box, shown in Figure 4-13, enables you to apply the reflected texture image as a spherical map or a ray trace reflection. A *spherical map* reflects the texture image about the selected object as if it were inside a large sphere. A *ray trace reflection* uses a special rendering technique to follow each light ray as it bounces about the scene to create perfect reflections. More on raytracing is covered in

Chapter 12, "Rendering Scenes." Of these two methods, the Spherical Map method renders much quicker, but the Ray Trace Reflection method results in higher quality reflections. You can multiply the reflected image by enabling the Lights and the Object Color options under the Reflection texture image. These options will tint the reflected image with the object color and dim the reflected image due to the direct lighting applied to the reflection.

NOTE

Reflection maps aren't visible in the Document Window. You can see them only after rendering the scene.

FIGURE 4-14
Bump material

Adding Bump Maps

A **bump map** texture image adds a relief to the surface of the material. This is accomplished by making the light areas of the bump appear to be raised from the surface and the darker areas to be indented. You can use the Amount dial to set the depth of the bumps. You can also enable the Displacement option, which applies the texture as a displacement map. A **displacement map** is different from a bump in that is actually changes the geometry of the object to include the affected bumps. Figure 4-14 shows a simple material with a bump texture applied.

FIGURE 4-13
Choose a reflection type

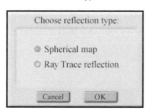

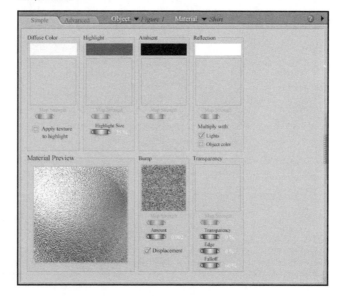

QUICKTIP

You can set the Amount value to a negative number to make the lighter areas of the bump map indented and the darker areas raised.

Using Transparency

You can use the Transparency value to make your entire material transparent. Transparency means that you can see through the material, like glass, to the objects behind it. The Edge value sets how transparent the edges of the material are and the Falloff value causes the areas closer to the edges to become less transparent. You can also select a texture map to define the areas where the material is transparent with light areas being transparent and dark areas **opaque** (or non-transparent). Figure 4-15 shows a transparent material applied to the shirt material group of a figure. Notice how you can see the ground plane lines through the shirt area.

FIGURE 4-15

Transparent material

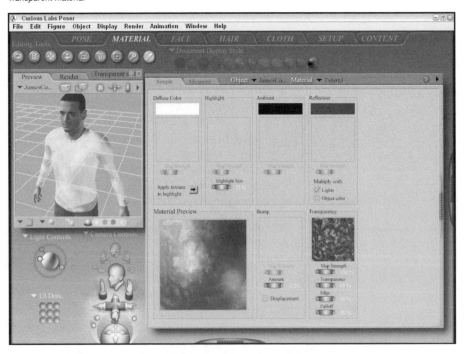

FIGURE 4-16

Simple green material with highlights

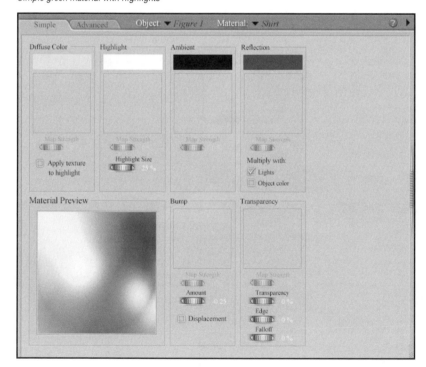

1. Open Poser and click the Material tab to access the Material Room.

2. In the Shader Window, click the color swatch beneath the Diffuse Color property and select a green color from the pop-up color palette.

3. Click the color swatch beneath the Highlight property and select a white color from the pop-up color palette.

4. Drag the Highlight Size dial to 25%.

   The new green material with highlights is shown in the Preview pane of the Shader Window, as shown in Figure 4-16.

5. Select File, Save As and save the file as **Green material with highlights.pz3**.

Add a reflection map

1. Open Poser and click the Material tab to access the Material Room.

2. In the Shader Window, click the texture map area beneath the Reflection property.

   A simple Choose Reflection Type dialog box appears.

3. Select the Spherical Map option and click OK.

   The Texture Manager dialog box opens.

4. Click the Browse button and locate the Downtown San Francisco.jpg image file. Click OK.

The reflection map image is displayed in the map area under the Reflection property and in the Preview pane using spherical mapping, as shown in Figure 4-17.

5. Select File, Save As and save the file as **Reflection map.pz3**.

Add a bump map

1. Open Poser and click the Material tab to access the Material Room.

2. In the Shader Window, click the texture map area beneath the Bump property.

The Texture Manager dialog box opens.

3. Click the Browse button and locate the Veins on blue.tif image file. Click OK.

The bump map image is displayed in the map area under the Bump property and in the Preview pane, as shown in Figure 4-18.

> NOTE Notice that the actual bump map colors aren't used, but the bright areas of the bump map are raised and the dark areas of the bump map are indented.

4. Select File, Save As and save the file as **Bump map.pz3**.

FIGURE 4-17

Reflection map

FIGURE 4-18

Bump map

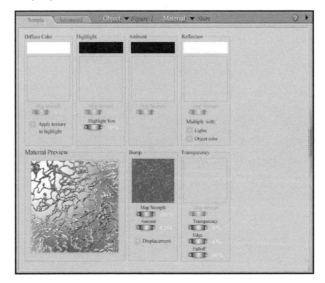

FIGURE 4-19

Transparent shirt

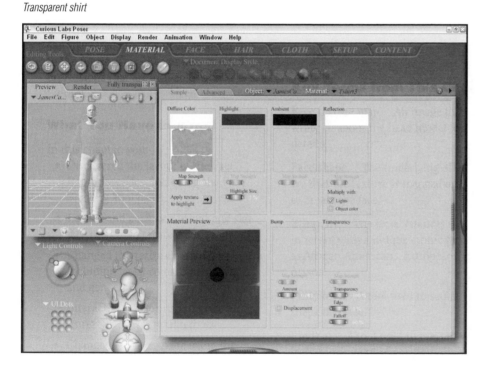

1. Open Poser and click the Material tab to access the Material Room.

2. Select the TShirt3 material group from the Material List at the top of the Shader Window, if it isn't already selected.

3. In the Shader Window, drag the Transparency dial to 100%.

   The shirt material turns invisible in the Document Window, as shown in Figure 4-19.

4. Select File, Save As and save the file as **Fully transparent shirt.pz3**.

USE MATERIAL NODES

What You'll Do

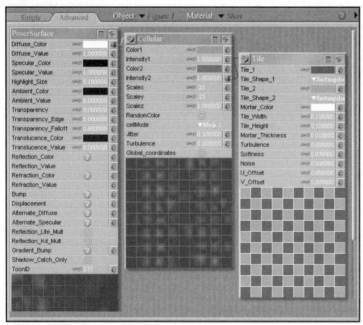

In this lesson, you learn how to work with material nodes.

To create advanced materials, select the Advanced tab at the top of the Shader Window to open the Advanced Material Panel. Within this panel, you can select and edit the various nodes, link nodes together, and create new nodes. All nodes plug into the **root node** that is applied to the selected object. Learning to work with **material nodes** is the key to creating complex materials.

Selecting and Moving Nodes

The Shader Window is an open space for positioning and connecting material nodes. Click a node to select it. The selected node can be moved to a new position by dragging its title bar. You can select several nodes at the same time by holding down the Shift key and clicking on their title bars. You can also select all nodes by clicking the pop-up menu in the upper-right corner or by right-clicking in the Shader Window and choosing the Select All command.

TIP

To save space in the Shader Window, click the buttons in the upper-right corner of the node to hide both the attribute list and the preview window. Only the title bar will remain.

Viewing the Root Node

The root node is titled *PoserSurface*, as shown in Figure 4-20, and is always the final surface that is applied to the material group. The root node has no Output value. Different root nodes exist depending on the type of item that you can create a material for. Poser includes four root nodes:

- **Material/Hair root node:** Used to define materials for figures, props, and hair-styles.
- **Light root node:** Used to define the materials applied to the selected light.

- **Background root node:** Used to define the materials applied to the scene background.
- **Atmosphere root node:** Used to define atmospheric materials such as fog and haze.

NOTE

Material attributes for the Light, Background, and Atmosphere root nodes are discussed in Chapter 6, "Establishing a Scene."

Changing Material Attribute Values

The root node includes many values that you can edit. Some of these values have color swatches, others have numeric values, and some are merely check boxes. Next to some of the attributes is a question mark button. Clicking this button opens a window providing some help with the attribute. The attributes found in the material/hair root node include the following:

- **Diffuse Color:** Defines the surface color of the object.

FIGURE 4-20
Root material node

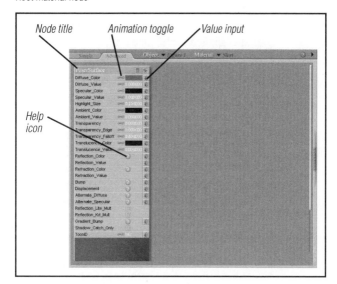

- **Diffuse Value:** Defines the strength of the diffuse color. A value of 0 makes the diffuse color black, whereas a value of 1 matches the defined diffuse color.
- **Specular Color:** Defines the color the highlights.
- **Specular Value:** Defines the strength of the specular color.
- **Highlight Size:** Defines how sharp or fuzzy the highlight is. Shiny surfaces have smaller, sharper highlights and rough surfaces have larger highlights.
- **Ambient Color:** Defines the ambient color for the scene. This color shades all objects in the scene including shadows.
- **Ambient Value:** Defines the strength of the ambient color.
- **Transparency:** Defines the amount of transparency of the material. A value of 1 is fully transparent and a value of 0 is fully opaque.
- **Transparency Edge:** Defines the amount of transparency applied to the edges of the object.
- **Transparency Falloff:** Defines how quickly the transparency fades as you approach the object edge.
- **Translucence Color:** Defines the color of light passing through a transparent object.
- **Translucence Value:** Defines the strength of the translucence.

NOTE

Most of the remaining material attributes have no value, but can be connected to other nodes such as a texture or variable node.

- **Reflection Color:** Defines a color reflected off the surface.
- **Reflection Value:** Defines the strength of the reflection color or texture.
- **Refraction Color:** Defines a color refracted or bent through a transparent surface.
- **Refraction Value:** Defines the strength of the refraction color.
- **Bump:** Defines a bump map that is applied to the material.
- **Displacement:** Defines a displacement that is applied to the material to change its geometry.
- **Alternate Diffuse:** An alternative attribute for applying diffuse colors and/or textures.
- **Alternate Specular:** An alternative attribute for applying specular highlights.
- **Reflection Lite Mult:** An option to multiply the lighting effects into the reflection map.
- **Reflection KD Mult:** An option to tint the reflection map by the diffuse color.
- **Gradient Bump:** An attribute to use gradient maps as bump maps. This attribute isn't used by the current

renderer and is only included for backwards compatibility.
- **Shadow Catch Only:** An option to make all transparent surfaces appear opaque for shadows. The result is to cast a shadow onto a transparent surface such as shadow puppets on a sheet.
- **ToonID:** When rendering using the cartoon shader each edge is outlined. By giving each separate material a different ID, multiple outlines will not be applied to a single object.

NOTE

All values assigned in the Simple Material Panel are automatically transferred to the material in the Advanced Material Panel.

Animating Material Attribute Values

The values with key icons can be animated. Clicking the key icon opens a pop-up menu where you can select to enable animation mode, view the Parameter Settings dialog box for the given attribute, or open the attribute's animation graph. When animation mode is enabled, you can animate the parameter by selecting an animation frame and changing the parameter value. More on animating materials is covered in Chapter 11, "Animating Figures."

Creating New Material Nodes

There are several ways to create a new material node, such as clicking a Value Input icon, clicking the Shader Window's pop-up menu, or right-clicking in the Shader Window. All of these methods open a pop-up menu that includes a Create New Node option.

Figure 4-21 shows a newly created 3D Texture node called Marble. This new node includes several additional values and a Value Output icon in its upper-left corner.

Connecting Material Nodes

To the right of every value is a plug socket icon, known as a Value Input icon. Clicking this icon opens a pop-up menu where you can create and attach a new node. You can connect any two material nodes using the Value Input and Value Output nodes. To connect two nodes, simply drag from the Value Output node to the Value Input node or vice versa. When connected, a light blue line (or cord) is shown connecting the two nodes and the node with the value output controls the value of the node with the value input. For example, connecting a Marble output node to the root node's Diffuse Color value makes the marble texture

FIGURE 4-21

New material node

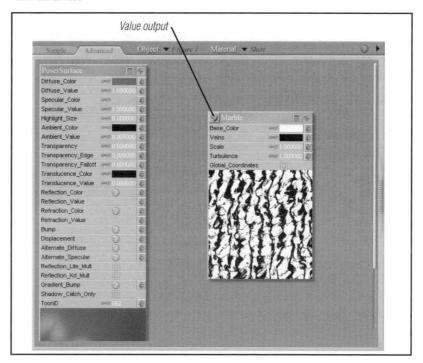

appear as part of the root material, as shown in Figure 4-22. You can disconnect nodes by clicking the Value Input icon and selecting Disconnect from the pop-up menu. Each Value Input and Value Output icon can be connected to multiple different nodes.

Copying and Pasting Nodes

The Shader Window pop-up menu includes commands for deleting, cutting, copying, and pasting the selected nodes. The pasted nodes are given the same name as their original with a different number attached on the end.

FIGURE 4-22

Two connected material nodes

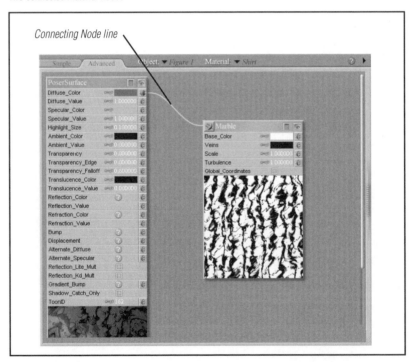

Use texture nodes

1. Open Poser and click the Material tab to access the Material Room.

2. Click the Advanced tab in the Shader Window.

3. Click the Value Input icon 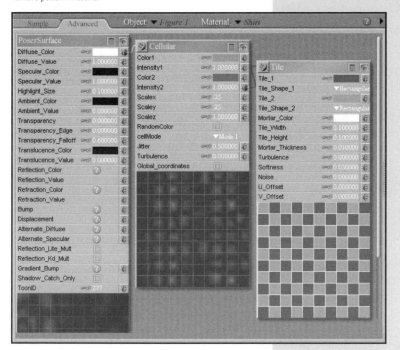 for the Diffuse Color value and select New Node, 3d Textures, Cellular from the pop-up menu.

   The Cellular material node is added to the Shader Window with a line connected to the Diffuse Color's Value Input icon.

4. Click the color swatch for the Color 1 value in the Cellular node and select a red color from the pop-up color palette. Then, click the color swatch for the Color 2 value in the Cellular node and select a blue color from the pop-up color palette. Change the Scale X and Scale Y values to 0.25.

5. Click the Value Input icon for the Intensity 2 value in the Cellular node and select New Node, 2d Textures, Tile from the pop-up menu.

   The Tile material node is added to the Shader Window with a line connected to the Cellular node's Intensity 2 Value Input icon.

6. Click the Node Preview button in the upper-right corner of both texture nodes.

   The preview pane for the Cellular node shows several red-colored cells among a light blue grid pattern, as shown in Figure 4-23.

7. Select File, Save As and save the file as **Texture pattern.pz3**.

FIGURE 4-23

Texture pattern material

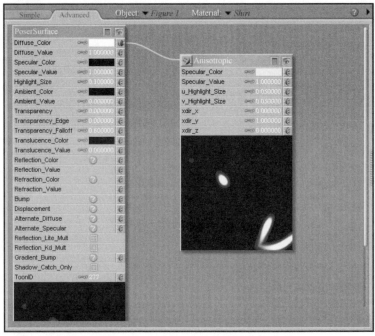

LESSON 5

LEARN THE VARIOUS
MATERIAL NODES

What You'll Do

In this lesson, you learn how to create a custom material group.

When creating a new material node, there are several categories of nodes available, each with its own unique attributes. The available nodes are divided into the following categories:

- **Math:** Used to mathematically manipulate values such as adding, subtracting, and multiplying values together.

- **Lighting:** Used to alter the scene lighting method to change highlight shapes, or to specify a certain effect like toon shading.

- **Variables:** Used to add variable values to the material values such as the current frame number, the dimensions of the current point, or the current pixel.

- **3D Textures:** Includes several preset 3D texture maps such as Noise, Clouds, Marble, and Granite.

- **2D Textures:** Includes several preset 2D texture maps such as Brick, Tile, and Weave. It also includes nodes for loading image files and movies.

Using Math Nodes

You can use math nodes to combine two values using several different mathematical functions. The available math nodes include:

- **Blender:** Used to blend between two colors.
- **Edge Blend:** Used to blend between an inner color and an outer color where the inner color faces the camera and the outer color faces away from the camera.
- **Component:** Used to extract red, green, or blue components from a color based on the Component value where Red = 1, Green = 2, and Blue =3.
- **Math Functions:** Used to combine two values using a mathematical function. Available functions include Add, Subtract, Multiply, Divide, Sin, Cos, Tan, Sqrt, Pow, Exp, Log, Mod, Abs, Sign, Min, Max, Clamp, Ceil, Floor, Round, Step, Smoothstep, Bias, and Gain.
- **Color Math:** Includes the same mathematical functions as the Math Functions node, except it works with two colors instead of two values.
- **User Defined:** Used to define a color using numeric color values. It lets you choose from Red, Green, Blue (RGB); Hue, Saturation, Lightness (HSL); and Hue, Saturation, Value (HSV) color models.

- **Simple Color:** Lets you select a single color using the pop-up color palette.
- **Color Ramp:** Includes four colors that are used to create a gradient ramp.
- **HSV:** Defines colors using Hue, Saturation, and Value color attributes.

QUICKTIP

Holding down the Alt key while clicking a color swatch automatically opens the Color Selector dialog box.

Using Lighting Nodes

The Lighting nodes let you specify a very specific lighting model for the current material. For example, the Special, Hair node lets you select colors for the hair roots, hair tips, and the root's transparency. Each light node listed here includes a submenu of available nodes.

- **Specular:** Used to select from several types of highlights, each with their own shape, color, size and intensity values. The available options include Anisotropic, Phong, Glossy, Blinn, and Specular.
- **Diffuse:** Used to alter how the diffuse color is affected by the lighting. The options include Clay, Diffuse, Probe Light, and Toon.
- **Special:** Several additional specialized lighting models. The options include Skin, Velvet, Hair, and Fast Scatter.

- **Ray Trace:** Several ray trace options used to create photo-realistic scenes. The options include Reflect, Refract, Ambient Occlusion, Gather, and Scatter.
- **Environment Map:** Includes a single option of Sphere Map for creating a reflection sphere map.

Using Variables Nodes

These nodes are used to represent specific scene values such as the current point. The available Variable nodes include:

- **N:** Includes the X, Y, and Z values of the normal at the current point used to determine the polygon's orientation.
- **P:** Includes the X, Y, and Z values of the current point.
- **Frame Number:** The current frame number for animation sequences.
- **u, v:** References the texture location of the pixel currently being rendered.
- **Du, Dv:** References the change rate of the texture coordinates or how fast the rendering is progressing.
- **dPdv, dPdu:** References the change rate of the current point.
- **dNdv, dNdu:** References the change rate of the surface normals.

Using Texture Nodes

The texture nodes are divided into two categories—3D and 2D. 3D textures maintain their material properties regardless of the shape of the object they are applied to, whereas 2D textures are simply images that are wrapped about the object. All of these textures are convenient because they can be selected and applied without having to load an image. The available 3D textures include:

- **Fractal Sum:** Creates a fractal-based texture.
- **FBM:** Creates a texture based on multiple fractals.
- **Turbulence:** Creates another variant fractal texture.
- **Noise:** Creates a static texture useful for adding variety to materials.
- **Cellular:** Creates a texture of repeating cells.
- **Clouds:** Creates a texture that resembles clouds.
- **Spots:** Creates a texture of random spots.
- **Marble:** Creates a texture that resembles a marble rock surface.
- **Granite:** Creates a texture that resembles a granite rock surface.
- **Wood:** Creates a texture that resembles a wood grain.
- **Wave 3d:** Creates a texture of concentric circles.

Figure 4-24 shows each of the available 3D texture nodes.

FIGURE 4-24

3D texture nodes

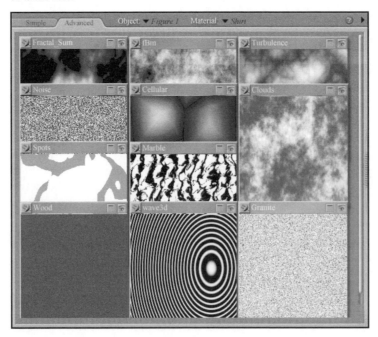

The available 2D textures include:

- **Wave 2d:** A texture map of concentric circles.
- **Image Map:** An image map loaded from the hard disk.
- **Brick:** An image map of a set of bricks.

- **Tile:** An image map of alternating checkerboard patterns.
- **Weave:** An image map of a basket weave pattern.
- **Movie:** A movie file loaded from the hard disk.

Figure 4-25 shows each of the available 2D texture nodes.

FIGURE 4-25

2D texture nodes

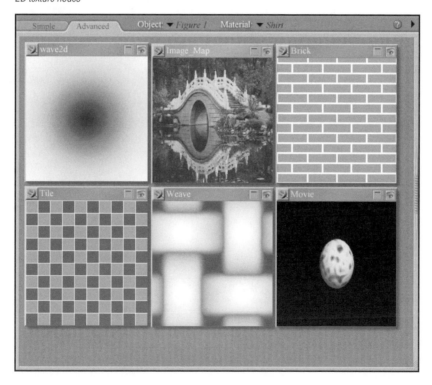

Use a math node

1. Open Poser and click the Material tab to access the Material Room.

2. Click the Advanced tab in the Shader Window.

3. Click the Value Input icon for the Diffuse Color value and select New Node, Math, Blender from the pop-up menu.

   The Blender material node is added to the Shader Window with a line connected to the Diffuse Color's Value Input icon.

4. Click the color swatch for Input 1 in the Blender node and select a red color from the pop-up color palette. Then, click the color swatch for the Input 2 value in the Blender node and select a yellow color.

5. Click the Node Preview button 🔲 in the upper-right corner of the Blender node.

   The preview pane for the Blender node shows a bright orange color created by blending together the red and yellow colors, as shown in Figure 4-26.

6. Select File, Save As and save the file as **Blended color.pz3**.

FIGURE 4-26

Math node material

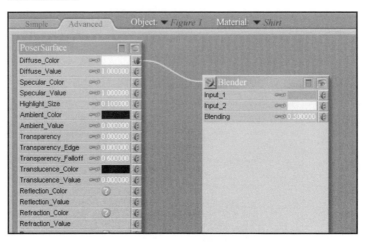

FIGURE 4-27

Lighting node material

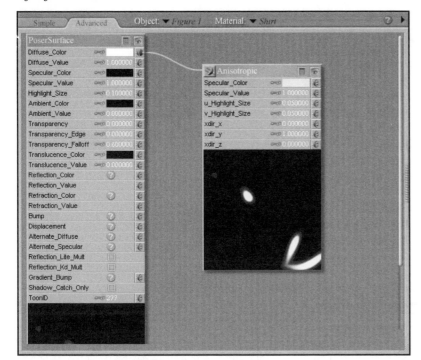

1. Open Poser and click the Material tab to access the Material Room.

2. Click the Advanced tab in the Shader Window.

3. Click the Value Input icon for the Diffuse Color value and select New Node, Lighting, Specular, Anisotropic from the pop-up menu.

   The Anisotropic material node is added to the Shader Window with a line connected to the Diffuse Color's Value Input icon. Anisotropic highlights are elliptical rather than circular.

4. Click the color swatch for the Specular Color value in the Anisotropic node and select a gold color from the pop-up color palette.

5. Click the Node Preview button in the upper-right corner of the Anisotropic node.

   The preview pane for the Anisotropic node shows a gold-colored elliptical highlight, as shown in Figure 4-27.

6. Select File, Save As and save the file as **Anisotropic highlight.pz3**.

CREATE A
MATERIAL GROUP

What You'll Do

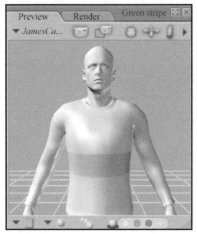

In this lesson, you learn how to create a custom material group.

Figure elements are divided into objects that align with the figure's bones to allow for easy figure posing, but the materials don't often follow these groupings. For example, the elements covered by the shirt area could include multiple elements including the chest, abdomen, and both collars and upper arms, whereas the head as a single element can require separate material groups for the scalp, lips, cheeks, teeth, and tongue.

Using the Grouping Tool

The Grouping Tool found in the Editing Tools opens the Group Editor panel, shown in Figure 4-28. Within this panel are buttons for creating a material group that can be recognized in the Shader Window. By dragging over polygons in the Document Window with the Grouping Tool, you can select polygons as part of the group. The selected polygons are highlighted in red in the Document Window.

FIGURE 4-28
Group Editor panel

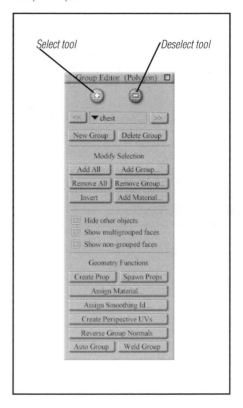

Deselecting Polygons

To remove polygons from the current selection, click the Deselect button at the top of the Group Editor and click the polygons you want to remove.

Creating a Material Group

Once all the polygons for the material group are selected, click the Assign Material button in the Group Editor. This opens the Assign Material dialog box, shown in Figure 4-29, where you can type a name for the new material group. After you click OK, you can select the new material group from the Material List in the Shader Window.

FIGURE 4-29

Assign Material dialog box

Create a material group

1. Open Poser and click the Material tab to access the Material Room.

2. Click the Grouping Tool button in the Editing Tools controls.

   The Group Editor panel appears and the figure in the Document Window goes dark.

3. Click the Hidden Line button in the Display Styles controls.

4. Click the chest object in the middle of the Document Window.

   All the polygons that make up the chest element are highlighted in red.

5. Click the Deselect button in the Group Editor panel and drag over the top polygons in the Document Window to remove them from the selected polygons.

6. When just a single band of polygons surrounds the mid-section of the figure in the Document Window, click the Assign Material button in the Group Editor panel.

   The Assign Material dialog box appears.

7. Type the name, **Shirt stripe**, in the Assign Material dialog box and click OK.

8. Select the Shirt stripe material group from the Material List at the top of the Shader Window and change the Diffuse Color to green.

9. Click the Smooth Shaded button in the Display Styles controls.

   The material group is colored green, as shown in Figure 4-30.

10. Select File, Save As and save the file as **Green stripe.pz3**.

FIGURE 4-30
Green stripe

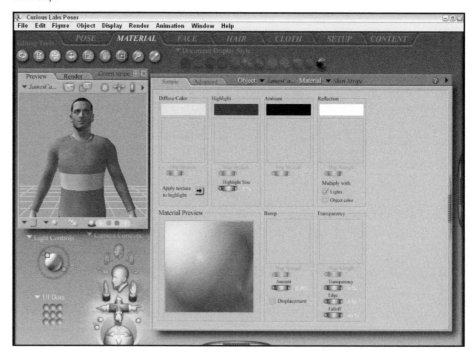

This chapter explained how materials can be used to define how the surface looks when rendered. Materials are created in the Material Room, and the Library includes an assortment of preset materials you can apply to material groups. Simple materials include properties such as color, highlight, reflection, and transparency and you create advanced materials by connecting material nodes together within the Shader Window. Finally, the chapter showed how new material groups can be created using the Group Editor.

What You Have Learned

In this chapter, you

- Discovered the layout of the Material Room interface including the Shader Window.
- Learned how to load preset materials into the current scene and how to save custom materials to the Library.
- Learned the properties used to create simple materials, including color, highlight, ambient, reflection, bump, and transparency.
- Added texture images to materials.
- Reviewed a list of the available material nodes and learned how to connect them together.

- Created a new material group using the Group Editor.

Key Terms from This Chapter

Shader Window. An interface found in the Material Room where new custom materials can be created.

Material group. A group of selected polygons that defines a region where similar materials are applied, such as a shirt or pants group.

Wacro. A custom PoserPython script used within the Shader Window to create new material types.

Diffuse color. The surface color emitted by an object.

Highlight. The spot on an object where the light is reflected with the greatest intensity. Also known as a *specular* highlight.

Ambient color. A global pervasive light color that is applied to the entire scene.

Texture map. A 2D image file that is wrapped about a surface.

Bump map. A 2D bitmap image that adds a relief texture to the surface of an object like an orange rind.

Displacement map. A 2D bitmap image that controls the displacement of geometry objects.

Transparency. A material property that defines how easy an object is to see through like glass.

Opaque. The opposite of transparency. When objects cannot be seen through.

Material node. A dialog box of material properties that can be connected to control another material value.

Root node. The top-level material node.

chapter

5

DEALING WITH
Props

1. Load Library props.

2. Import external props.

3. Select and position props.

4. Attach props to elements.

5. Create props from a selected group.

6. Use the Content Room.

chapter 5 DEALING WITH
Props

Although posing figures is the main purpose behind Poser, you aren't limited only to populating scenes with figures. Poser also supports objects known as **props** that can be placed anywhere within the scene. Props can be used to enhance the scene such as the ground plane, a tree, or a light post; interact with a figure, such as a chair, a weapon, or a basketball; or enhance the figure directly, such as a hairdo, clothing, or jewelry.

Props can be loaded into a scene from the Library palette or created in another 3D package and imported into Poser. Once in Poser, the prop can be edited using the same Editing Tools that are used to edit figures. Props can also be grouped and given materials.

By parenting props to figure elements, you can make the prop move along with a figure element. You can also replace figure body parts with props to create some interesting characters.

New props can be created using the Group Editor dialog box. Any selection of polygons can be converted into a prop using the Create Prop button.

Finally, you can download and install new content using the Content Room.

Tools You'll Use

LOAD LIBRARY
PROPS

What You'll Do

In this lesson, you learn how to load props into the scene from the Library.

In addition to figures, poses, and materials, the Library palette also includes many props that you can add to the scene. Externally loaded props can also be easily saved back into the Library.

Loading Props from the Library

To access the available props from the Library, click the Props category and navigate to the folder containing the types of props you want to add to the scene. Prop folders included in the default installation include a variety of clothing and generic scene items. Within each folder are thumbnails of the various props. With a prop thumbnail selected, click the Add Prop button at the bottom of the Library palette to load the selected prop into the scene. Figure 5-1 shows several material thumbnails contained in the James Clothing folder.

FIGURE 5-1

Prop Library folder

Saving Materials to the Library

You can save the current prop to the Library using the Add to Library button located at the bottom of the Library palette. This button opens a simple dialog box where you can name the current prop. The thumbnail for the current material is added to the open Library folder, where it is listed in alphabetical order.

Removing Props from the Library

The Remove from Library button in the Library palette permanently deletes the selected thumbnail prop.

FIGURE 5-2

Default figure with prop sunglasses

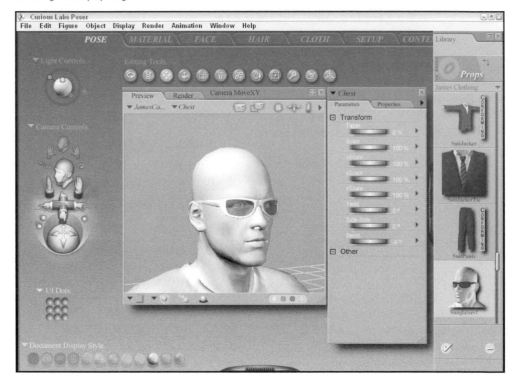

1. Open Poser with the default man visible.

2. Click the Face Camera button in the Camera controls.

3. Click the side control to the right of the interface to open the Library palette or select Window, Libraries.

4. Click the Props category at the top of the Library palette and navigate to the Clothing folder.

5. Select the Sunglasses 1 thumbnail and click the Add Prop button at the bottom of the Library palette.

   The selected prop is loaded into the Shader Window, as shown in Figure 5-2.

6. Select File, Save As and save the file as **Figure with cap.pz3**.

IMPORT
EXTERNAL PROPS

What You'll Do

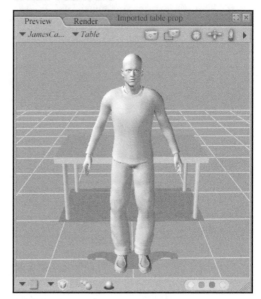

In this lesson, you learn how to import external props.

Although the Library palette contains some great props, it doesn't include all the props you may want to use. Any 3D object can be used as a prop, including objects created in external 3D packages. You simply import the object into Poser.

CAUTION

The imported objects must be in one of the 3D formats that Poser supports in order to be imported. The supported formats include QuickDraw 3DMF, 3D Studio 3DS, DXF, LightWave LWO, and Wavefront OBJ. Also, Poser can only import polygon models.

Preparing Prop Models for Importing into Poser

When building external models to be imported into Poser, keep the following in mind:

- The coordinate origin for the external 3D package corresponds the center of the floor in Poser. To have your props correctly positioned above the floor when imported, move them so they are above the origin along the Y-axis.

- Eliminate any duplicate polygons from the 3D model. Most external 3D packages include tools for automatically identifying and eliminating duplicate polygons.

- Avoid any internal polygons within the model. For example, creating a cylinder object that intersects with a sphere object leaves several polygons embedded within the sphere object. Using Boolean commands can eliminate these internal polygons. If left, the polygons will appear in their original place when bones are applied and the object is posed.

- Convert the model to polygons before saving. Poser's import features cannot handle NURBS, patches, or splines.

- Include enough resolution for the object if it needs to be posed. If an imported figure has an arm made from an extended cube, the object will not have enough polygons to bend.

- If you import a prop with groups, make sure each polygons is only included in a single group. If you're unsure whether polygons are in isolated groups, eliminate the groups and use Poser's grouping functions.

- Material definitions aren't imported along with the model, but material groups are recognized and imported.

Loading External Props

To load an external 3D object as a prop, select File, Import and choose the 3D format that matches your 3D object. The available 3D formats that Poser can import include QuickDraw 3DMF, 3D Studio 3DS, DXF, LightWave LWO, and Wavefront OBJ. After you select an import format, a file dialog box appears where you can locate the specific file to open. After you click the Open button, the Prop Import Options dialog box, shown in Figure 5-3, is displayed.

Setting Import Options

The Prop Import Options dialog box is used to set the initial position and scaling of the imported prop object and includes options for fixing problems. The Centered option cause the imported prop to appear centered within the Document Window. The Place on Floor option causes the imported prop to be set on the floor. The Percent of Standard Figure Size option lets you scale the imported prop based on the size of the current figure. Setting this value to 100 will import the prop roughly the same size as

FIGURE 5-3

Prop Import Options dialog box

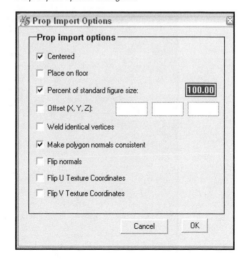

the figure. You can use the **Offset** value to move the prop's initial position from the center.

The **Weld Identical Vertices** option reduces the total number of vertices by combining any vertices that have the same coordinates.

If the prop appears inside out, all of its **normals** are pointing inward. Using the Make Polygon Normals Consistent option causes all normals to point inward or outward and the Flip Normals option changes their direction if necessary. You can also flip U and V texture coordinates if the textures appear backwards.

QUICKTIP

Don't be too concerned if the imported prop isn't in the exact position or scaled to the right size because you can use the Editing Tools to change its position and scale.

Saving Imported Props to the Library

You can save imported props to the Library using the Add to Library button located at the bottom of the Library palette. This button opens a simple dialog box where you can name the current prop and the thumbnail for the current prop is added to the open Library folder. Figure 5-4 shows an imported chair prop that has been added to the Library.

CAUTION

When saving a prop to the Library, the current figure is included with the prop thumbnail. To capture a thumbnail without a figure, simply hide the figure with the Figure, Hide Figure menu command before clicking the Add to Library button.

Importing Figures

You can also import figures using the File, Import menu commands. Figures that are imported appear in Poser initially as props, but are converted to figures when the Setup Room is opened. The Setup Room is covered in more detail in Chapter 10, "Working with Bones."

FIGURE 5-4
Imported chair prop

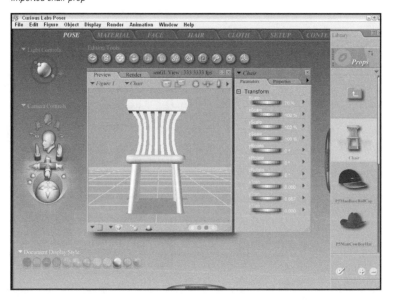

Loading Props from the Content Room

Another source for loading external props is to use the Content Room. Clicking the Content tab at the top of the interface opens the Content Room where you can access additional content via a connection to the Internet and Poser's Content Paradise Web site. To locate the available props for downloading, click the Prop category or search for the prop that you want to download. After you download the requested file, a dialog box of installation options appears with choices to install, copy, or cancel each downloaded file.

FIGURE 5-5

Imported table prop

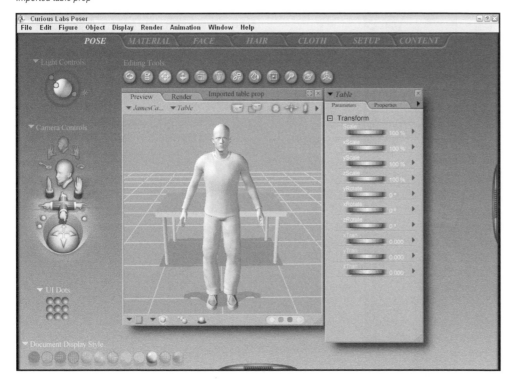

Import props

1. Open Poser with the default man visible.

2. Select File, Import, Wavefront OBJ.

   A file dialog box appears.

3. Locate and import the Table.obj file and click Open.

   The Prop Import Options dialog box opens.

4. In the Prop Import Options dialog box, enable the Centered, Place on Floor, and Off-set options. Set the Z-Axis Offset values to **-0.5** and click OK.

   The imported table object is displayed behind the figure, as shown in Figure 5-5.

5. Select File, Save As and save the file as **Imported table prop.pz3**.

Save an imported prop to the Library

1. Select File, Open and open the Imported table prop.pz3 file (if necessary).

2. Select James Casual from the Figure List at the top of the Document Window.

3. Select Window, Parameter Dials to open the Parameters/Properties palette, if it isn't already open. Click the Properties tab and disable the Visible option.

   The scene figure is hidden, leaving only the table prop object.

4. Drag on the Camera Controls until the table is centered within the Document Window.

5. Select the table prop from the Actor List at the top of the Document Window.

6. Click the side interface tab to open the Library palette and select a folder where you want to save the prop thumbnail.

7. Click the Add to Library button ⊕ at the bottom of the Library palette.

   The Set Name dialog box appears.

8. Enter **Table** as the name of this prop and click OK.

   The new prop appears in the folder of thumbnails, as shown in Figure 5-6.

FIGURE 5-6

New material added to the Library

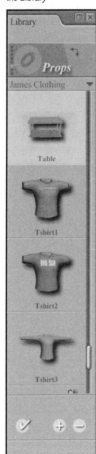

SELECT AND
POSITION PROPS

What You'll Do

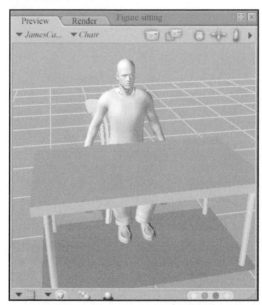

In this lesson, you learn how to select and position props.

You an select props by using the Props submenu of the Actor List located at the top of the Document Window. You can also select props from the Hierarchy Editor, which is opened using the Window, Hierarchy Editor menu command.

Using the Editing Tools

Once selected, props can be edited using all the standard buttons found in the Editing Tools. After selecting a tool, drag within the Document Window when the prop is highlighted in white.

Using the Parameter Dials

The position and orientation of the selected props can also be controlled using the various parameter dials found in the Parameter/Properties palette.

Dropping to the Floor

Selected props can also be aligned with the ground floor using the Figure, Drop to Floor (Ctrl+D) menu command.

Locking Props

When the prop is positioned exactly where you want it to be, you can lock its position and orientation using the Object, Lock Actor menu command. This prevents the prop from being accidentally moved. To unlock a locked prop, just select Object, Lock Actor again to disable the toggle.

Naming Props

Imported props carry the name assigned to them in the external 3D program, but you can change this name in the Name field found in the Properties palette. You can open the Properties palette by selecting the Object, Properties menu command. The other properties are the same as those for figures.

Select and position props

1. Select File, Open and open the Imported table prop.pz3 file.

2. Select File, Import, Wavefront OBJ and import the chair.obj file into the current scene.

3. With the chair prop selected, click the Scale tool 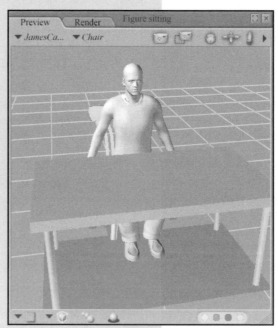 in the Editing Tools control. Hold down the Shift key and drag within the prop circle to uniformly reduce the size of the chair prop.

4. Select Figure, Drop to Floor (or press Ctrl+D).

   The chair prop should now be aligned with the floor like the table.

5. Select the Translate In/Out tool from the Editing Tools and drag the chair prop behind until it is positioned behind the table.

6. Select the From Left camera from the Camera Controls to see the scene from a side view.

7. Click the Translate/Pull tool in the Editing Tools, select the figure's hip element, and drag backwards until the figure is in a sitting position. Then, drag on the figure circle to move the entire figure backward until it is sitting in the chair.

8. Select the main camera from the Camera Controls and rotate and move the camera until the figure is zoomed in to the figure.

   The figure is positioned about the table and chair props, as shown in Figure 5-7.

9. Select File, Save As and save the file as **Figure sitting.pz3**.

FIGURE 5-7

Figure sitting at table and chair props

ATTACH PROPS
TO ELEMENTS

What You'll Do

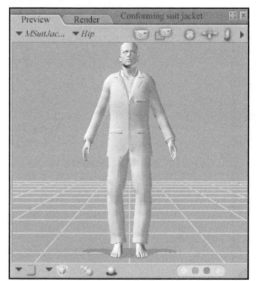

▶ In this lesson, you learn how to attach props to elements.

If you look through the types of props that are included in the Library, you'll find many figure accessories such as clothing items, jewelry, watches, hats, and ties. These props won't help you much if you need to reposition them every time you change a figure's pose. Luckily, you can attach and conform these props to the figure, so that when the figure is posed, the prop moves with it.

Attaching a Prop to a Figure Element

You attach a prop to a figure element by making the figure element the prop's **parent** with the Object, Change Parent menu command or by clicking the Set Parent button in the Properties panel. Once parented to an element, the prop will move with the element as the element is posed. Figure 5-8 shows a figure with a microphone prop attached to its left hand element. As the hand element is posed, the prop is moved with it.

FIGURE 5-8
Microphone prop attached to the figure's hand

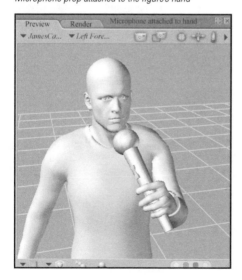

Replacing an Element with a Prop

Another way to attach a prop to an element is to actually replace an element with a prop. A good example of this is modeling a pirate who has a hook for a hand or a peg instead of a leg. To replace an element with a prop, load the prop into the scene, position the prop where it should be in place of the body part, select the body part that you want to replace, and choose the Object, Replace Body Part with Prop menu command. This opens a Replace Body Part dialog box where you can select the prop to replace the selected element. Figure 5-9 shows a silly figure where the head has been replaced by a hatchet prop.

FIGURE 5-9

Hatchet head

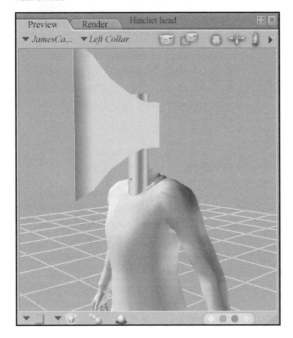

Conforming Clothing Props to a Figure

Another way to attach props to an object is to make clothing props conform to a figure's shape using the Figure, Conform To menu command. **Conforming clothes** are best applied to naked figures. All conforming props in the Library are easily identified with the Conforming label. Most clothes are loaded as figures and can be selected from the Figure List at the top of the Document Window. Selecting the Figure, Conform To menu command opens the Conform To dialog box, shown in Figure 5-10, where you can select the figure to which to conform the clothing. Figure 5-11 shows a shirt and pair of pants conforming to a figure.

QUICKTIP

When loading a clothing item from the Library, use the Add New Item button instead of the Replace Figure button or the current figure will be removed.

FIGURE 5-10
Conform To dialog box

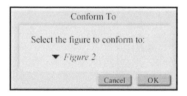

FIGURE 5-11
Conforming pants

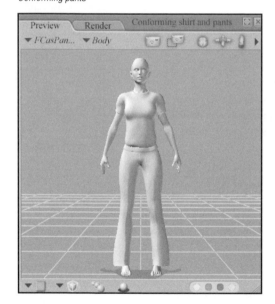

Attach a prop to a figure element

1. Open Poser with the default figure visible.

2. Select File, Import, Wavefront OBJ and import the Rolling pin.obj file into the current scene.

3. With the rolling pin item selected, click the Scale tool in the Editing Tools control. Hold down the Shift key and drag within the prop circle to uniformly reduce the size of the rolling pin prop.

4. Select the Rotate tool 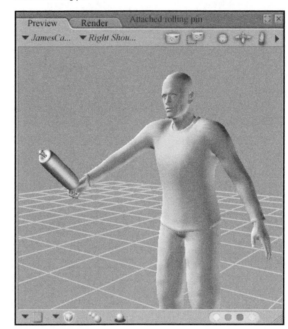 from the Editing Tools and rotate the rolling pin prop until it is parallel to the figure's right hand. Select the Translate/Pull tool to move the rolling pin prop close to the right hand.

5. Select the right hand element and drag the Grasp and Thumb Grasp dials in the Parameters palette to close the hand's fingers.

6. Position and orient the rolling pin prop within the right hand. Select the right hand camera from the Camera Controls to see it up close.

7. Select the rolling pin prop and select Object, Change Parent.

8. Select the Right Hand element in the Change Parent dialog box that appears and click OK.

   The prop will now move with the attached element, as shown in Figure 5-12.

9. Select File, Save As and save the file as **Attached rolling pin.pz3**.

FIGURE 5-12

Attached rolling pin

FIGURE 5-13

Clothing mismatched with figure

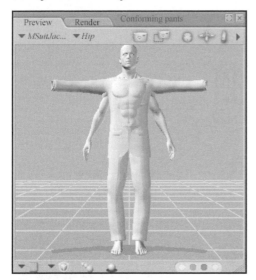

FIGURE 5-14

Conforming suit jacket

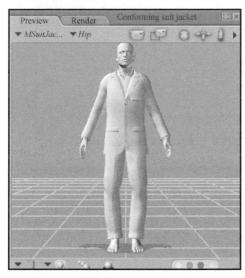

1. Select File, Open and open the Conforming pants.pz3 file.

2. Click the side control to the right of the interface to open the Library palette or select Window, Libraries.

3. Click the Props category at the top of the Library palette and navigate to the Clothing folder.

4. Select the Suit Jacket thumbnail and click the Add New Item button at the bottom of the Library palette.

   The selected clothing item is loaded into the Shader Window, but it doesn't match the figure, as shown in Figure 5-13.

5. With the Suit Jacket item selected in the Figure List at the top of the Document Window, select Figure, Conform To.

6. In the Conform To dialog box that appears, select the Figure 1 object and click OK.

   The clothing item is conformed to fit the figure, as shown in Figure 5-14.

7. Select File, Save As and save the file as **Conforming suit jacket.pz3**.

CREATE PROPS FROM
A SELECTED GROUP

What You'll Do

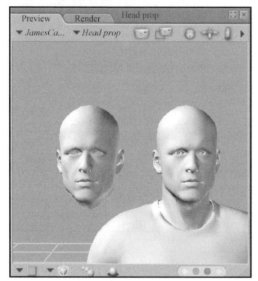

In this lesson, you learn how to create new props using the Group Editor.

If you want to create a prop from part of a figure, you can use the Group Editor, shown in Figure 5-15, to select the exact polygons that make up the prop. You open the Group Editor by clicking the Grouping tool in the Editing Tools control.

Selecting Polygons

Within the Group Editor dialog box are two buttons for selecting polygons—one for selecting and one for removing selected polygons. By dragging over polygons in the Document Window with the Grouping tool, you can select polygons as part of the group. The selected polygons are highlighted in red in the Document Window. To remove polygons from the current selection, click the Deselect button at the top of the Group Editor and click the polygons to remove.

FIGURE 5-15

Group Editor dialog box

You can also access the Deselect button by holding down the Ctrl key.

Creating a Prop

Clicking the Create Prop button converts the selected polygon group into a prop. A dialog box opens where you can name the new prop. Figure 5-16 shows a new prop that was created using the polygons that make up the chest element.

Spawning Multiple Props

Clicking the Spawn Prop button creates multiple props by converting all newly created groups into props.

FIGURE 5-16
New prop

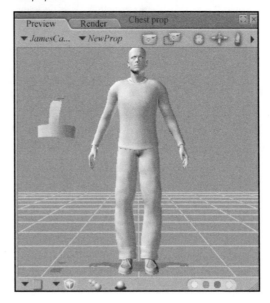

Create a new prop

1. Open Poser with the default figure visible.

2. Click the Grouping tool button ⊞ in the Editing Tools controls.

   The Group Editor panel appears and the figure in the Document Window goes dark.

3. Click the Hidden Line button in the Document Styles controls.

4. Click the head object in the Document Window.

   All the polygons that make up the head element are highlighted red.

5. Click the Create Prop button in the Group Editor panel.

   The New Prop Name dialog box appears.

6. Type the name, **Head shell**, in the New Prop Name dialog box and click OK.

7. Select the Head shell prop from the Actor List at the top of the Document Window and move it to the side of the original head object.

8. Click the Smooth Shaded button in the Display Styles controls.

   The head shell prop is positioned next to the figure's head, as shown in Figure 5-17.

9. Select File, Save As and save the file as **Head prop.pz3**.

FIGURE 5-17

Head prop

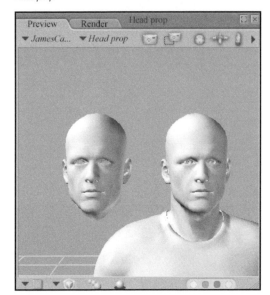

USE THE CONTENT ROOM

What You'll Do

▶ In this lesson, you learn how to use the Content Room.

If you've used all the presets in the Library and you're ready for some new content, you can open the Content Room, which gives you access to a ton of new content via an online connection and the Content Paradise Web site.

Accessing Content Paradise

When the Content Room is opened, the Content Paradise Web pages appear within the Content Room. Using these pages, you can search for objects by Partner, category or type in a text search. Each of the various

categories is displayed as a tab at the top of the pages. The categories include Figures, Clothing, Hair, Poses, Props and Other. When you open a category of objects, thumbnails of the available objects are displayed, as shown in Figure 5-18.

FIGURE 5-18
Paradise Content props

CAUTION

On Macintosh systems, Content Paradise opens within a separate window and the Auto Install feature is not available.

Purchasing Content

Below each object is the object's cost. Clicking the thumbnail displays a page with more detailed information on the selected object, such as the one in Figure 5-19. To purchase the item, click the shopping cart icon to add it to your cart. Clicking the Cart tab in the top-right corner lets you check out and pay for your selected objects. You need an account in order to purchase content online.

FIGURE 5-19
Detailed item information

Downloading and Installing Content

Once you have purchased the selected content, a download progress box appears for each selected object. Once all items are downloaded, the Install Options dialog box, shown in Figure 5-20, appears. Clicking the Install button automatically installs the content into the selected directory. Clicking the Copy button opens a file dialog box where you can select to save the content to the hard drive.

QUICKTIP

If the Web page fails to load for some reason, you can click the Reset Content Paradise button at the top of the Content Room and the first page will be reloaded.

Installing from a Zip Archive

Files that are downloaded are contained within a compressed archive with a .ZIP file extension. If a friend sends you a figure via an email, you can save the zip file to your hard drive and auto install it using the Install from Zip Archive button at the top of the Content Room. This button opens a file dialog box where you can select a zip file to auto install using the same Install Options dialog box.

Accessing Downloaded Content

Files that are auto installed are placed by default in the Downloads folder where Poser6 is installed. You can access the downloaded content by double-clicking the Up arrow folder at the top of the Library palette. At the top of each category are several folders including a folder labeled *Poser 6* and another labeled *Downloads,* as shown in Figure 5-21. The red circle marks the active folder. All downloaded content by default is in the Downloads folder.

FIGURE 5-21
Top Library folders

FIGURE 5-20
Install Options dialog box

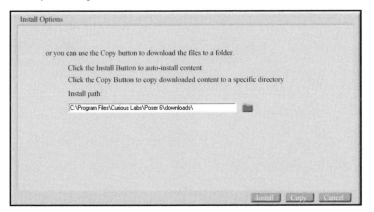

Add new content

1. Open Poser with the default figure visible.

2. Click the Content tab at the top of the interface to open the Content Room.

   The Content Paradise pages are displayed.

3. Click the Free Stuff link button at the top of the Content Paradise Web page.

4. Select a free object and click the shopping cart icon underneath its thumbnail.

   One item is added to the cart.

5. Click the Cart tab in the upper-right corner of the Web page.

   The selected item appears in the Web page.

6. Click the Checkout Go button.

   An account login page appears.

7. Enter your username and password or register to create a new account.

8. Click the Go button to complete your registration.

   After you purchase the item, the selected item is downloaded to the default folder and the Install Options dialog box appears.

9. Click the Install button.

   The item is automatically installed.

10. Click the side control to the right of the interface to open the Library palette or select Window, Libraries.

11. Click the category at the top of the Library palette for the item that you selected and then double-click the Up arrow folder until you reach the Poser 6 folder.

12. Double-click the Downloads folder to access the downloaded item, as shown in Figure 5-22.

FIGURE 5-22
Downloaded item

CHAPTER SUMMARY

This chapter explained how prop objects can be used to enhance the scene. Props can be loaded from and saved to the Library and can include external objects such as a mail box or a motorcycle or figure accessories such as watches, jewelry, hairstyles, or clothes. Props can also be created in an external package and imported into Poser. Props are selected and positioned just like figure elements using the Editing Tools. Finally, props can be attached to existing figure elements or created from existing body parts.

What You Have Learned

In this chapter, you
- Learned how props can be loaded from the Library.
- Discovered how external props can be imported into Poser using a number of different formats and options and how imported props can be saved to the Library for future use.

- Selected and positioned props using the various Editing Tools.
- Attached props to figure elements using the Set Parent feature, replaced body parts with props, and made clothes conform to the figure.
- Created new props from a selected group of polygons.

Key Terms from This Chapter

Prop. Any external object added to the scene to enhance the final image. Props may include scenery, figure accessories, clothes, and hair.

Weld. An import option used to combine vertices with the same coordinates together.

Offset. The location of an imported prop as measured from the scene's origin point.

Normal. A non-rendered vector that extends from the center of each polygon face and is used to indicate the direction the polygon face is pointing.

Locked prop. A prop whose position and orientation is set and cannot be changed unless the object is unlocked.

Parent. The controlling object that a child object is attached to. When the parent moves, the child object moves with it.

Conforming prop. An object that is deformed in order to fit the designated figure.

chapter

6 ESTABLISHING
a Scene

1. Load light and camera Library presets.

2. Work with lights.

3. Set light materials.

4. Work with cameras.

5. Aim and attach lights and cameras.

6. Change the background.

7. Add atmosphere effects.

chapter 6 ESTABLISHING a Scene

Poser enables you to work with figures, but you can also dress up the scene that the figure resides in. By establishing a scene, you can use Poser to create images without requiring any other software. Several items are involved in establishing a scene and learning to control each of these various elements will help you as you begin to create rendered images. These items can include cameras, lights, a background image, and atmospheric elements.

If you don't know where to start in configuring your lights and cameras, you can look in the Library palette for several examples of lighting and camera presets that can help you as you start out. From these presets, you can begin to explore the various controls contained with the Light and Camera Controls. You can control both also by using the parameter dials and the Editing Tools.

Poser also includes some specialized features that let you point lights and cameras at specific items in the scene. For example, you can quickly animate the rotations of a camera by pointing the camera towards the figure's head or torso. Spotlights can also be pointed at a figure's head or hands to always keep them in the light during an animation.

You can change the background of the Document Window to display a color, a picture, a movie, or particular texture and atmospheric effects. Effects such as depth cueing and volume fog can add to the ambience of a scene.

Tools You'll Use

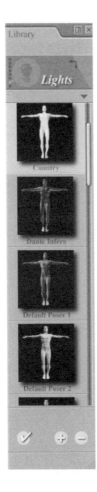

LOAD LIGHT AND CAMERA
LIBRARY PRESETS

What You'll Do

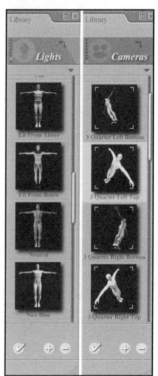 In this lesson, you learn how to use the Library to load and save light and camera presets.

The last two categories in the Library palette are Lights and Cameras. These presets can save you some time manipulating settings to create a certain look. You can also easily save new lights and cameras back into the Library.

Loading Lights and Cameras from the Library

To access the available lights and cameras from the Library, click either category and navigate the folders until you find just the light or camera you want to apply to the current scene. Each light and camera thumbnail shows the default figure using the lighting or camera setup.

With the desired thumbnail selected, click the Change Item button at the bottom of the Library palette and the selected light or camera set is loaded into the Document Window. Figure 6-1 shows several light and camera thumbnails found in the Library.

FIGURE 6-1

Some available Library lights and cameras

Saving Light and Camera Settings to the Library

You can also save the current light and/or camera settings to the Library using the Add to Library button located at the bottom of the Library palette. This button opens a simple dialog box where you can name the current light or camera; Poser then adds the thumbnail for the current settings to the open Library folder.

Removing Presets from the Library

The Remove from Library button in the Library palette permanently deletes the selected thumbnail.

Using the Camera Dots

If you want to temporarily remember a specific camera setting for use during the current session, you can use the **camera dots** to place the current camera settings. To remember camera settings, select the Camera Dots option from the pop-up menu at the top of the Memory Dots control. Clicking a dot once adds the current camera to the selected dot where you can recall it at any time by clicking the dot that holds the camera settings. Holding down the Alt key while clicking a camera dot clears the dot.

Load light and camera settings from the Library

1. Open Poser with the default man visible.

2. Click the side control to the right of the interface to open the Library palette or select Window, Libraries.

3. Click the Lights category at the top of the Library palette and locate the Lit from Below light setting. Then click the Change Item button at the bottom of the Library palette.

   The scene is updated with the new light settings.

4. Click the Cameras category at the top of the Library palette and locate the 3 Quarter Left Top camera setting. Then click the Change Item button at the bottom of the Library palette.

   The scene is updated with the new camera settings, as shown in Figure 6-2.

5. Select File, Save As and save the file as **Loaded lights and camera.pz3**.

FIGURE 6-2

Scene with preset lights and camera

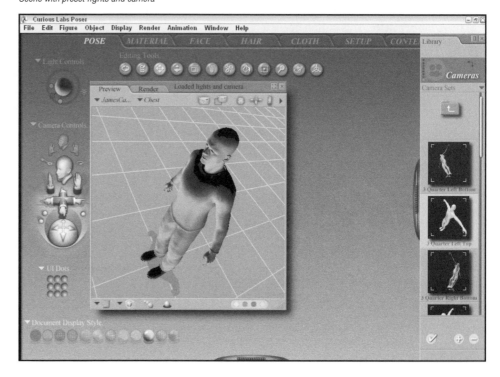

FIGURE 6-3

New camera setting added to the Library

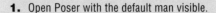

1. Open Poser with the default man visible.

2. Click the side control to the right of the inter-face to open the Library palette or select Window, Libraries.

3. Click the Lights category at the top of the Library palette and open a Lights folder.

4. Change the lighting configuration using the Light Controls.

5. Click the Add to Library button ⊕ at the bottom of the Library palette and name the custom light setting in the Set Name dialog box that appears. Then click OK. Click OK again in the Save Frames dialog box.

6. Repeat steps 3-5 for a custom camera setting.

   The new camera setting appears in the folder thumbnails, as shown in Figure 6-3.

WORK WITH LIGHTS

What You'll Do

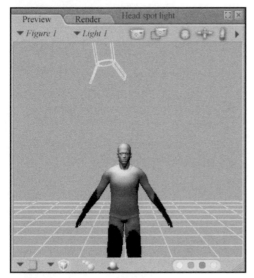

In this lesson, you learn how to work effectively with lights.

If a scene contained no lights, all scene items wouldn't be visible, but Poser has three default lights that are available. You can easily add more light sources to the scene. Poser works with four light sources—**infinite lights**, **spotlights**, **point lights**, and **diffuse image-based lights** (IBLs).

> **NOTE**
>
> Not every display style displays the effects of lights.

Learning the Light Types

Infinite lights shine from a distance so all its rays are parallel when they strike the scene objects. This causes all scene elements to receive an equal amount of light. Spotlights are focused, casting light only to those scene objects that are within the cone of influence; objects farther away receive less light than closer objects. Point lights cast light in all directions from a single point such as a light bulb or a candle in a room. Diffuse image-based lights (IBLs) define the scene lighting by building an image of the scene that holds all the lighting information. Using light, image maps can speed up rendering times because the light information doesn't need to be recomputed.

> **NOTE**
>
> When using point lights and diffuse IBLs, realistic shadows can be computed only using raytracing.

Creating New Lights

All scene lights are displayed within the Light Controls by clicking the Create Light button, but the type of light is set using the options in the Properties palette. Poser lets you switch easily between the various light types.

Using the Light Controls

The Light Controls offer a convenient way of creating and positioning lights, and setting light properties. To open the Light Controls, select Window, Light Controls. The Light Controls, shown in Figure 6-4, include a large sample sphere in the center that shows the lighting effects; surrounding it are three smaller circles. These smaller circles are the lights. You can change their locations by dragging them about the larger sphere. When you select a circle representing a light, controls for changing its intensity, color, and properties appear. There are also buttons for removing the selected light and creating new lights.

Selecting and Positioning Lights

You can select lights by clicking their circular icons in the Light Controls, by selecting a light from the Actor List located at the top of the Document Window, or by choosing a light from the Hierarchy Editor. When a light is selected, an indicator of the light, shown in Figure 6-5, becomes visible within the Document Window. You can position lights by dragging their circular icons with the Light Controls or by dragging their indicator in the Document Window using the Editing Tools. Each indicator is different depending on the light type that is selected. You also can position lights using the parameter dials found in the Parameters palette.

FIGURE 6-4
Light controls

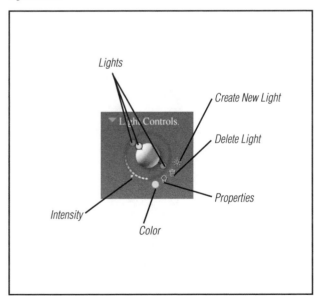

FIGURE 6-5
Light indicators appear in the Document Window

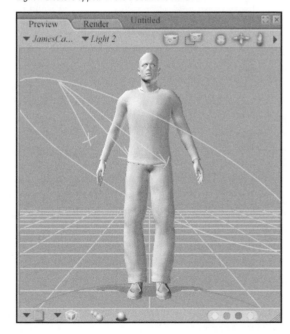

NOTE

When the spotlight type is selected, the parameter dials include values for setting the spotlight's cone distance and angle.

Setting Light Properties

You can set several light properties in the Light Controls, but an extended set of properties is available in the Properties palette, as shown in Figure 6-6. The Name field lists the light's name, which is simply Light, and a number by default, but you can type a new name. The Visible property makes the visual indicator of the light appear in the Document Window, the Animating property enables the light to be animated, and the On property turns the light on and off. The Properties palette also includes a set of radio

FIGURE 6-6
Light properties

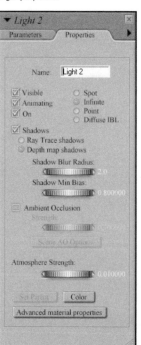

buttons for selecting the light type and controls for shadows and **ambient occlusion**.

Enabling Shadows

Shadows are computed when the scene is rendered and two methods exist for creating shadows—**Ray Trace** and **Depth Map**. Ray Trace shadows are much more realistic because they are created by following each light ray as it bounces about the scene, but the drawback is that they can take a considerable amount of time to render. Shadow Map shadows are blurrier, but they can be rendered very quickly. You can set the amount of blur that a shadow has using the Shadow Blur Radius setting. The Shadow Min Bias setting prevents the scene objects from casting shadows on themselves. Figure 6-7 shows two rendered images side by side in the Render panel with Shadow Map shadows with different Blur Radius settings. Notice how the left half of the figure has a blurry shadow and the right half is clean.

FIGURE 6-7
Shadows can be blurred

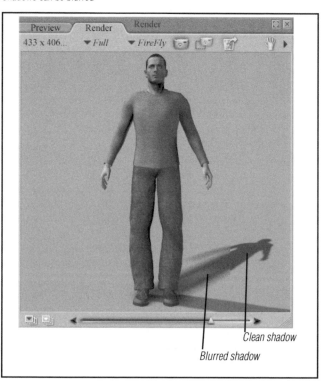

Clean shadow

Blurred shadow

QUICKTIP

If multiple lights are included in a scene, only enable shadows for one light in the scene.

Using Ambient Occlusion Settings

Ambient light, as specified for the various surfaces in the Material Room, is a general lighting that lights all scene objects without radiating from a particular source. It occurs naturally by light that bounces off the surfaces of objects. Ambient light in particular affects shadows. *Ambient occlusion* is an effect that diminishes ambient light from the scene, thus causing shadows to appear darker and providing more contrast for the rendered image. In addition to the Strength value, you can open the Scene Ambient Occlusion Options dialog box, shown in Figure 6-8, using the Scene Ambient Occlusion Options button in the Properties palette. This dialog box includes three additional values—Max Distance, which defines the distance that raytraced rays are allowed to travel; Bias, which defines where the light rays originate from; and Number of Samples, which determines how many light rays are cast into the scene.

CAUTION

Using high Max Distance or Number Samples values can result in a very long rendering time.

FIGURE 6-8

Scene Ambient Occlusion Options dialog box

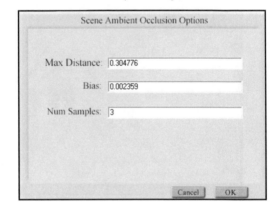

Create and position a spotlight

1. Open Poser with the default man visible.

2. Select each of the light circles in the Light Controls and click the Delete Light button 🗑 to remove the default lights. Click OK in the Delete confirmation dialog box that appears.

3. Click the Create Light button 🔆 in the Light Controls.

   A new light circle is added to the Light Controls and a spotlight indicator appears in the Document Window.

4. Drag the light circle in the Light Controls to roughly position the new spotlight above the scene figure.

5. Drag the Move XZ control in the Camera Controls to zoom out the scene until the spotlight indicator is visible in the Document Window.

6. Select Window, Parameter Dials to open the Parameters palette, if it isn't already open, and set the Angle End value to 30.

7. Click and drag on the spotlight indicator in the Document Window and position it so the spotlight is positioned to light the head.

   The spotlight is positioned to light the head from above, as shown in Figure 6-9.

8. Select File, Save As and save the file as **Head spot light.pz3**.

FIGURE 6-9

Spotlight focused on the figure's head

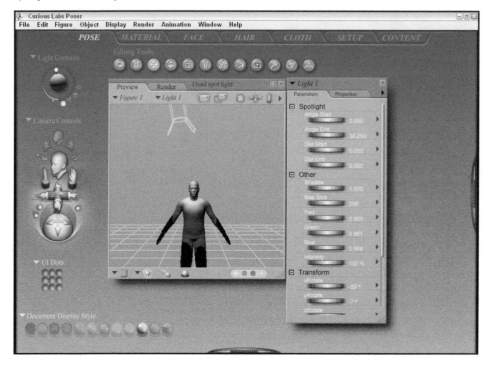

FIGURE 6-10
Rendered figure with shadow

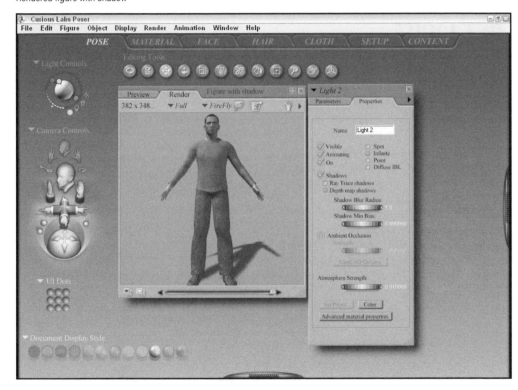

1. Open Poser with the default man visible.

2. Select Lights, Light 1 from the Actor List at the top of the Document Window.

3. Select Window, Parameter Dials to open the Parameters/Properties palette, if it isn't already open. Click the Properties tab and disable the Shadows option to turn off shadows for this light. Repeat this step for Light 3.

4. Select Light 2 and enable the Shadows option in the Properties palette. Then select the Depth Map Shadows option and set the Shadow Blur Radius to 5.0.

5. Click the Render button ⬛ in the Document Window.

   The scene is rendered and the rendered image is displayed in the Document Window with shadows, as shown in Figure 6-10.

6. Select File, Save As and save the file as **Figure with shadow.pz3**.

SET LIGHT
MATERIALS

What You'll Do

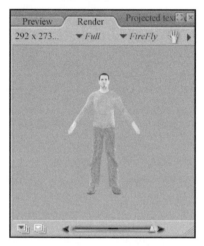

In this lesson, you learn how to use the Material Room to set light materials.

If you look closely at the Properties palette when a light is selected, you'll notice that there is a button labeled Advanced Material Properties. Clicking this button opens the Advanced panel in the Material Room with the selected light's nodes visible. Although you can set a light's color and intensity in the Light Controls, the Material Room offers many more options for controlling the look of a light.

Accessing Light Material Properties

If you select a light from the Actor List in the Material Room, you can view a node listing all the light's material values in the Advanced panel of the Shader Window, as shown in Figure 6-11.

FIGURE 6-11
Light material values

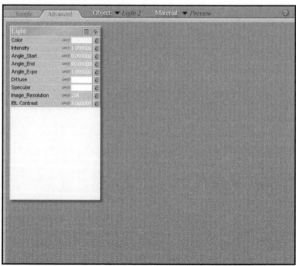

Projecting a Textured Light

If you change a light's color, the entire scene is affected by the light color and the light color is mixed with any diffuse surface colors, but using the light material values, you can also have the light project a texture. This effect is like shining a light through a transparent image. To create such an effect, simply add a texture to the light material. You can do this in either the Simple or Advanced panels of the Material Room. Figure 6-12 shows a texture image added to a light in the Simple panel of the Material Room.

Enabling Image-Based Lights

One of the available light types is the Diffuse IBL light. This light type lets you add a loaded texture as the light source or any shader tree. The controlling shader tree can even be animated to show effects like a flashing light or a disco-ball light. The Wacros panel includes a preset for loading textures for an IBL light.

FIGURE 6-12

Light projected image

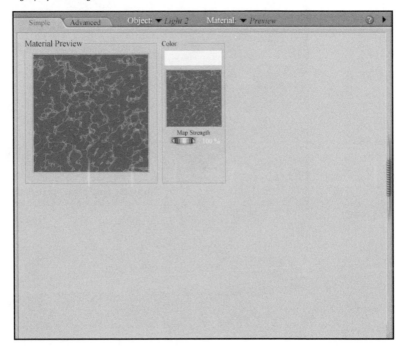

Project a textured light

1. Open Poser with the default man visible.

2. Select Lights, Light 2 from the Actor List at the top of the Document Window.

3. Select Window, Parameter Dials to open the Parameters/Properties palette, if it isn't already open. Click the Diffuse IBL option to make the selected light an image-based light.

4. With the Light 2 object still selected, click the Material tab to open the Material Room.

5. Select the Simple tab in the Shader Window and click the image area under the color swatch. In the Texture Manager that opens, click the Browse button and load the Banana Husk.tif image. Then click OK.

6. From the Document Window's pop-up menu, select the Render option.

   The scene is rendered and the rendered image is displayed in the Document Window, as shown in Figure 6-13. Notice how the figure is colored using the texture image for a light source.

7. Select File, Save As and save the file as **Projected texture light.pz3**.

FIGURE 6-13

Projected texture light

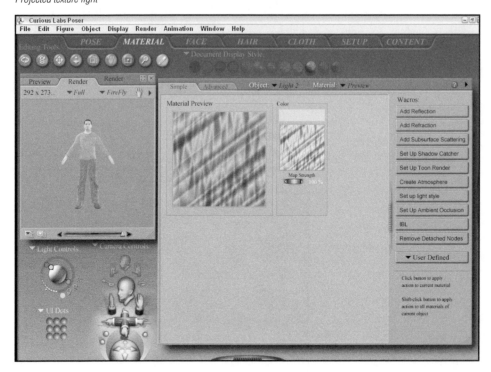

WORK WITH
CAMERAS

What You'll Do

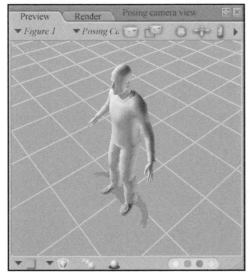

In this lesson, you learn how to work with cameras.

Cameras provide you a view of the scene and can be manipulated to show you the exact portion of the scene that you want to concentrate on. You can select cameras from the Actor List at the top of the Document Window and can manipulate them using the Camera Controls.

FIGURE 6-14
Camera controls

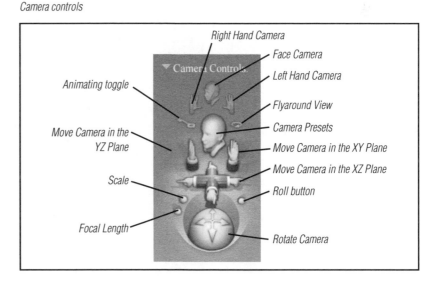

Using the Camera Controls

The Camera Controls allow you to pan, rotate, and zoom in on the scene. These controls, shown in Figure 6-14, have an immediate impact on the scene displayed in the Document Window. By using these controls, you can control precisely which part of the scene is displayed.

The top three icons focus the view on the right hand, the left hand, and the face. Figure 6-15 shows the scene from the Face camera. The key icon toggles animating on and off. The key icon is colored red when animating is enabled. The Flyaround button spins the camera about the figure's center.

Using Camera Presets

The centered head icon lets you switch between preset camera views including the Main, Auxiliary, Left, Right, Front, Back, Top, Bottom, Face, Pose, Right Hand, and

Left Hand cameras. You can also select each of these cameras from the Camera Control's pop-up menu and by using the Display, Camera View menu command. Each of these cameras has its own icon, which you can access by clicking the icon or by clicking and dragging to the left or right.

The Main and Auxiliary cameras are rotated about the scene, but the Posing camera is different in that it is rotated about the selected figure. The Face and Hand cameras also rotate about the face and hands of the selected figure.

FIGURE 6-15
Face Camera

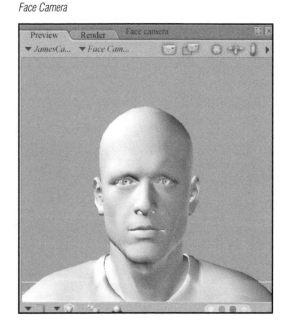

Using Orthogonal and Shadow Cameras

The Left, Right, Front, Back, Top, and Bottom cameras are all orthogonal cameras that are located at the end of each axis. Orthogonal cameras are special views that show the scene as a 2D image without any perspective and all dimension measurements are correct. Figure 6-16 shows the scene using the Left camera preset. Orthogonal cameras also cannot be rotated and the Rotation sphere in the Camera Controls is disabled when any of these cameras are selected.

The pop-up menu in the Camera Controls also includes a **Shadow camera** for each light in the scene. These cameras are positioned and oriented to point the same direction as its light and provide a look at how the shadows will be cast when rendered. Shadow cameras, like orthogonal

FIGURE 6-16

Left camera

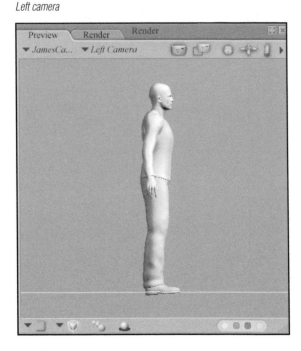

cameras, cannot be rotated. Figure 6-17 shows the Shadow camera for Light 1.

Moving and Rotating a Camera

The hand icons in the Camera Controls are used to move the camera view within the YZ plane, the XY plane, or XZ plane. To use these icons, just click them and drag. The view in the Document Window is updated as you drag. The sphere with arrows on it at the bottom of the Camera Controls is used to rotate the camera. It is used like the

FIGURE 6-17
Shadow camera

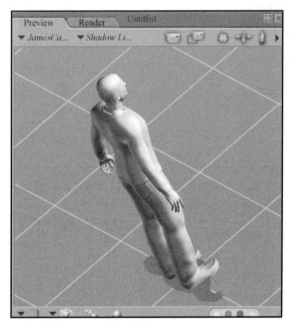

move icons by clicking and dragging in the direction you want to rotate the camera. The Roll button spins the figure within the Document Window about its center. You can also change the camera's position and rotation by dragging the parameter dials in the Parameters palette.

Changing a Camera's Scale and Focal Length

The final two Camera Controls buttons to the left of the Rotate Camera control are for adjusting the camera's scale and **focal length**. Dragging on the Scale button changes the size of the figure within the view pane and dragging with the Focal

Length button changes the center focus point for the camera, which results in the how close or far the figure appears from the camera.

Using Display Guides

The Display, Guides menu command includes several useful display guides that can help as you begin to move the cameras about the scene. In addition to the two guides used to indicate the relative size and proportions of the figure, the Display, Guides menu command also includes the following guides:

- **Ground Plane:** Can be turned on and off. It is useful to help set the vertical alignment of objects in the scene. The Material Room can also be used to apply a unique material to the ground plane.

- **Horizon Line:** Adds a set of horizontal dashed lines across the Document Window to show where the horizon in the distance is located.

- **Vanishing Lines:** Marks the point off in the distance where all objects converge to show perspective.

- **Focus Distant Guide:** Marks the point where the camera is in focus. This is used to determine the center point for the Depth of Field render effect.

FIGURE 6-18
Posing camera view

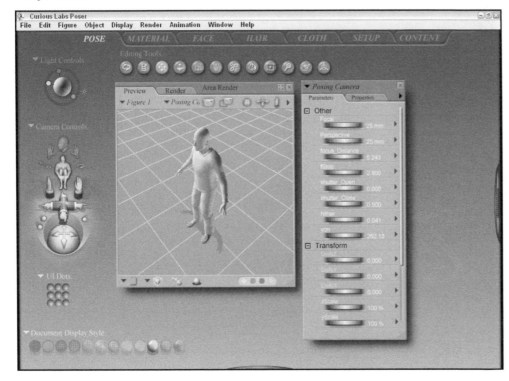

1. Open Poser with the default figure visible.

2. From the Camera Controls pop-up menu, select Posing Camera. Then, from the Actor List at the top of the Document Window, select the Cameras, Posing Camera option.

3. Select Window, Parameter Dials to open the Parameters/Properties palette, if it isn't already open.

4. Drag the Pitch dial to -45 and the Yaw dial to 50.

   Notice how the Posing camera rotates about the figure, as shown in Figure 6-18.

5. Select File, Save As and save the file as **Posing camera view.pz3**.

Use a Shadow camera

1. Open Poser with the default figure visible.

2. From the Camera Controls pop-up menu, select Shadow Camera 2. Then, from the Actor List at the top of the Document Window, select the Cameras, Shadow Lite 2 Cam option.

3. Drag on the Zoom parameter dial to see the scene up closer.

   Notice how the figure is completely bathed in light, as shown in Figure 6-19.

4. Select File, Save As and save the file as **Shadow camera view.pz3**.

FIGURE 6-19
Shadow camera view

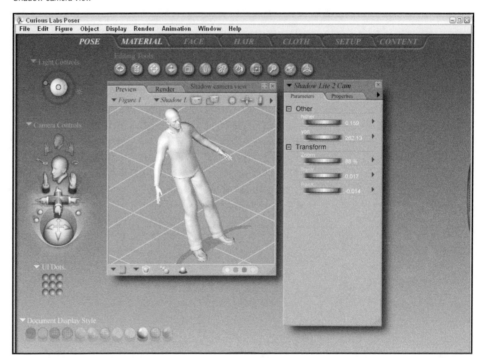

AIM AND ATTACH
LIGHTS AND CAMERAS

What You'll Do

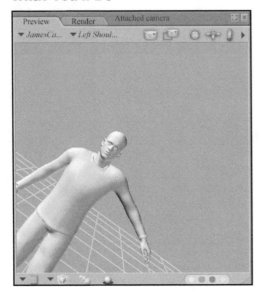

▶ *In this lesson, you learn how to use the Point At menu command to aim cameras and attach cameras to figure elements.*

In addition to the many controls, parameters, and properties available for lights and cameras, there are also controls available for making lights and cameras point at specific items and for attaching lights and cameras to other scene items.

Pointing Lights and Cameras

You can aim lights and cameras to point at a specific scene item. This item can be any body part, prop, or even another light or camera. To point a light or a camera at a specific item, first select the item using the Actor List at the top of the Document Window or the Parameters/Properties palette. Then, choose Object, Point At and the Choose Actor dialog box, shown in Figure 6-20, appears with a hierarchical list of the scene items. From the Choose Actor dialog box, select the item that you want the selected item to point at and click OK.

To remove the Point At feature, select the item and the Object, Point At menu command again and choose the None button in the Choose Actor dialog box.

Attaching Cameras to Items

You can attach cameras to scene items using Object, Change Parent. This menu command opens the Change Parent dialog box, which looks the same as the Choose Actor dialog box, where you can choose an item to be the camera's parent. Once attached, the camera moves along with the attached item.

FIGURE 6-20
Choose Actor dialog box

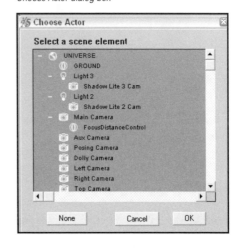

Point a spotlight

1. Open Poser with the default man visible.

2. Select the Lights, Light 2 item from the Actor List at the top of the Document Window.

3. Open the Properties palette and enable the Spotlight option.

4. With the Light 2 item selected, choose Object, Point At.

   The Choose Actor dialog box opens.

5. Select the Head element in the Choose Actor dialog box and click OK.

6. Select and move the figure about the Document Window.

   Notice how the spotlight stays focused on the head element as the figure is moved about the scene, as shown in Figure 6-21.

7. Select File, Save As and save the file as **Pointing spot light.pz3**.

FIGURE 6-21
Pointing spotlight

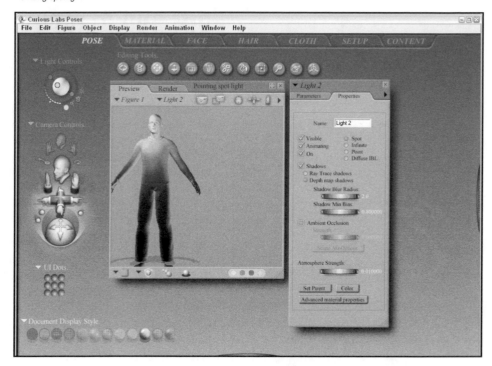

FIGURE 6-22
Attached camera

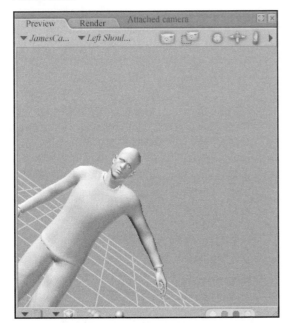

1. Open Poser with the default figure visible.

2. From the Actor List at the top of the Document Window, select the Cameras, Main Camera option.

3. With the Main Camera item selected, choose Object, Change Parent.

   The Change Parent dialog box opens.

4. Select the Left Hand element in the Change Parent dialog box and click OK.

5. Select and rotate the left arm in the Document Window.

   Notice how the camera changes as the left hand moves, as shown in Figure 6-22.

6. Select File, Save As and save the file as **Attached camera.pz3**.

CHANGE THE
BACKGROUND

What You'll Do

In this lesson, you learn how to change the Document Window background.

Adding a background image or movie can often help you as you pose a figure. Imagine loading the movie of a dancer as a background. You could then animate the dance steps by matching the figure to the background movie. You can also render background images to add a nice backdrop to your scene.

Changing the Background Color

Changing the background color is accomplished easily using the color dots found at the bottom of the Document Window. There are color dots for changing the foreground, background, shadow, and ground colors. Clicking any of these dots opens a pop-up color palette where you can select a new color.

Loading a Background Image

You load **background images** using the File, Import, Background Picture menu command. This makes the Open dialog box appear where you can select the image file to open as a background. The file formats that can be imported include SGI, 8BP, BMP, DIP, Flash Pix, GIF, JPEG, MAC, PICT, PIC, PNG, PNTG, PSD, TGA, and TPIC files. If the Document Window is set at a resolution different from the loaded background image, a warning dialog box appears asking if you want to change the Document Window to match the image resolution. Figure 6-23 shows the Document Window with a background image loaded.

FIGURE 6-23
Loaded background image

> **NOTE**
>
> If a background image is loaded, but doesn't appear, select Display, Show Background Picture (Ctrl+B) to make the background image visible.

Loading a Background Movie

In addition to static images, Poser can also load movie files as a background. Windows systems use a File, Import, AVI Footage menu command and Macintosh systems use a File, Import, QuickTime Footage menu command. Either command makes an Open dialog box appear where you can select the appropriate file to open. Figure 6-24 shows the Document Window with a background movie.

Clearing the Background

To remove the background picture or movie, use the Display, Clear Background Picture or the Display, Clear Background Footage menu commands, respectively.

Using a Background Shader

If you open the Material Room, you can select the Background option from the Material List at the top of the Shader Window. This opens the nodes used for the background in the Shader Window, as shown in Figure 6-25. Using these nodes, you can define a shader that is rendered along with the background image or movie. To enable the designated background shader, choose the Display, Use Background Shader Node menu command.

FIGURE 6-24

Loaded background movie

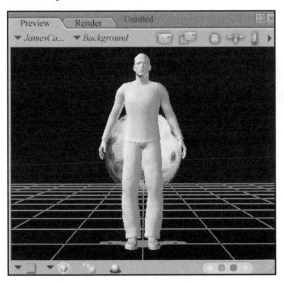

FIGURE 6-25

Background shader

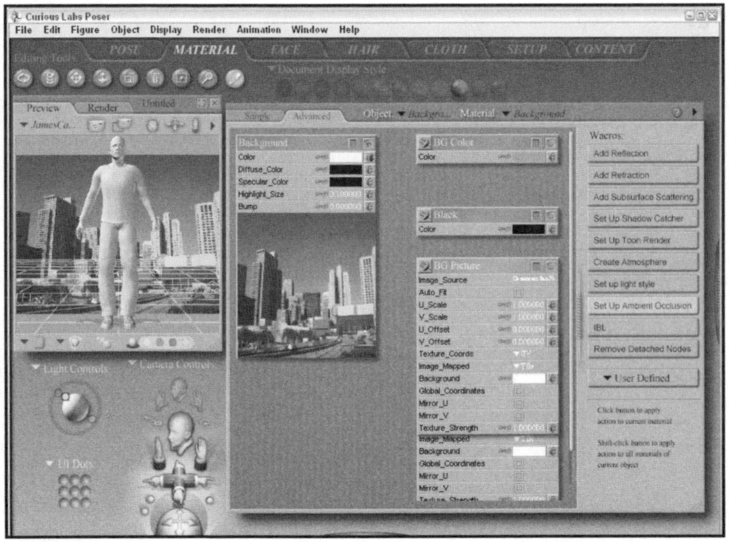

Load a background picture

1. Select File, Import, Background Picture.

   The Open dialog box appears.

2. Select and open the Oregon coast.jpg image file and click Open.

   A warning dialog box appears stating that the Document Window is different than the image resolution. Click the Yes button to match the window to the image. The image appears in the background of the Document Window, as shown in Figure 6-26.

3. Select File, Save As and save the file as **Background image.pz3**.

Load a background movie

1. Open Poser with the default figure visible.

2. Select File, Import, AVI Footage.

   The Open dialog box appears.

3. Select and open the Exploding planet.avi movie file and click Open.

   A warning dialog box appears stating that the width/height ratio is different than the Document Window. Click Yes to continue. The first frame of the movie appears in the background of the Document Window, as shown in Figure 6-27.

4. Select File, Save As and save the file as **Background movie.pz3**.

FIGURE 6-26
Background image

FIGURE 6-27
Background movie

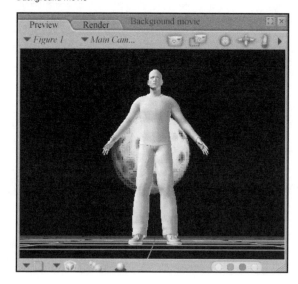

ADD ATMOSPHERE
EFFECTS

What You'll Do

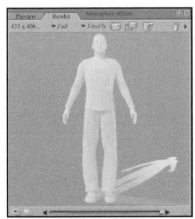

In this lesson, you learn how to add atmosphere effects to the scene.

If you look in the Material List found at the top of the Shader Window in the Material Room, you'll find an Atmosphere option directly below the Background option. Selecting this option opens the Atmosphere root node in the Advanced panel of the Shader Window, as shown in Figure 6-28. Using this node, you can add depth cue and volume atmosphere effects to the rendered scene.

CAUTION

Enabling atmosphere effects can add a substantial amount of time to the rendering process.

Enabling Depth Cueing

By selecting the Depth Cue option in the root Atmosphere node, you can turn on the **depth cueing** atmosphere effect. This works just like the Depth Cue option in the Document Window by making objects farther back in the scene appear hazier.

FIGURE 6-28
Atmosphere root shader

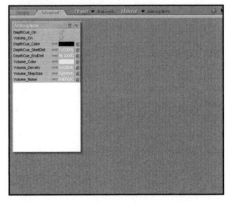

Adding a Volume Effect

The Volume atmosphere effect adds a fog and haze to the scene by coloring all scene objects with the designated color. Figure 6-29 shows a figure rendered with a **volume effect**. Notice how the figure details are washed out by the fog effect. The volume effect also affects shadows.

FIGURE 6-29
Rendered volume effect

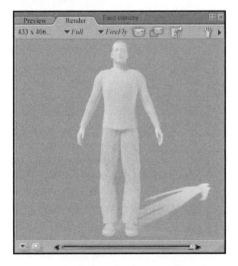

Enable atmosphere effects

1. Open Poser with the default figure visible.

2. Click the Material tab at the top of the interface to open the Material Room and click the Advanced tab in the Shader Window, if necessary.

3. Select the Atmosphere option from the Object List at the top of the Shader Window.

   The Atmosphere root node appears in the Shader Window.

4. Enable the Depth Cue On and Volume On values in the Atmosphere root node.

5. Click the Pose tab to move back to the Pose Room.

6. Click the Render button at the top of the Document Window.

   The scene is rendered using the atmosphere effects, as shown in Figure 6-30.

7. Select File, Save As and save the file as **Atmospheric effects.pz3**.

FIGURE 6-30

Rendered atmosphere effects

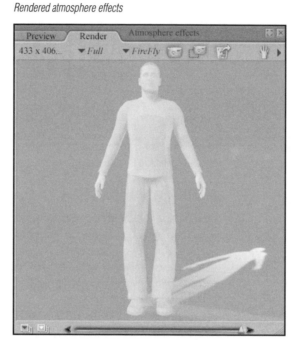

CHAPTER SUMMARY

This chapter covered many of the elements that are used to create a scene other than a posed figure and props, including lights, cameras, backgrounds, and atmosphere effects. This chapter also included an in-depth look at how to use lights and cameras, including aiming lights and cameras at specific scene objects. The various background and atmosphere effects were also covered, including background images and movies and volume effects.

What You Have Learned

In this chapter, you
- Loaded and saved lights and cameras to and from the Library.
- Learned about the different light types.
- Enabled shadows for the selected light.
- Changed light materials, including projecting textures onto the scene.
- Attached and aimed lights and cameras to and at objects.
- Created a new background with colors, images, materials, and movies.

- Added depth cueing and volume atmosphere effects to the scene.

Key Terms from This Chapter

Camera dots.   An interface control used to remember and recall camera position and properties.

Infinite light.   A light that simulates shining from an infinite distance so all light rays are parallel.

Spotlight.   A light that projects light within a cone of influence.

Point light.   A light that projects light rays in all directions equally.

Image-based light (IBL).   A light that illuminates the scene by recording all light information into an image map.

Ray trace shadows.   Shadows that are calculated using an accurate raytracing method that results in sharp edges.

Depth map shadows.   Shadows that are calculated and the shadow information is saved in a depth map, resulting in shadows with blurred edges.

Ambient occlusion.   An effect that diminishes ambient light from the scene, thus causing shadows to appear darker and providing more contrast for the rendered image.

Textured light.   A light that projects a texture map onto the scene.

Shadow camera.   A camera that is positioned in the same location as a light.

Focal length.   A camera property that changes the center focus point for the camera.

Background image.   An image that is set to appear behind the scene.

Depth cueing.   An atmosphere effect that makes objects farther in the scene appear hazier.

Volume effect.   An atmosphere effect that colors all scene objects with the designated color, much like fog.

chapter

7

CREATING
a Face

1. Learn the Face Room interface.

2. Create a face from photos.

3. Change texture variation.

4. Use the Face Shaping tool.

5. Add the face to the figure.

6. Work with expressions.

213

chapter 7 CREATING a Face

If you've ever wanted to place your face on a superhero's body, now is your chance. The Face Room includes several sets of controls for creating and modifying the look of the figure face. These modified faces are then applied to the figure model.

There are two ways to modify faces in the Face Room and controls to use each way. One way is to change the face texture, which can include color, shading, highlighting, beard, and so on. Another way to alter the face is to change the head's geometry by deforming the head model.

A number of parameters are available for changing the face's texture, including the ability to load custom face images. Using the Photo Lineup panel in the Face Room,

you can load custom front- and side-view face images and map them to the head geometry for the current figure. You can also save the existing texture map and edit it within an image-editing package.

Even more parameters are available to change the head geometry, including an interface Face Shaping tool, which lets you deform the head geometry by dragging in a separate pane.

You can apply the resulting face to the current figure by simply clicking a button. This chapter also looks at the parameters available for working with **expressions**.

Tools You'll Use

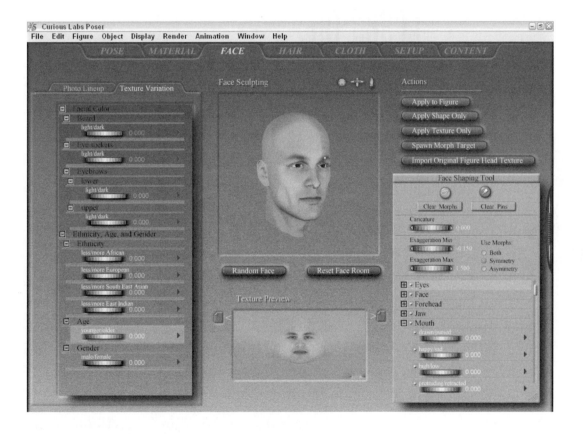

LEARN THE
FACE ROOM INTERFACE

What You'll Do

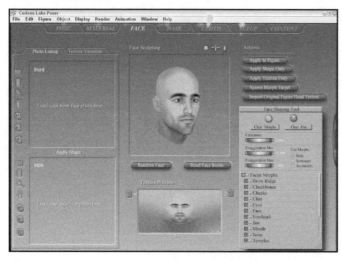

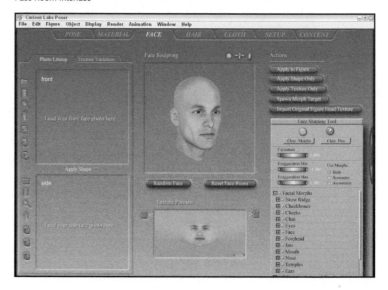

You open the Face Room by clicking the Face tab at the top of the Poser interface. This opens an interface setup that is different from the Pose Room, as shown in Figure 7-1.

The main interfaces within this room are the Photo Lineup panel, the Face Sculpting

FIGURE 7-1
Face Room interface

In this lesson, you learn how to using the Face Room interface.

Preview pane, and the Face Shaping Tool dialog box.

CAUTION

You cannot access the File, Save menu command when the Face Room is open. To save the current scene, click the Pose tab to access the Pose Room again.

Using the Photo Lineup Panel

You use the Photo Lineup panel, shown in Figure 7-2, to load custom front and side face images into the Face Room. These images can then be matched to a 3D head using a series of walkthrough steps. To the left side of the panes are several buttons used to load, remove, and manipulate the face images.

Using the Texture Variation Pane

You access the Texture Variation pane, shown in Figure 7-3, by clicking the Texture Variation tab at the top of the Photo Lineup panel. Using this pane, you can adjust the parameters of the loaded face images. The parameters contained within this pane include facial colors for the beard, eye sockets, and eyebrows, along with parameters to define the ethnicity, age, and gender of the face.

FIGURE 7-2

Photo Lineup panel

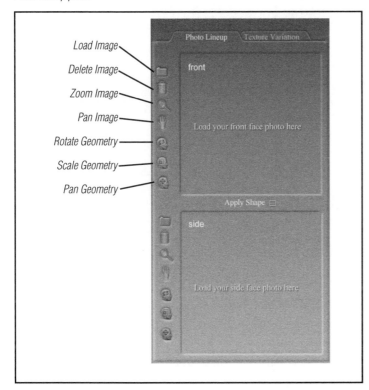

FIGURE 7-3

Texture Variation pane

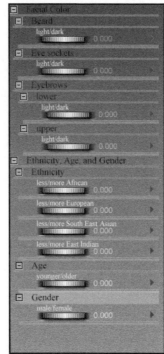

Using the Face Sculpting Pane

The Face Sculpting pane, shown in Figure 7-4, shows a preview of the current images mapped onto 3D geometry. You can move and rotate the face within the preview pane using the three view controls at the top-right corner of the pane. The Face Sculpting pane also lets you interactively change the face's shape by dragging with the Putty and Pin tools located in the Face Shaping Tool panel or by changing the parameters located in the Face Shaping Tool panel. The Face Sculpting pane also includes Random Face and Reset Face Room buttons.

Using the Texture Preview Pane

The Texture Preview pane, shown in Figure 7-5, shows the actual 2D texture that is generated by the Face Room and is mapped onto the 3D geometry to create a completed head. Using the buttons to the left and right of the Texture Preview pane, you can load and save the texture map to the hard drive where you can edit it using an external image-editing package.

FIGURE 7-4

Face Sculpting pane

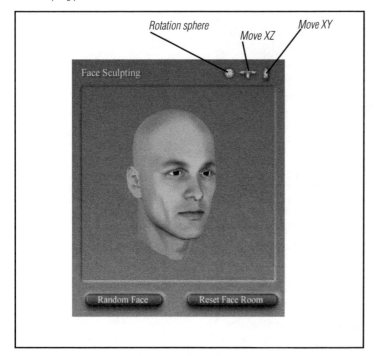

FIGURE 7-5

Texture Preview pane

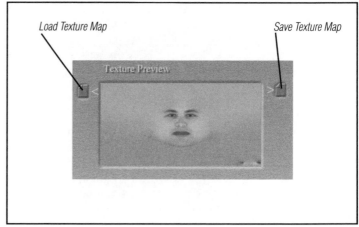

Using the Actions Buttons

You can use the Actions buttons, shown in Figure 7-6, to perform several specific tasks such as applying the finished face to the current figure.

Using the Face Shaping Tool Panel

The Face Shaping Tool panel, shown in Figure 7-7, includes two buttons for accessing the Putty and the Pin tools. These tools alter the shape of the face in the Face Sculpting pane. The Face Shaping Tool panel also includes a long list of parameters that you can use to precisely alter almost every aspect of the face such as the brow ridge, cheekbones, eyes, forehead, mouth, and nose.

FIGURE 7-7
Face Shaping Tool panel

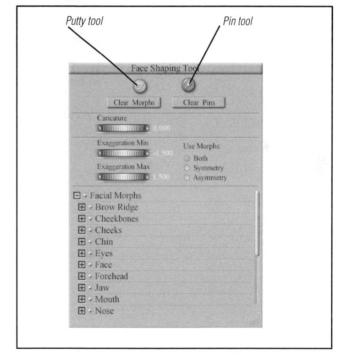

FIGURE 7-6
Actions buttons

Access the Face Room controls

1. Open the Poser interface with the default figure visible.

2. Click the Face tab to access the Face Room.

   A new interface appears with a unique set of controls, as shown in Figure 7-8.

3. Click the Random Face button to load a random face.

4. Click the Pose tab to access the Pose Room again.

5. Select File, Save As and save the file as **Face room.pz3**.

FIGURE 7-8

Face Room

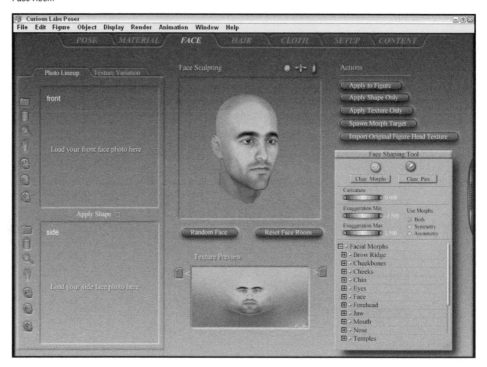

CREATE A FACE
FROM PHOTOS

What You'll Do

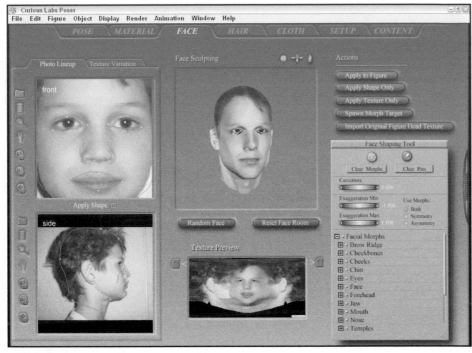

In this lesson, you learn how to create a custom face from loaded front- and side-view images.

The Face Room includes the capability to create a custom face from digital photos. The needed photos are a front view and a profile view. You can map these images onto the current head element.

Loading the Front Face Image

To load a front face image, click the Load Image button to the left of the front pane in the Photo Lineup panel. This opens the Load Front Face Image dialog box to help in the alignment of the photo, shown in Figure 7-9. This panel lets you position the front image by clicking once to locate the corner of the right eye and again to locate the corner of the left lip. This dialog box also includes a Flip button that you can use to flip the image about its vertical center. After you click to locate the left corner of the lip, the image is placed in the front pane of the Photo Lineup panel. If you make a mistake, use the Delete Image button to remove the loaded image.

Loading the Side Face Image

To load a side face image, click the Load Image button to the left of the side pane in the Photo Lineup panel. This opens the Load Side Face Image dialog box to help in the alignment of the photo, shown in Figure 7-10. This panel lets you position the side image by clicking once to locate the top of the right ear and again to locate the front of the chin. This dialog box also includes a Flip button that you can use to flip the image about its vertical center. After you click to locate the front of the chin, the image is placed in the side pane of the Photo Lineup panel.

Aligning the Face to the Images

Once the face images are loaded into the Photo Lineup panel, a red outline of the 3D head element is projected on top of the images with green dots to mark the key features such as the corners of the eyes, mouth, and nose. Using the Zoom and Pan Image tools to the left of the front and side panes, you can resize and move the images

FIGURE 7-9
Front image placement

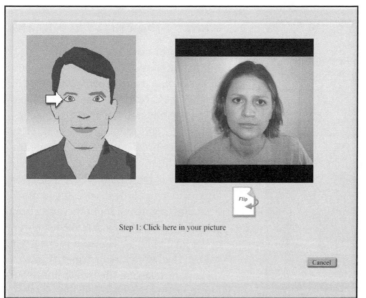

FIGURE 7-10
Side image placement

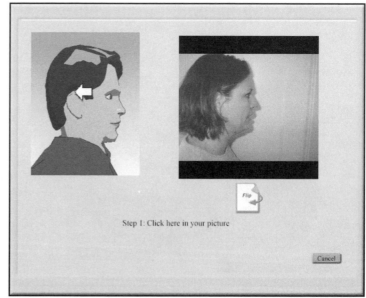

and using the Rotate, Scale, and Pan Geometry tools, you can change the outlines to match the images. For detailed work, drag the green dots to their correct location. Figure 7-11 shows the results after matching the outline points to the images.

Applying the Face Shape from Photos

Moving the alignment dots in the Photo Lineup panel not only aligns the image with the current head model, but it also defines the shape of the head model. To see the shape changes, enable the Apply Shape option located between the front and side panes. This updates the Preview window with the new head shape.

FIGURE 7-11
Aligned face images

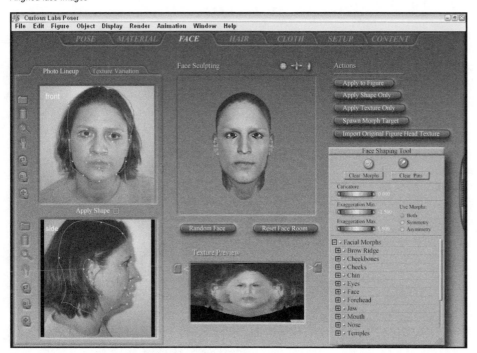

Create a face from photos

1. Open the Poser interface with the default figure visible.

2. Click the Face tab to access the Face Room.

3. Click the Load Image button 📁 to the left of the front pane in the Photo Lineup panel and select the Thomas – front.jpg file from the file dialog box. Click Open.

   A placement dialog box opens.

4. Click in the photo, as the placement dialog box instructs, on the corner of the right eye and at the corner of the left lips.

5. Click the Load Image button to the left of the side pane in the Photo Lineup panel and select the Thomas – side.jpg file from the file dialog box. Click Open.

6. Click in the photo, as the placement dialog box instructs, at the top of the ear and at the front of the chin.

   The placement dialog box closes automatically and the photos appear in the Photo Lineup panel with red outlines on top of each.

7. Drag the Zoom Image tool 🔍 in the front pane to show the details of the eyes and mouth photo up close.

8. Drag the Scale Geometry tool 🔍 in the side pane until the outline roughly matches the image, and then select the Pan Geometry tool 🔍 to align the outline with the photo.

9. Drag the green placement points in the front and side panes to align with the photos.

   The Preview pane shows the resulting face, as shown in Figure 7-12.

10. Click the Apply to Figure button, switch back to the Pose Room, select File, Save As, and save the file as **Custom photo face.pz3**.

FIGURE 7-12
Custom photo face

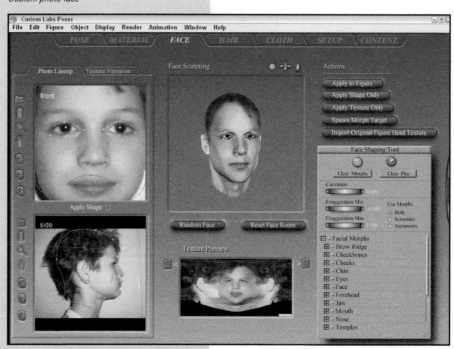

CREATE
TEXTURE VARIATION

What You'll Do

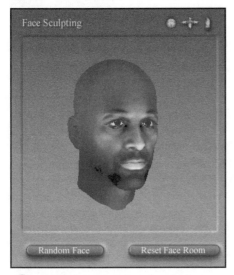

In this lesson, you learn how to change the texture parameters for the face.

Clicking the Texture Variation tab next to the Photo Lineup tab opens a panel of options that you can use to change the texture for the current face. You can apply these texture variations to both custom-loaded photos or to the default face textures. The changes are immediately visible in the Face Sculpting and Texture Preview panes.

FIGURE 7-13
Darkened and lighten face features

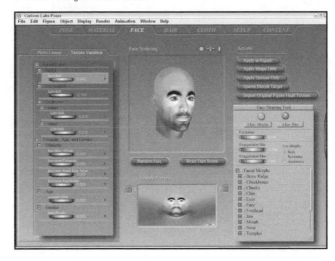

Changing Facial Color

The Facial Color options can lighten or darken the beard, eye sockets, or upper and lower eyebrows. Positive values will darken and negative values will lighten the selected areas. Figure 7-13 shows the default face with a darkened beard and eyebrows and lightened eye sockets.

Changing Ethnicity

Within the Ethnicity, Age, and Gender options are the Ethnicity options. You can use these parameters to make the face more or less African, European, South East Asian, and East Indian. Each of these options will change the skin color in a different manner and add highlights about the face. Figure 7-14 shows the East Indian option. Notice the darker highlights about the eyebrows.

Changing Age

The Age parameter changes the highlighting on the face to display wrinkles and lighting to make the face appear younger or older. Figure 7-15 shows a face that has been aged.

FIGURE 7-14

Altered ethnicity

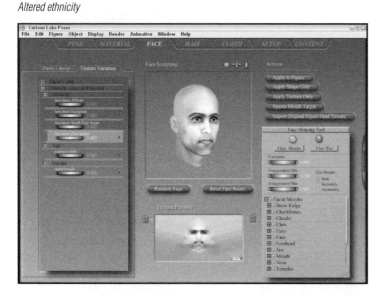

FIGURE 7-15

Aged face

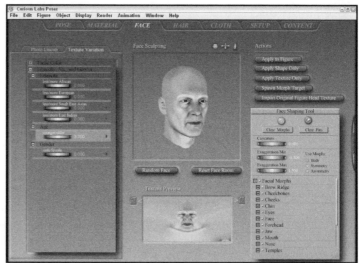

Changing Gender

The final face texture option enables you to change the current face from male to female and vice versa. Female features have redder lips and lighter skin tones, whereas male faces feature darker skin tones and darker highlights around the beard and brows. Figure 7-16 shows the female features.

FIGURE 7-16

Female face features

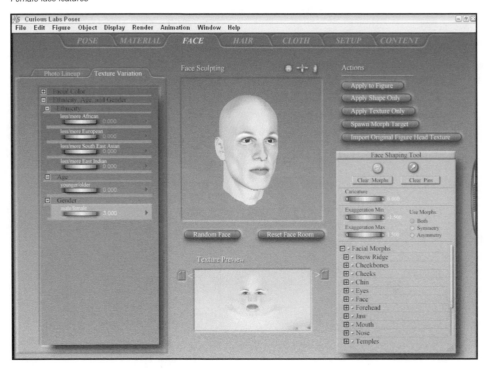

Add texture variation

1. Open the Poser interface with the default figure visible.

2. Click the Face tab to access the Face Room.

3. Click the Texture Variation tab to open the Texture Variation panel.

4. Open the Facial Color set of parameters and set the Beard parameter to 3.0.

5. Open the Ethnicity, Age, and Gender set of parameters and set the Less/More African parameter to 1.0 and the Age parameter to 0.5.

   The face texture is updated in the other Face Room panes, as shown in Figure 7-17.

6. Click the Apply to Figure button, switch back to the Pose Room, select File, Save As, and save the file as **Texture variation.pz3**.

FIGURE 7-17

Face texture variation

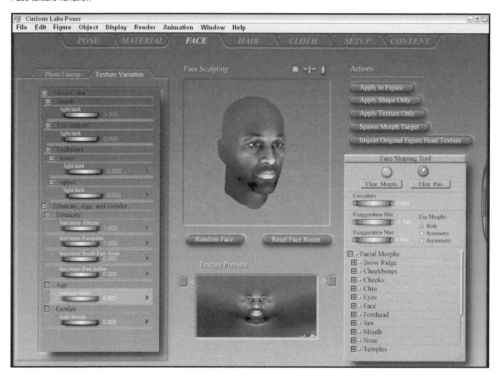

USE THE FACE
SHAPING TOOL

What You'll Do

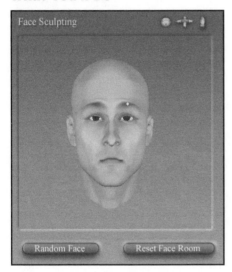

In this lesson, you learn how to use the Face Shaping tool and parameters to distort the face's shape.

The various options found in the Texture Variation panel change the look of the face by changing only the texture of the face, but you can change the face also by modifying the shape of the head model. This is accomplished using the Face Shaping tool and the Face Sculpting pane.

Using the Putty Tool

The **Putty tool** is selected by default in the Face Shaping Tool panel. It allows you to sculpt the current face by dragging in the Face Sculpting pane. When you first click the face, the vertex closest to where you click is selected and appears as a green dot. With a single vertex selected, you can drag the vertex to a new location. When dragging a vertex, its movement is made based on the current camera view. You can use the camera tools in the upper-right corner of the Face Sculpting pane to rotate, pan, and zoom the face camera. If you make a mistake, you can remove all modifications using the Clear Morphs button.

Pinning Vertices

As you drag a single vertex with the Putty tool, adjacent vertices and body parts are moved along with the vertex. For example, dragging a vertex in the forehead region also moves the eyebrows. If you want to keep a specific set of vertices positioned relative to each other, you can use the **Pin tool** to click the vertices that you want to remain in position. Pinned vertices are displayed as red dots, as shown in Figure 7-18. The Clear Pins button will remove all current pins.

FIGURE 7-18
Pinned vertices

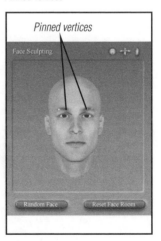

Setting Exaggeration Limits

If you want to set a limit on how far face vertices can be deformed, you can use the Exaggeration Min and Exaggeration Max parameters to set limits to the face deformation. If you try to move a face feature that has reached its boundary, the deformation will still stop.

QUICKTIP

A good place to use exaggeration limits is to prevent the face from collapsing in on itself.

Using the Caricature Parameter

The **Caricature** parameter emphasizes any existing deformation to a greater extent. This is helpful for creating cartoon-like faces. Negative values can be used to de-emphasize a particular feature. Figure 7-19 shows a figure with an over-emphasized nose and chin that was created by increasing the Caricature value.

Making Symmetrical Deformations

To the right of the Exaggeration parameters are options for using morphs. When the **Symmetry** option is selected, all deformations applied to one half of the face are mirrored on the other half, but when the Asymmetry option is selected, you can change one side of the face differently from the other.

Altering Face Parameters

At the bottom of the Face Shaping Tool panel are many parameters divided into categories that you can use in conjunction with the Putty tool to deform the **face shape**. Each category includes several parameters and changing these parameters provides a more focused way to deform the facial features. The available face categories and their parameters are listed in Table 7-1.

FIGURE 7-19

Caricature emphasized face

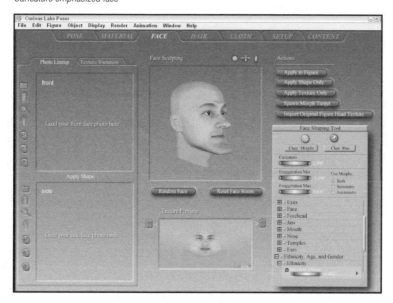

TABLE 7-1: FACE PARAMETERS

Category	Parameters
Eyes	Up/Down, Small/Large, Tilt Inward/Outward, Together/Apart, Height Disparity, Transverse Shift
Face	Brow-Nose-Chin Ratio, Forehead-Sellion-Nose Ratio, Light/Heavy, Round/Gaunt, Thin/Wide, Coronal Bend, Coronal Shear, Vertical Axis Twist
Forehead	Small/Large, Short/Tall, Tilt Forward/Back, Forward Axis Twist
Jaw	Retracted/Jutting, Wide/Thin, Jaw-Neck Slope High/Low, Concave/Convex
Mouth	Drawn/Pursed, Happy/Sad, High/Low, Protruding/Retracted, Tilt Up/Down, Underbite/Overbite, Mouth-Chin Distance Short/Long, Corners Transverse Shift, Forward Axis Twist, Transverse Shift, Twist and Shift
Mouth, Lips	Deflated/Inflated, Large/Small, Puckered/Retracted
Nose	Up/Down, Flat/Pointed, Short/Long, Tilt Up/Down, Frontal Axis Twist, Tip Transverse Shift, Transverse Shift, Vertical Axis Twist
Nose, Bridge	Shallow/Deep, Short/Long, Transverse Shift
Nose, Nostrils	Tilt Up/Down, Small/Large, Thin/Wide, Frontal Axis Twist, Transverse Shift
Nose, Sellion	Up/Down, Shallow/Deep, Thin/Wide, Transverse Shift
Temples	Thin/Wide
Ears	Up/Down, Back/Front, Short/Long, Thin/Wide, Vertical Shear, Forward Axis Shear
Ethnicity	Less/More African, Less/More European, Less/More South East Asian, Less/More East Indian
Age	Younger/Older
Gender	Male/Female

Locking Face Parameters

To the immediate left of each parameter title is a small green dot. Clicking this green dot changes it to a lock icon, as shown in Figure 7-20. This lock icon locks the given parameter so it cannot be changed with the Putty tool.

FIGURE 7-20
Locked parameter

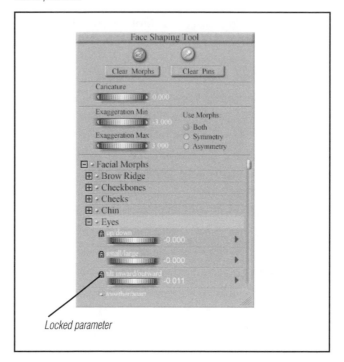

Locked parameter

Creating a Face   Chapter 7

FIGURE 7-21
Surprised face

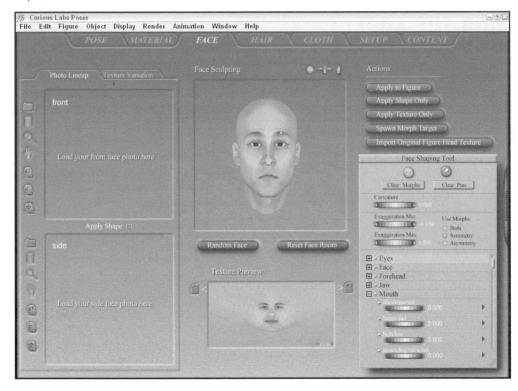

1. Open the Poser interface with the default fig- ure visible.

2. Click the Face tab to access the Face Room.

3. Drag on the Rotate control ◉ in the upper-right corner of the Face Sculpting pane until the front of the default face is visible.

4. With the Putty tool ◉ selected, drag upward on the left eyebrow.

 Both eyebrows are moved upward together.

5. In the Face Shaping Tool panel, expand the Mouth category and set the Happy/Sad parameter to 2.0.

 The face is altered to show a look of surprise, as shown in Figure 7-21.

6. Click the Apply to Figure button, switch back to the Pose Room, select File, Save As and save the file as **Surprised face.pz3**.

ADD THE FACE
TO THE FIGURE

What You'll Do

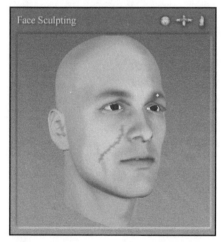

In this lesson, you learn how to apply the face to the current figure.

If you spent some time creating a perfect-looking face, you may be frustrated to notice that the File, Save menu command is disabled from the Face Room. To save the face (no pun intended), you need to apply the existing face to the current figure and save the figure from within the Pose Room.

Applying a Face to the Current Figure

To apply the current face texture and shape to the current figure, simply click the Apply to Figure button. This replaces the existing head element with the one defined in the Face Room. The Apply Shape Only button places only the new head shape onto the figure without the face texture and the Apply Texture Only button causes only the defined texture to be placed on the current figure head, without any shape changes.

CAUTION

After you click the Apply to Figure or the Apply Shape Only buttons, a warning dialog box will appear stating that applying a modified head shape to an older figure model may result in unmatched polygons around the neck.

Importing the Original Figure Texture Face Map

If you want to import the existing face texture from the current figure into the Face Room, click the Import Original Figure Head Texture button. This loads the texture used by the existing figure into the Face Room, as shown in Figure 7-22.

Loading and Saving Texture Maps

On either side of the Texture Preview pane are small buttons that you can use to load (the one on the left) and save (the one on the right) the existing texture map. Both of these buttons open a file dialog box where you can select the file to open or give the file a name. Saved texture maps are saved to a 512 x 512 pixel image using the image format that you select. The saved texture map can then be loaded within an image-editing package such as Photoshop to be edited and reloaded into Poser. Figure 7-23 shows the default face texture map loaded within Photoshop.

CAUTION

Although you can save texture maps in Photoshop's PSD file format, you cannot load them back into Poser using this format.

Synching Face and Body Color

When a face with a different skin color is applied to a figure, a warning dialog box appears identifying that the face and body skin colors are different and asking whether you want to synchronize the two. Clicking Yes will change the body skin color to match the face.

FIGURE 7-22

Imported face texture

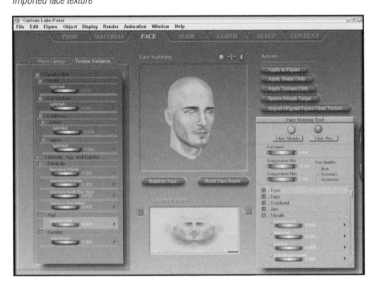

FIGURE 7-23

Texture map loaded in Photoshop

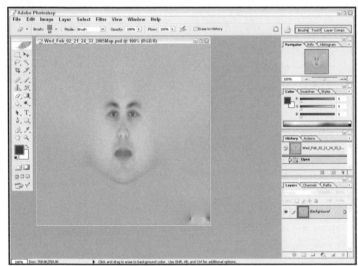

Save, edit, and load a face texture map

1. Open the Poser interface with the default figure visible.

2. Click the Face tab to access the Face Room.

3. Click the Save Texture button 🔲 to the right of the Texture Preview pane. In the Save As dialog box, choose the PSD file format and click Save.

4. Locate the saved texture file and open it in Photoshop.

5. Within Photoshop, edit the texture image by adding a scar to the image with the Paint Brush tool. Then save the texture file as Texture map with the name scar.jpg.

6. Back within Poser, click the Load Texture button 🔲 to the left of the Texture Preview pane in the Face Room. Then locate and load the saved file.

   The face is updated with the edited texture map, as shown in Figure 7-24.

7. Click the Apply to Figure button, switch back to the Pose Room, select File, Save As, and save the file as **Face with scar.pz3**.

FIGURE 7-24

Edited texture map

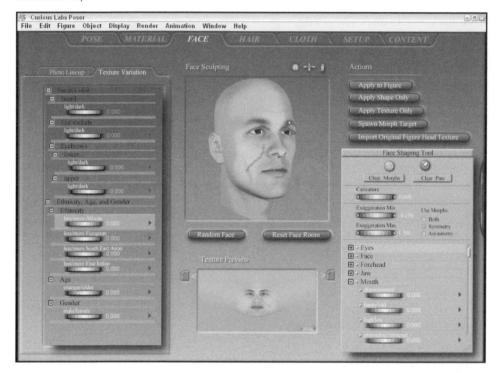

WORK WITH
EXPRESSIONS

What You'll Do

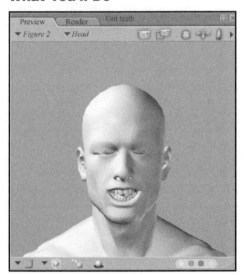

In this lesson, you learn how to work with the Library to load and save expressions.

Before leaving this chapter, you need to look closely at the thumbnails located within the Expressions category of the Library. These expressions give the character a different facial look and are different from the faces created in the Face Room.

Loading Expressions from the Library

To access the available expressions from the Library, click the Expression category and navigate to the folder containing the types of expressions you want to apply to the current figure. Within each folder are thumbnails of the various expressions. With an expression thumbnail selected, click the Change Expression button at the bottom of the Library palette. The selected expression is loaded onto the figure.

Creating a Custom Expression

When the head element is selected, the Parameter/Properties palette includes all the parameters for creating a custom expression. The available parameters for the head element for creating expressions include those listed in Table 7-2.

TABLE 7-2: HEAD PARAMETERS

Category	Parameters
Brow	Brow Up All, Brow Up Left, Brow Up Right, Brow Up Center, Scowl, Scowl Left, Scowl Right
Eyes	Blink, Blink Left, Blink Right, Eyes Up-Down, Eyes Side-Side, Eyes Smile
Nose	Nose Wrinkle
Jaw	Mouth Open, Jaw Shift Left, Jaw Shift Right
Lips	Smile, Smile Left, Smile Right, Smile Thin, Smile Teeth, Smile Small, Snarl, Snarl Left, Snarl Right, Lip Corner Depressors, Lip Lower Depressor, Lip Upper Raiser, Pucker, Lip Stretch, Lip Stretch Left, Lip Stretch Right
Tongue	Tongue Roll, Tongue Tip Up-Down, Tongue Curl Up-Down
Phonemes	Mouth A, Mouth CH, Mouth E, Mouth F, Mouth TH, Mouth O, Mouth U, Tongue L, Mouth M, Mouth W

Saving Expressions to the Library

You can save the current expression to the Library using the Add to Library button located at the bottom of the Library palette. This button opens a simple dialog box where you can name the current expression. A thumbnail for the current expression is added to the top of the open Library folder.

Removing Expressions from the Library

The Remove from Library button in the Library palette permanently deletes the selected thumbnail expression.

FIGURE 7-25

Random expression loaded from the Library

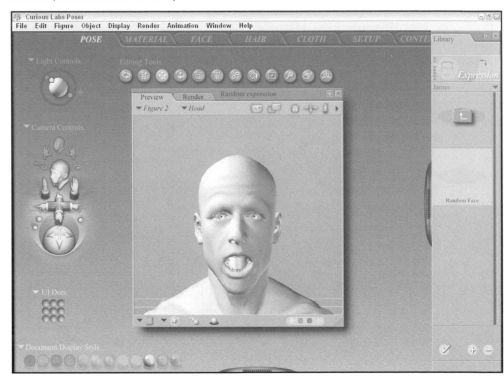

1. Open Poser with the default man visible.

2. Select the Face Camera ⬚ from the Camera Controls.

3. Click the side control to the right of the interface to open the Library palette or select Window, Libraries.

4. Click the Expression category at the top of the Library palette and navigate to the James folder.

5. Select the Random Face thumbnail and click the Replace Expression button ⬚ at the bottom of the Library palette.

   The expression you see will likely vary from the figure. A new expression is generated every time the Random Face expression is applied. The selected expression is loaded into the Shader Window, as shown in Figure 7-25.

6. Select File, Save As and save the file as **Random expression.pz3**.

Save a material to the Library

1. Open Poser with the default man visible.

2. Select the Face camera from the Camera Controls.

3. Select the head element in the Document Window and select Window, Parameter Dials to open the Parameters/Properties palette (if necessary).

4. Expand the Eyes category in the Parameters palette and set the Blink parameter to 1.0. Then expand the Phonemes category and set the Mouth A parameter to 1.0.

5. Click the side control to the right of the interface to open the Library palette or select Window, Libraries.

6. Click the Expression category at the top of the Library palette and navigate to the James folder.

7. Click the Add to Library button [+] at the bottom of the Library palette.

   The Set Name dialog box appears.

8. Enter **Grit Teeth** as the name of this expression and click OK to accept the name and click OK again in the Save Frames dialog box.

   The new expression appears in the folder thumbnails, as shown in Figure 7-26.

9. Select File, Save As and save the file as **Grit teeth.pz3**.

FIGURE 7-26
New expression added to the Library

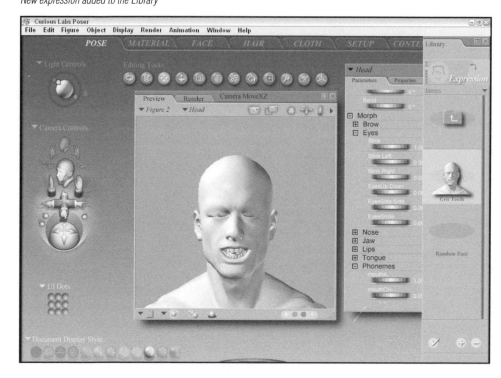

CHAPTER SUMMARY

This chapter covers all the features found in the Face Room, including the capability to create a face from loaded images. Using the parameters found in the Texture Variation panel, you can change the texture for the current face or, using the Face Shaping tool, you can deform the geometry of the actual head model. You can then apply the resulting face directly to the figure. This chapter also covered expressions that are available in the Library.

What You Have Learned

In this chapter, you:

- Discovered the layout of the Face Room interface, including the Face Shaping Tool panel.
- Loaded and positioned front and side face images to create a custom face.
- Changed the texture parameters including facial color, ethnicity, age, and gender.
- Interactively deformed the face model using the Putty and Pin tools.
- Changed the face shape using the parameters found in the Face Shaping Tool panel.
- Applied the finished face to the current figure.

- Saved and loaded texture maps for editing in an external image-editing package.
- Loaded expressions from the Library and saved expressions back to the Library.
- Saved and loaded texture maps for editing in an external image-editing package.

Key Terms from This Chapter

Face texture map. An image that is wrapped about the head model to show details.

Face shape. The underlying 3D geometry that the texture is mapped on in order to create the face.

Ethnicity. The facial features that are inherent with a unique ethnic group such as African-Americans, Europeans, and Asians.

Putty tool. A tool used to sculpt the shape of a face.

Pin tool. A tool used to prevent vertices from moving out of position.

Caricature. A silly drawing of a face that overemphasizes a person's prominent features such as a large nose, big ears, or a small mouth.

Symmetry. A property of faces that makes all features on one side of the face the same as features on the opposite side.

Sellion. That part of the nose that extends from its tip up between the eyes.

Temples. The portion of the face that lies between the ears and the eyes.

Expression. When the face features are saved in a unique position to show different emotions.

Phonemes. Facial expressions that occur when different speaking sounds are made.

chapter

8

WORKING WITH
Hair

1. Load hair from the Library.

2. Learn the Hair Room interface.

3. Grow hair.

4. Style hair.

5. Use hair dynamics.

6. Add a wind force deformer.

7. Change hair material.

chapter 8 WORKING WITH
Hair

Unless you're partial to bald heads, nothing can add more to the details of your figure than a nice head of hair. However, a bad hairstyle can detract quite a bit from your figure. Another tricky part of working with hair is that it can add significantly to the complexity of your scene, which increases file size and update and render times, but the power made possible by the Poser Hair Room is definitely worth it.

Poser offers two ways to add hair to your figures. The first is using prop-based hair that can be loaded from the Library. This hair is loaded as a prop and is designed to fit perfectly on certain figures. Prop hair can be moved and positioned just like other props in the scene. The second method for adding hair deals with strand-based hair and can only be manipulated in the Hair Room.

The Hair Room includes a robust interface for adding hair to your figures, allowing you to add hair anywhere to the figure using a hair group selected using the Group Editor. Once a hair group is defined, you can grow **guide hairs**, which are a simply representation of the full set

of hair. With guide hairs in place, you can control their length and relative position.

Poser's styling tools let you control hair parameters such as **hair density**, root and tip width, **clumpiness**, and **kinkiness**. In addition to these parameters, the **Hair Style Tool** panel includes tools for selecting individual hairs or groups of hair and interactively applying transformations, curls, and twisting.

You can also define dynamic parameters that are used to compute the position and motions of hairs through all animated frames. These dynamic parameters include gravity, **springiness**, and **stiffness**, and can even include collision detection. In addition to gravity, you can add wind force to the simulation using the wind force deformer.

Finally, you can use the Material Room to change the material values used to shade the hair. By manipulating these values, you can change the hair's color, softness, and highlights.

244

Tools You'll Use

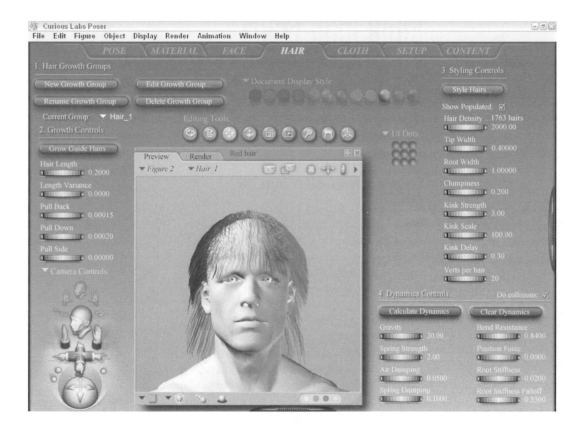

LOAD HAIR FROM
THE LIBRARY

What You'll Do

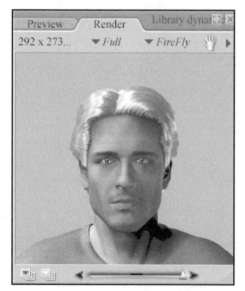

In this lesson, you learn how to load hair from the Library.

The Hair category in the Library includes both prop-based hair examples and strand-based dynamic hair for each of the available figures.

Loading Prop Hair from the Library

If you're not sure where to start, you can check the Library for several preset prop hairstyles that you can apply directly to the current figure. To access the available hair from the Library, click the Hair category and navigate to the folder containing the prop hairstyles you want to apply. Within each folder are thumbnails of the various hairstyles. With a prop hairstyle thumbnail selected, click the Change Hair button at the bottom of the Library palette and the selected hairstyle is loaded into the Shader Window. Figure 8-1 shows several hair thumbnails. You can select prop hairstyles from the Figure List and conform them to the current figure.

FIGURE 8-1
Loaded Library prop hair

Loading Dynamic Hair from the Library

Dynamic hair is also available within the Hair category of the Library. When applied to a figure, only the sparse guide hairs are displayed in the Document Window. These guide hairs can be controlled using the controls found in the Hair Room.

Saving Hairstyles to the Library

You can save the current hairstyle to the Library using the Add to Library button located at the bottom of the Library palette. This button opens a simple dialog box where you can name the current hairstyle and the thumbnail for the current hairstyle is added to the open Library folder.

Removing Hair from the Library

The Remove from Library button in the Library palette permanently deletes the selected thumbnail hairstyle.

Load prop hair from the Library

1. Open Poser with the default man visible.

2. Click the side control to the right of the interface to open the Library palette or select Window, Libraries.

3. Click the Hair category at the top of the Library palette and navigate to the Kozaburo/James folder.

4. Select the Messy Hair_James thumbnail and click the Apply Library Preset button 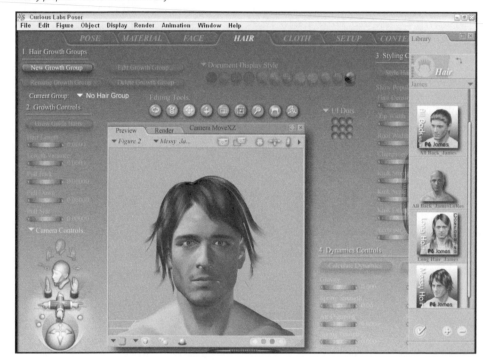 at the bottom of the Library palette.

5. Click the Texture Shaded style from the Display Styles controls or select the Display, Document Style, Texture Shaded menu command.

   The selected prop hairstyle is loaded into the Document Window, as shown in Figure 8-2.

6. Select File, Save As and save the file as **Library prop hair.pz3**.

FIGURE 8-2

Messy prop hair loaded from the Library

FIGURE 8-3

Messy dynamic hair loaded from the Library

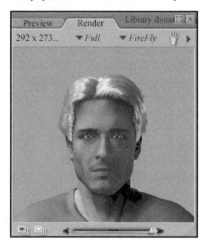

1. Open Poser with the default man visible.

2. Click the Hair tab to access the Hair Room.

3. Click the side control to the right of the interface to open the Library palette or select Window, Libraries.

4. Click the Hair category at the top of the Library palette and navigate to the James Hair folder.

5. Select the James_Messy thumbnail and click the Apply Library Preset button at the bottom of the Library palette.

6. Click the Face camera in the Camera controls.

7. Click the Render button at the top of the Document Window.

   The loaded dynamic hairstyle is rendered into the Document Window, as shown in Figure 8-3.

8. Select File, Save As and save the file as **Library dynamic hair.pz3**.

LEARN THE
HAIR ROOM INTERFACE

What You'll Do

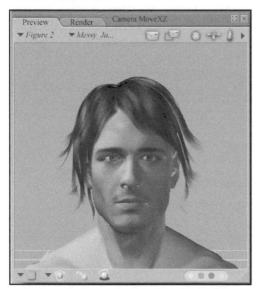

In this lesson, you learn how to use the Hair Room interface and select a hair group that defines where the hair is located.

You open the Hair Room by clicking the Hair tab at the top of the Poser interface. This opens an interface setup, as shown in Figure 8-4, that is different from the Pose Room, although it includes all of the same controls as the Pose Room, including the Document Window, the Camera and Light controls, and the Display Styles and Editing Tools button sets. The Hair Room interface also includes four additional sets of buttons that are used to group, create, style, and move hair.

FIGURE 8-4
Hair Room interface

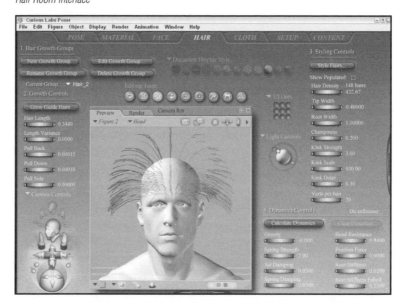

Using the Hair Controls

When the Hair Room is first opened, only the New Growth Group button in the **hair growth groups** set of controls is enabled. Before you can set any hair properties, you must create a hair growth group. This allows you to select, name, and create several different areas where hair is located. Once you create a hair growth group, the parameters in the Hair Growth controls become active. The remaining two sets of parameters—the Styling controls and Dynamics controls—only become active once you click the Grow Guide Hairs button.

Accessing the Hair Style Tool

Within the Editing tools is a special tool that is only available within the Hair Room. The Hair Style tool opens a panel, shown in Figure 8-5, where you can style individual selections of hair. Each of the tools available on the Hair Style Tool panel is explained the Hair Styling lesson to follow.

Specifying Hair Location

The first step in adding hair to a figure is to select the figure polygons where the hair will be located. Each separate occurrence of hair is grouped and named. You create groups using the Group Editor.

FIGURE 8-5
Hair Style Tool panel

Creating a Hair Growth Group

You use the four buttons located in the Hair Growth Group controls to create and manage separate groups of hair. To create a hair growth group, click the New Growth Group button. This opens a simple dialog box where you can give the growth group a name. The default name is *Hair* followed by a sequential number. Each new growth group is added to the Current Group list where you can select the current group. You can rename the current growth group by clicking the Rename Growth Group button. This makes the same naming dialog box appear.

Deleting Hair Growth Groups

You can delete the current hair growth group by clicking the Delete Growth Group button. This button causes a confirmation dialog box to appear asking if you are sure that you want to delete the current growth group.

Editing Hair Growth Groups

If you click the Edit Growth Group button, the Group Editor, shown in Figure 8-6,

opens with the current growth group listed as the current group. When the Group Editor is opened, the figure appears dark gray.

Selecting a Hair Growth Group

You can add new polygons to the group by clicking polygons or dragging an outline over the polygons to select in the Document Window with the Select Polygons tool. All polygons that are selected with the Select Polygons tool are highlighted in red. You can remove polygons from the current

group with the Deselect Polygons tool. The Add All button adds all polygons that belong to the body part listed in the Actor List at the top of the Document Window and the Remove All button removes all polygons. The Invert button inverts the selection for the current body part.

QUICKTIP

Holding down the Ctrl key while clicking the Select Polygons tool lets you remove polygons from the selection and vice versa.

FIGURE 8-6
Group Editor

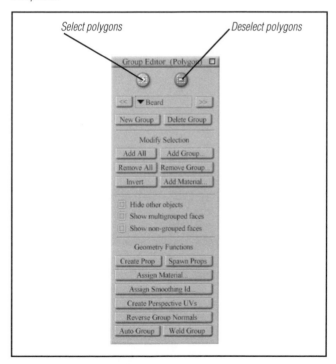

FIGURE 8-7

Mustache group

1. Open Poser with the default man visible.

2. Click the Hair tab at the top of the interface to open the Hair Room.

3. Select the Head element in the Document Window, and then click the New Growth Group button and name the new group **Mustache**. Click OK.

   The new growth group name appears in the Current Group list.

4. Select the Face camera from the Camera tools to zoom in on the face in the Document Window.

5. Click the Edit Growth Group button to open the Group Editor panel.

6. Select the Head element from the Actor List at the top of the Document Window.

7. With the Select Polygons tool selected in the Group Editor panel, drag over the polygons between the nose and mouth in the Document Window.

   The selected polygons are highlighted in red, as shown in Figure 8-7.

8. Select File, Save As and save the file as **Mustache group.pz3**.

GROW
HAIR

What You'll Do

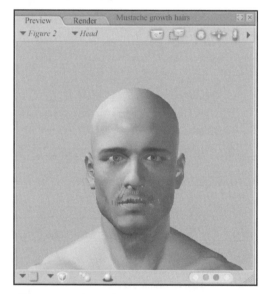

In this lesson, you learn how to grow guide hairs and set the hair's length and initial position.

After you define a hair growth group, the buttons in the Growth Controls become active. These buttons let you grow guide hairs and define the hair's initial parameters.

Growing Guide Hairs

Clicking the Grow Guide Hairs button will add hairs to the selected hair group and

these hairs become visible in the Document Window, as shown in Figure 8-8. Don't be alarmed if the new hairs stick straight out or if they appear to be too thin; you can relax and thicken them during the styling phase.

FIGURE 8-8
Guide hairs

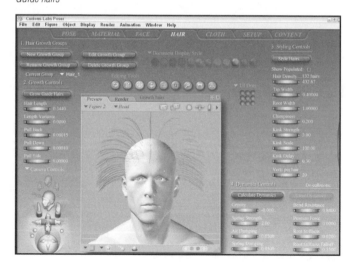

Setting Hair Length

Once the guide hairs are visible (or even before they are visible), you can change their length using the Hair Length parameter. If you change the Hair Length parameter after the guide hairs have been created, the hairs displayed in the Document Window will change as the parameter is changed.

Setting Hair Variance

The Length Variance parameter changes the range of different hair lengths that are possible. Setting this value to 0.0 results in a hairstyle where every hair strand is equal in length. Increasing this value causes the hair to become more wild, messy, and shaggy, as shown in Figure 8-9.

Moving Hair

Although most of the hair movement is accomplished during the styling phase, you can use the Pull Back, Pull Down, and Pull Side parameters to move all the hairs a given direction. You can set these parameters to positive and negative values. The Pull Back parameter can move the hairs towards the back of the head or forward with a negative value. The Pull Down parameter can move the hairs vertically straight up with a negative value, as shown in Figure 8-10, or straight down with a positive value. The Pull Side parameter will move the hairs to the figure's left with a negative value and to the figure's right with a positive value.

FIGURE 8-9
Messy hair

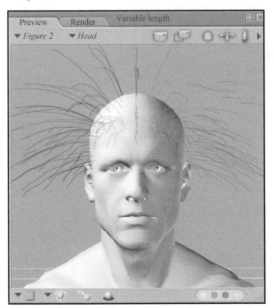

FIGURE 8-10
Hair straight up

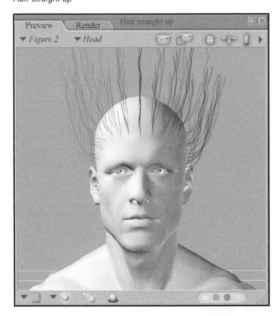

Create guide hairs

1. Select File, Open and open the Mustache group.pz3 file.

2. Click the Hair tab at the top of the interface to open the Hair Room.

3. Click the Head element in the Document Window and select the Mustache group from the Growth Group controls.

4. Click the Grow Guide Hairs button.

   Several long hairs are displayed for the mustache group in the Document Window.

5. Set the Hair Length parameter to 0.0076, the Length Variance, Pull Back, and Pull Side parameters to 0.0, and the Pull Down parameter to 0.1.

6. Select the Texture Shaded button in the Display Styles controls.

   The short guide hairs are displayed in the Document Window, as shown in Figure 8-11.

7. Select File, Save As and save the file as **Mustache guide hairs.pz3**.

FIGURE 8-11
Mustache guide hairs

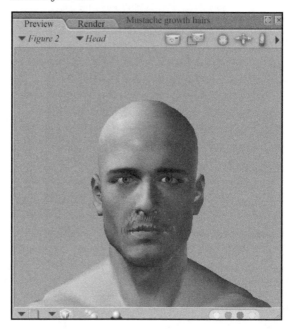

STYLE HAIR

What You'll Do

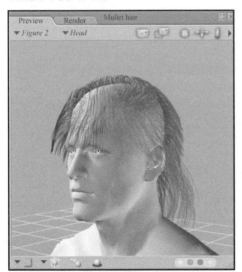

In this lesson, you learn how to style hair using parameters and the Hair Style Tool panel.

Once you add the guide hairs to the hair growth group, you can style them collectively using the parameters found in the Styling controls. For further modification, you can use the Hair Style tool to select and individually style and change single hairs or groups of hair.

Setting Hair Density

At the top of the Styling controls is a Show Populated option. When this option is enabled, all designated hairs are shown in Document Window, but when this option is disabled, only a sampling of the total number of hairs is displayed. If the hairstyle includes a large number of hairs, updating the Document Window may take some time. This option offers a way to speed up the refresh rate of the Document Window. The total number of hairs is displayed directly beneath the Show Populated option. You can change the total number of hairs using the Hair Density parameter. Figure 8-12 shows a figure with a full head of hair.

CAUTION

Adding hairs to a figure will greatly increase the total number of polygons for the figure and will also increase the time to render the scene.

FIGURE 8-12
Dense hair

Using Hairstyle Parameters

Beneath the Hair Density parameter are several additional style parameters. These parameters are applied to all hairs within the current hair group and you can use them to customize the look of the hair. The additional hairstyle parameters include the following:

- **Tip Width:** Defines the width of the hair at its tip.
- **Root Width:** Defines the width of the hair at its root. For normal hair, the root width value is typically greater than the tip width value. Hairs with equal root and tip width values are more coarse and stringy.
- **Clumpiness:** Causes hair strands to group together into clumps like dread-locks. You can set this value to a negative value to make hair more feather-like. Figure 8-13 shows some hair with a maximum Clumpiness value.
- **Kink Strength:** Defines how wavy and curly the hair is.
- **Kink Scale:** Defines the size of the wave and curl applied to the hair. This value can range between 1 and 1000.

QUICKTIP

If you increase the Kink Strength value and nothing happens, check to make sure that the Kink Scale value isn't set to 0.

- **Kink Delay:** Defines the point along the hair length from the **hair root** where the wave and curl begins. This value can range from 0 for hair that curls at the root to 1.0 for hairs that curl at the tip. Figure 8-14 shows some hair with the Kink Scale and Kink Delay values set to their maximum values.

- **Verts Per Hair:** Defines the number of vertices used to represent each strand of hair. This value can range from 4 for straight hairs to 100 for smooth hair. The default of 20 is enough for most hairstyles.

CAUTION

Increasing the Verts Per Hair value above the default of 20 can increase the render time significantly.

FIGURE 8-13
Clumpy hair

FIGURE 8-14
Curls at hair tips

Using the Hair Style Tool

You can open the Hair Style Tool panel, shown in Figure 8-15, by clicking the Style Hairs button in the Styling controls or by selecting the Hair Style tool from the Editing tools. When the Hair Style Tool panel first opens, only the Select Hairs button is enabled.

Selecting Hairs

With the Select Hairs tool, you can select a single hair or a group of hairs in the Document Window by clicking them or by dragging an outline around the hairs that you want to select. A single vertex at the end of each selected hair is highlighted when the hair is selected. Once some hairs are selected, the other tools in the Hair Style Tool panel become available. You can

deselect hairs using the Deselect Hairs tool or you can drop the entire selection by clicking the Clear Selection button.

QUICKTIP

Holding down the Ctrl key with the Select Hair tool selected lets you remove polygons from the selection, whereas holding down the Ctrl key with the Deselect Hair tool selected lets you add polygons to the selection.

FIGURE 8-15
Hair Style Tool panel

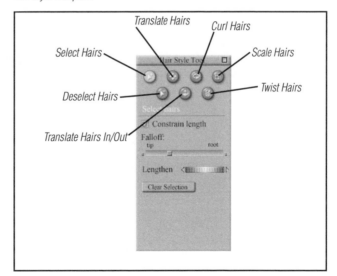

Styling Selected Hairs

The various styling tools included in the
Hair Style Tool panel let you translate,
rotate, scale, and twist the selected hairs.
The direction of the hair movement
depends on the current camera. The Constrain Length option causes all selected
hairs to remain the same length and the
Falloff setting controls whether the tool's
effect is applied to the root, tip, or some-
where in between. The Lengthen parameter
dial can lengthen or shorten the selected
hairs. Figure 8-16 shows a female figure
with some curls added to the tips of the
hair with the Rotate tool.

FIGURE 8-16

Curled hair

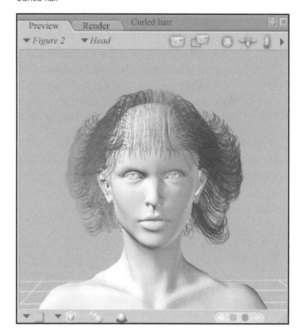

FIGURE 8-17

Mustache final

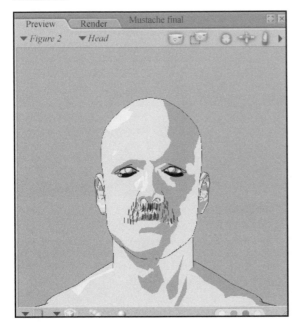

Use the hairstyle parameters

1. Select File, Open and open the Mustache guide hairs.pz3 file.

2. Click the Hair tab at the top of the interface to open the Hair Room.

3. Click the Head element in the Document Window and select the Mustache group from the Growth Group controls.

4. In the Styling controls, enable the Show Populated option.

   Many additional hairs are displayed for the mustache group in the Document Window.

5. Click the Hair Density parameter and set it to 100. Set the Clumpiness to 0.0, the Kink Strength to 2.0, the Kink Scale to 100, and the Kink Delay to 1.0.

6. Select the Cartoon with Lines option in the Display Styles controls.

   The mustache hairs in the Document Window are clearly visible, as shown in Figure 8-17.

7. Select File, Save As and save the file as **Mustache final.pz3**.

Lesson 4   Style Hair

Use the Hair Style tool

1. Open Poser with the default man visible.

2. Click the Hair tab at the top of the interface to open the Hair Room.

3. Select the Head element in the Document Window, then click the New Growth Group button and name the new group **Hair_1**. Click OK.

4. Select the Face camera from the Camera controls to zoom in on the face in the Document Window.

5. Click the Edit Growth Group button to open the Group Editor panel.

6. Drag over the top half of the skull in the Document Window with the Select Polygons tool. Then, drag on the rotate sphere in the Camera controls to make the side of the head visible and drag over the side of the head above the ear. Repeat for the back and opposite side of the head until the entire area where hair belongs on the head is selected. If you make a mistake, you can remove polygons with the Deselect Polygons tool.

7. Once the hair group is selected, close the Group Editor and click the Grow Guide Hairs button.

   Some sample guide hairs are displayed for the current hair group.

8. Set the Hair Length parameter to 0.2, the Pull Down parameter to .0002, and the Hair Density parameter to 2000. Enable the Show Populated option.

9. Click the Style Hairs button to open the Hair Style Tool panel.

10. Drag the rotate sphere in the Camera tools until the side of the head is visible. Drag over the hairs located at the back of the neck with the Select Hairs tool to select them.

    The vertices at the **hair tips** are displayed as yellow dots for the selected hairs.

11. Drag the Lengthen parameter dial to the right in the Hair Style Tool panel to lengthen the hairs.

12. Drag the rotate sphere in the Camera controls until the back of the head is visible. Select the Scale Hairs tool and drag in the Document Window to the left to pull the hairs at the back of the neck in towards the midline of the head.

13. Drag the rotate sphere in the Camera controls until the front side of the head is visible again.

    The hairstyle is displayed in the Document Window, as shown in Figure 8-18.

14. Select File, Save As and save the file as **Mullet hair.pz3**.

FIGURE 8-18
Mullet hair

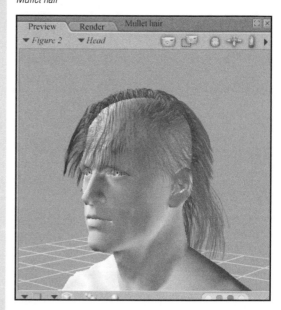

Working with Hair   Chapter 8

USE HAIR DYNAMICS

What You'll Do

In this lesson, you learn how to use hair dynamics.

In real life, hair doesn't just stick up in the air unless you use a lot of styling gel. Another way to position hair is to define the hair properties with the **Dynamics Controls** parameters and let the software calculate where the hair should fall for every animated frame using gravity, collisions, and **damping**.

Defining Hair's Dynamic Parameters

The dynamic parameters are used to define how the hair reacts to the motion of the body part to which it is attached. These parameters define how springy, stiff, and resistant to bending the hairs are. The available dynamic parameters for hair include:

- **Gravity:** Defines the strength of the gravity force that acts on the hair. A negative gravity value pulls hair towards the ground and a positive value pushes it away from the ground.

- **Spring Strength:** Defines how springy hair reacts to motion. Hair with a high Spring Strength value will bounce in response to motion.

- **Air Damping:** Defines how resistant the hair is to the air. Hair with a low Air Damping value won't be affected by wind as much as hair with a higher Air Damping value.

- **Spring Damping:** Defines how quickly springy hair quits bouncing. Hair with high Spring Strength and low Spring Damping values will bounce longer than hair with a higher Spring Damping value.

- **Bend Resistance:** Defines the hair's ability to resist folding in on itself.

- **Position Force:** Causes hair to stay in its place and defy the hair dynamics. This value, like hairspray, keeps each hair separated.

- **Root Stiffness:** Defines how stiff the hair is at its root and how quickly the hair roots move with the head.

- **Root Stiffness Falloff:** Defines how far the root stiffness carries up the length of the hair. A value of 0.0 causes the entire hair to maintain the same Root Stiffness value and a value of 1.0 makes the hair less stiff immediately beyond the root.

NOTE

Some dynamic objects such as wind can add an additional force to the dynamics of hair. More on using these dynamic objects is covered in Chapter 11, "Animating Figures."

Enabling Collisions

The Do Collisions option in the Dynamics controls enables collisions to be calculated as part of the dynamic simulation. This computes whether the hair collides with other polygons such as props, ears, hands, and the like. Enabling collisions can add to the time required to compute the hair dynamics.

Calculating Dynamics

Once you set the dynamic parameters, you can click the Calculated Dynamics button. This computes the positions and movements of each hair for every animation frame. A simple progress dialog box, shown in Figure 8-19, appears when the calculations are initiated. This dialog box includes a Cancel button that you can use to cancel the calculations at any time. The Clear Dynamics button removes all saved dynamic calculations.

FIGURE 8-19

Calculate Dynamics process dialog box

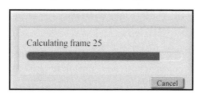

FIGURE 8-20

Dynamic hair

1. Select File, Open and open the Mullet hair.pz3 file.

2. Click the Hair tab at the top of the interface to open the Hair Room.

3. Click the Head element in the Document Window and select the Hair_1 group from the Growth Group controls.

4. In the Dynamics controls, enable the Do Collisions option.

5. Click the Gravity parameter and set it to 0.3. Set the Spring Strength to 2.0 and the Spring Damping to 0.1.

   Setting the Gravity value to a high positive value will act like a fan blowing the hair upward and the Spring Strength value will make the hair spring slightly as it reaches its top position.

6. Click the Calculate Dynamics button.

   A progress dialog box appears and lists each frame as it is calculated. At the completion of the calculations, the resulting hair for the current frame is displayed, as shown in Figure 8-20.

7. Select File, Save As and save the file as **Dynamic hair.pz3**.

ADD A WIND
FORCE DEFORMER

What You'll Do

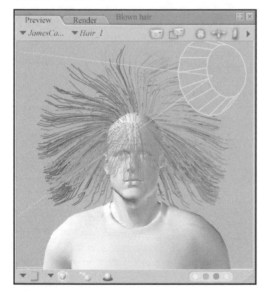

In this lesson, you learn how to add wind with the wind force deformer object.

Hair simulations include the force of gravity by default, but you can also add a directional wind force to the simulation using the Object, Create Wind Force menu command.

Positioning the Forcefield

When the wind force deformer is added to the scene, it is represented by a simple indicator that has two diagonal lines projecting from it, as shown in Figure 8-21.

FIGURE 8-21
Wind force deformer indicator

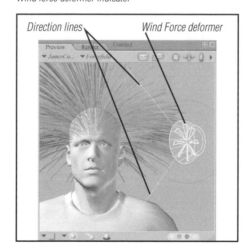

You can position and orient the wind indicator anywhere in the scene using the standard editing tools; the diagonal lines denote the direction of the wind from the center of the indicator outward towards the diagonal lines.

Changing the Forcefield's Parameters

When the wind force deformer is selected, several parameters are available in the Parameters/Properties palette, including the following:

- **Amplitude:** Sets the strength of the wind force.
- **Spread Angle:** Sets the angle for the diagonal lines, which is the area where the wind has influence.
- **Range:** Sets how far the wind force is projected.
- **Turbulence:** Sets the amount of variability applied to the wind.

The wind only affects hair that is within the Spread Angle and Range parameters.

NOTE

You can also use wind force deformers to deform dynamic cloth.

Add a wind force deformer

1. Choose File, Open and select and open the Hair in wind.pz3 file.

2. Click the Hair tab at the top of the interface to open the Hair Room.

3. Select the Object, Create Wind Force menu command to add a wind force deformer to the scene.

   The deformer appears at the scene origin.

4. Drag the deformer object with the Translate/Pull tool and the Rotate tool to position and orient the deformer in front and to the side of the figure's face so the direction lines are pointing towards the figure's head.

5. Select the Face camera from the Camera controls.

6. Select the Window, Parameter Dials menu command to open the Parameters/Properties palette. With the deformer selected, set the Amplitude to 10, the Spread Angle to 15, the Range to 1.0, and the Turbulence to 1.0.

7. Select the hair object and click the Calculate Dynamics button.

   A progress dialog box appears and every frame for the simulation is calculated. The result is that the hair is blown towards the back of the head, as shown in Figure 8-22.

8. Select File, Save As and save the file as **Blown hair.pz3**.

FIGURE 8-22

Blown hair

CHANGE
HAIR MATERIAL

What You'll Do

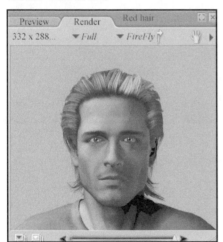

In this lesson, you learn how to change the hair's material values.

Selecting the hair group in the Material Room lets you change the material used to shade the hair, including its root color, tip color, highlights, and root softness.

Viewing Hair Material

To view the material used to shade hair, open the Material Room and select the hair group from the Props menu in the Object List at the top of the Shader Window. This will make the hair material visible in the Advanced panel of the Shader Window, as shown in Figure 8-23.

Setting Hair Material Properties

With the hair group selected, the Shader Window includes a specific node that includes several unique material properties, including:

- **Root Color:** Defines the hair color at the hair root.

- **Tip Color:** Defines the hair color at the hair tip.

- **Specular Color:** Defines the color used for specular highlights.

- **Highlight Size:** Defines how big the highlights are that reflect off the hair.

- **Root Softness:** Defines the transparency of the hair at its roots.

- **Opaque in Shadow:** Causes hair to be fully visible without any transparency when the hair is in the shadow.

The Hair node should always be connected into the Alternate Diffuse attribute.

FIGURE 8-23
Hair material in the Shader Window

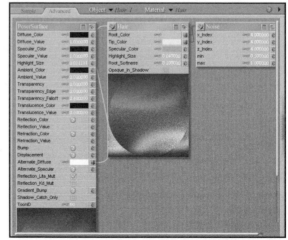

Change hair color

1. Open Poser with the default man visible.

2. Click the Hair tab to access the Hair Room.

3. Click the side control to the right of the interface to open the Library palette or select Window, Libraries.

4. Click the Hair category at the top of the Library palette and navigate to the James Hair folder.

5. Select the James_Med thumbnail and click the Apply Library Preset button at the bottom of the Library palette.

6. Click the Face camera in the Camera controls.

7. Select the Props, HairALLHEAD option from the Object List at the top of the Shader Window.

8. Click the Material tab at the top of the interface to open the Material Room.

9. Click the Advanced tab to open the Advanced panel in the Shader Window.

10. Click the color swatch for the Root Color value and select a dark red color. Then, click the color swatch for the Tip Color value and select a light red color.

    Changing the hair color won't change the color in the Document Window, but it will be visible when the scene is rendered.

11. Click the Render button 🖼 in the Document Window.

    The hair for the figure is rendered with red hair, as shown in Figure 8-24.

12. Select File, Save As and save the file as **Red hair.pz3**.

FIGURE 8-24

Red hair

CHAPTER SUMMARY

This chapter covered all the features found in the Hair Room, including the capabilities to define hair groups, to grow guide hairs, and to set their length. Styling hair is made possible with the Styling controls and the Hair Style Tool panel. You can also define the dynamic parameters used to compute the hair simulation. You can add wind forces to the scene to interact with the hair using the wind force deformer. Finally, you can also change the material used to shade the hair.

What You Have Learned

In this chapter, you:
- Discovered the layout of the Hair Room interface, including the Hair Style Tool panel.
- Learned how to load preset hairstyles into the current scene.
- Created unique hair groups using the Group Editor.
- Grew guide hairs and set the hair length and position.
- Styled hair using parameters and the Hair Style Tool panel.
- Defined the dynamic properties of hair and calculated the hair's dynamic positions.

- Changed the hair's material parameters in the Material Room.
- Added wind to the simulation using a wind force deformer.

Key Terms from This Chapter

Hair growth group. A grouped selection of polygons that define where the hair is to be located.

Guide hairs. A sampling of hairs that show where the full set of hair will be located.

Hair Style tool. A tool that is used to style individual hairs or groups of selected hairs.

Hair density. The total number of hairs for a given hair group.

Hair root. The end of the hair nearest the figure.

Hair tip. The end of the hair farthest away from the figure.

Clumpiness. The tendency of hair to clump together into groups.

Kinkiness. The amount of curl in each hair.

Dynamics. The study of the motions of connected objects.

Springiness. The tendency of an object to bounce after being set in motion.

Damping. The tendency of an object to resist bouncing after being set in motion. The opposite of springiness.

Stiffness. A property that makes hairs resist motion.

chapter

9

WORKING WITH
Cloth

1. Load cloth from the Library.

2. Create a cloth simulation.

3. Create cloth.

4. Create cloth groups.

5. Simulate cloth dynamics.

6. Add a wind force deformer.

chapter 9 WORKING WITH
Cloth

Many of the early Poser images featured many naked figures or figures with tight spandex. This was because adding realistic cloth with its folds and smooth flowing surfaces was so difficult to position so it looked right. The later versions of Poser now include the Cloth Room, where you can simulate the movement and **draping** of cloth.

Just like hair, Poser offers two ways to apply clothing to the figure. The first method is to apply prop clothes. These clothes are typically custom made to fit a specific figure and can be conformed to fit the figure exactly and to match the figure's pose as it changes. A detailed discussion of conforming clothes is found in Chapter 5, "Dealing with Props."

The second method uses dynamic cloth that can simulated to flow and interact with the figure and other scene props using the Cloth Room.

Clothing and various props can be used as cloth with a wide range of parameters for defining how the cloth folds on itself, how dense the cloth is, its **friction** parameters, how it is affected by the air, and how stretchy the cloth is. Using these parameters, you can define any type of cloth from soft fine silks to hard coarse leather.

You can also select which scene objects the cloth collides with. By enabling **collisions** between the cloth and the figure, you can realistically drape cloth over the figure or over other scene objects.

You can also divide cloth into groups using the Group Editor. Each group can have its own defined parameters, making it possible to simulate a single cloth object made from several different types of material.

Calculating a simulation actually creates animation keys for the cloth interacting with the figure and other scene objects.

Tools You'll Use

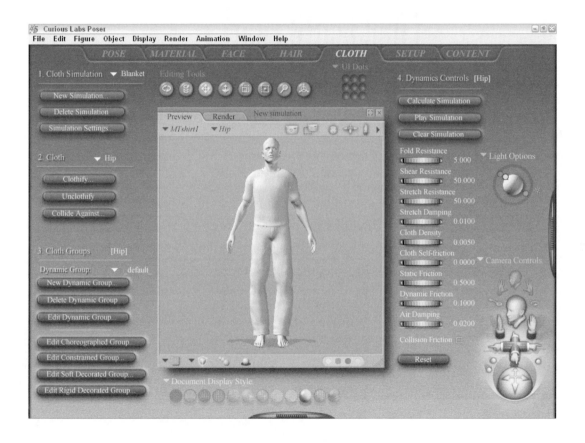

LOAD CLOTH FROM
THE LIBRARY

What You'll Do

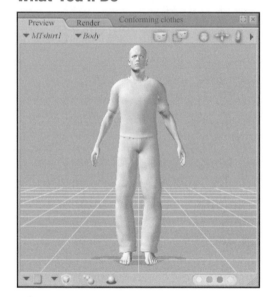

In this lesson, you learn how to use the
Cloth Room interface.

You can open the Cloth Room by clicking
the Cloth tab at the top of the Poser interface. This opens an interface setup that is
different from the Pose Room, as shown in
Figure 9-1, although it includes all of the
same controls as the Pose Room, including
the Document Window, the Camera and
Light controls, the Display Styles and the
Editing Tools button set. The Cloth Room
interface also includes four additional sets
of buttons that are used to group, load, and
dynamically simulate the motion of cloth
objects.

FIGURE 9-1

Cloth Room interface

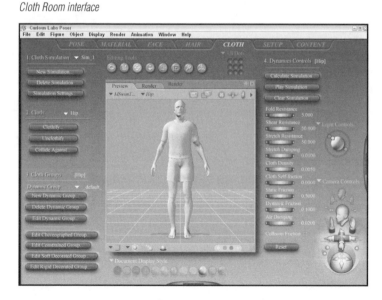

Using the Cloth Controls

When you first open the Cloth Room, only the New Simulation button in the **Cloth Simulation** set of controls is enabled. Before any cloth properties can be set, you must add a clothing prop to the scene. Once you create a new simulation, the **Clothify** button in the Cloth group becomes active. The remaining two sets of controls only become active once you select an object using the Clothify button.

Loading Cloth from the Library

Although almost any object, including body parts, can be treated as cloth, you'll typically want to look for cloth objects in the Props Library category. Within each folder are thumbnails of the various cloth objects. With a cloth object thumbnail selected, click the Change Prop button at the bottom of the Library palette and the selected object is loaded into the Shader Window. Figure 9-2 shows several clothing thumbnails.

> **NOTE**
>
> Cloth objects can actually be loaded from within any room.

Using Conforming Clothes

Many objects in the Props category of the Library are identified as **Conforming objects**. These objects are created to fit exactly on the matching figure. To conform a clothing prop to its matching figure, choose the Figure, Conform To menu command. This opens a dialog box where you can select the figure to conform the prop object to.

> **CAUTION**
>
> Prop clothes that are conformed to a figure shouldn't be used in a dynamic simulation. For cloth to be simulated properly, it needs to be free of any intersections with the scene objects. Also, conforming clothes are set to move with the body and including conforming clothes in a cloth simulation will make it so the clothes no longer move with the body.

Removing Cloth from the Library

The Remove from Library button in the Library palette permanently deletes the selected thumbnail cloth object.

FIGURE 9-2
Loaded Library clothing

Conform clothes to a figure

1. Open Poser with the default man visible.

2. Click the side control to the right of the interface to open the Library palette or select Window, Libraries.

3. Click the Props category at the top of the Library palette and navigate to the James Clothing folder.

4. Select the Jeans 1 thumbnail and click the Add New Item button at the bottom of the Library palette.

   The selected clothing item is loaded into the Shader Window, but it doesn't match the figure.

5. With the Jeans 1 item selected, select Figure, Conform To.

6. In the Conform To dialog box that appears, select the James Casual object and click OK.

7. Repeat steps 4-6 to add and conform the T-shirt 1 object.

   Both clothing items are conformed to fit the figure, as shown in Figure 9-3.

8. Select File, Save As and save the file as **Conforming clothes.pz3**.

FIGURE 9-3

Conforming jeans and T-shirt

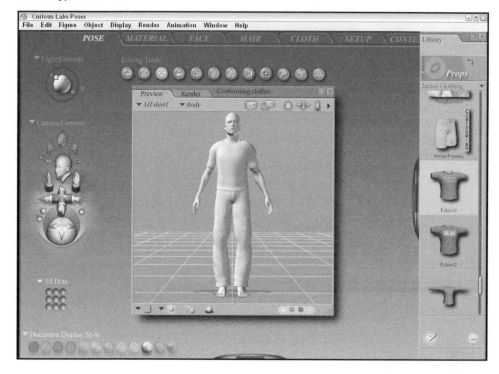

LESSON 2

CREATE A CLOTH SIMULATION

What You'll Do

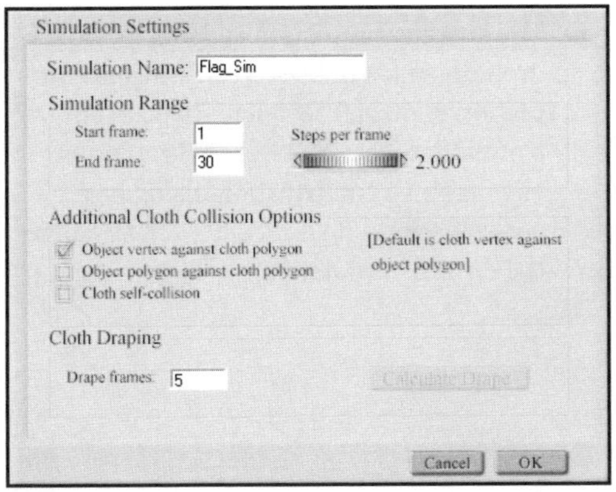
Simulation Settings
Simulation Name: Flag_Sim
Simulation Range
Start frame: 1
End frame: 30
Steps per frame
2.000
Additional Cloth Collision Options
Object vertex against cloth polygon
Object polygon against cloth polygon
Cloth self-collision
[Default is cloth vertex against object polygon]
Cloth Draping
Drape frames: 5
Calculate Drape
Cancel
OK

In this lesson, you learn how to create a new cloth simulation.

The first step in creating dynamic cloth effects is to create a simulation. A single Poser scene can include several different cloth simulations to control, for example, a figure's coat, or a flag being held by a figure. By separating each cloth effect into a separate simulation, you can control which effects are included with the current animation.

Creating and Naming a New Simulation

To create a new simulation, click the New Simulation button in the Cloth Simulation controls of the Cloth Room. This opens the Simulation Settings dialog box, shown in Figure 9-4. Using this dialog box, you can name the current simulation. All current simulations are listed in the drop-down menu next to the Cloth Simulation title. The default simulation names are Sim_1, Sim_2, and so on.

Setting Simulation Range

The Simulation Settings dialog box includes settings for controlling the precise range for the simulation using the Start and End Frame values. All animation frames prior to the start frame will display the cloth in its starting position and

FIGURE 9-4
Simulation Settings dialog box

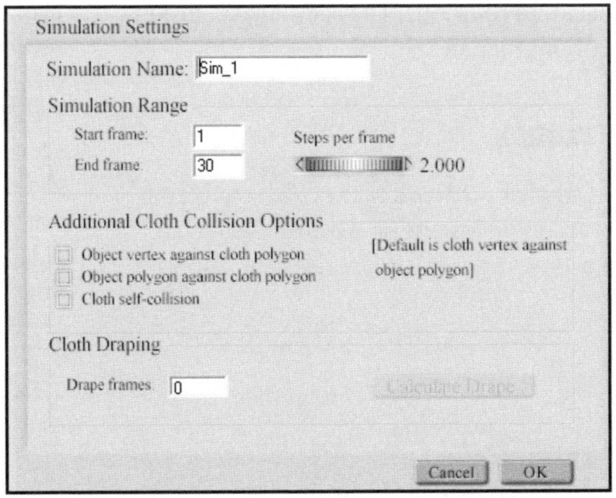
Simulation Settings
Simulation Name: Sim_1
Simulation Range
Start frame: 1
End frame: 30
Steps per frame
2.000
Additional Cloth Collision Options
Object vertex against cloth polygon
Object polygon against cloth polygon
Cloth self-collision
[Default is cloth vertex against object polygon]
Cloth Draping
Drape frames: 0
Calculate Drape
Cancel
OK

all frames that follow the end frame display the cloth in its final position. You can use Step Size to change how often the cloth simulation is calculated. A Steps Per Frame setting of 1 computes the cloth's position only once for every frame and a steps per frame setting of 2 computes the cloth's potition twice every frame. Higher step size values will result in a smoother simulation, but will require much longer to compute the simulation.

Setting Collision Options

Collisions between the cloth object and the figure and the other scene forces are the reactions that determine the cloth's dynamic motion. By default, these collisions are determined by watching the position of the cloth vertices relative to the scene polygon faces, but you can enable several additional collision checks in the Simulation Settings dialog box for more accurate collisions. The additional collision options include:

CAUTION

Enabling any of these additional collision options substantially increases the simulation computation time.

- Object Vertex against Cloth Polygon: This option is opposite of the default, but will help prevent having figure objects such as hands penetrate the center of the cloth.
- Object Polygon against Cloth Polygon: This option will help prevent large flat figure areas, such as the chest, penetrate the cloth when the two are placed parallel to each other.
- Cloth Self-Collision: This option keeps the cloth from folding in on itself by detecting when the cloth object intersects with itself.

Using Cloth Draping

When a cloth object is added to the scene, it is probably stiff and doesn't fit with its surroundings. You could manually place the cloth object to a more realistic setting, but it is easier to let the simulation do it for you using the Drape settings. The Drape Frames setting in the Simulation Settings dialog box lets you set the number of frames that are allowed to let the cloth settle into the scene. Once these frames are completed, the cloth's draped position is used as the starting point for the simulation. The Calculate Drape button lets you initiate the drape computations immediately.

Changing Simulation Settings

After clicking OK, the Simulation Settings dialog box closes and the simulation is added to the current list of simulations. The Clothify button also becomes active for selecting the cloth object. If you want to revisit the simulation settings, you can click the Simulation Settings button to open the dialog box again.

Deleting Simulations

The current simulation is listed in the drop-down list at the top of the Cloth Simulation controls. To delete this current simulation, click the Delete Simulation button and a confirmation dialog box appears asking if you really want to delete the current simulation.

FIGURE 9-5

New simulation settings

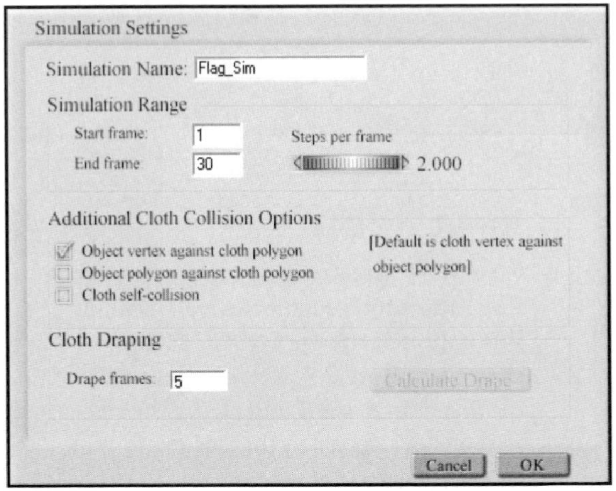

Simulation Settings

Simulation Name: Flag_Sim

Simulation Range

Start frame: 1   Steps per frame

End frame: 30   ◁▦▦▦▦▦▦▦▷ 2.000

Additional Cloth Collision Options

☑ Object vertex against cloth polygon   [Default is cloth vertex against
☐ Object polygon against cloth polygon   object polygon]
☐ Cloth self-collision

Cloth Draping

Drape frames: 5   Calculate Drape

Cancel   OK

Create a new simulation

1. Open Poser with the default man visible.

2. Click the Cloth tab at the top of the interface to open the Cloth Room.

3. Click the New Simulation button at the top of the Cloth Simulation controls.

   The Simulation Settings dialog box opens.

4. Change the name of the simulation to **Flag_Sim** and enable the Object Vertex Against Cloth Polygon option, as shown in Figure 9-5. Click OK.

5. Select File, Save As and save the file as **New simulation.pz3**.

CREATE
CLOTH

What You'll Do

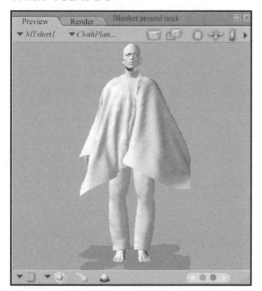

In this lesson, you learn how to convert clothing and prop objects into cloth objects.

The Cloth controls in the Cloth Room include buttons for creating cloth objects and for specifying which objects should be computed as collide objects. Any prop object, and even body parts, can be made into a cloth object using the Clothify button.

Using Primitives for Cloth

Within the Props category of the Library is a subfolder named Primitives that includes a collection of standard 3D objects such as a sphere, cube, cone, and cylinder. There is also an object labeled as a Hi-Res Square. By selecting, scaling, and clothifying these various objects, you can create an assortment of towels, blankets, scarves, shawls, and flags. The Hi-Res Square prop object actually shows up in the Actor List named Cloth Plane.

> **QUICK TIP**
>
> You can also import and use external objects as cloth objects. Make sure that the imported objects have a fairly high resolution so the deformations can be accurately represented.

Using Clothify

Once you've created a simulation, the Clothify button becomes active. Clicking this button opens the Clothify dialog box, shown in Figure 9-6, where you can select the object to make it into cloth. The current object selected in the Document Window is shown in the Clothify dialog box by default, but you can select any loaded body part or prop from the drop-down list.

FIGURE 9-6
Clothify dialog box

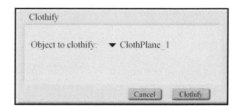

Removing Clothify

All clothified objects are listed in the drop-down list next to the Cloth controls title. You can change the current cloth object back into a normal object using the Unclothify button.

Enabling Collisions

When a simulation is calculated, the cloth object will fall under the weight of gravity straight to the ground plane unless you select an object to collide with the cloth.

Clicking the Collide Against button opens the Cloth Collision Objects dialog box, shown in Figure 9-7. At the top of the Cloth Collision Objects dialog box is a list of all the objects that the cloth will collide with. Clicking the Add/Remove button opens the Hierarchy Selection dialog box, shown in Figure 9-8, where you can select collision objects by selecting specific objects.

FIGURE 9-8

Hierarchy Selection dialog box

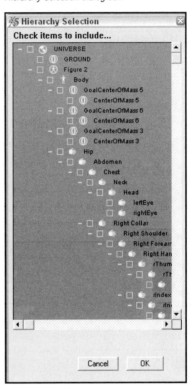

FIGURE 9-7

Cloth Collision Objects dialog box

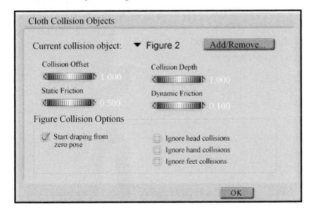

Setting Collision Options

If multiple specific objects are enabled as collision objects, each selection can have its own collision settings. To change the settings for the collision object listed at the top of the Cloth Collision Objects dialog box, drag the parameter dial or click and type a new value in the value field. The available collision parameters and options include:

- **Collision Offset:** The offset value provides some space between the cloth image and the object that it is colliding with in order to prevent the object from intersecting with the cloth.

- **Collision Depth:** The depth value defines how close the cloth vertices must be to the object polygons in order to be detected as a collision.

- **Static Friction:** This parameter defines the friction between the cloth and the colliding object to start the objects moving. For example, silk and hard plastic would have a very low Static Friction value because it would take very little force to start the two objects moving, whereas leather and denim would have a higher Static Friction value because a larger force would be required to start moving the two objects relative to one another.

- **Dynamic Friction:** This parameter defines the friction between the cloth and colliding object to keep the objects that are already moving in motion relative to one another. For example, a quilt moving over a rocky surface would have a fairly high Dynamic Friction value and would stop moving quickly, but a piece of ice on a smooth steel bar would continue sliding for some way, thus having a low Dynamic Friction value.

- **Start Draping from Zero Pose:** When conforming clothes are applied to a figure and the figure's pose is changed, the clothes will follow the figure's form, but they will be offset slightly. To make the cloth object drape over the figure for the new pose, enable this option.

- **Ignore Head, Hand and Feet Collisions:** When you slip on a shirt, you scrunch your hands together to slide your arm into the sleeve. In Poser, you can simply disable hand collisions from the simulation. The same can be done for the head and feet.

Create cloth

1. Choose File, Open and select and open the New simulation.pz3 file.

2. Click the side control to the right of the interface to open the Library palette or select Window, Libraries.

3. Click the Props category at the top of the Library palette and navigate to the Primitives folder.

4. Select the Square Hi-Res thumbnail and click the Add New Item button at the bottom of the Library palette.

   The square object appears under the figure in the Document Window.

5. With the Translate/Pull tool [image] selected in the Editing tools, drag the square object up above the figure's head.

6. Click the Cloth tab at the top of the interface to open the Cloth Room.

7. With the Square object still selected, click the Clothify button. In the Clothify dialog box, click the Clothify button.

8. Click the Collide Against button to open the Cloth Collision Objects dialog box. Click the Add/Remove button and select the James Casual object in the Hierarchy Selection dialog box. Then scroll down through the hierarchy list and deselect the Neck, Head, and Eye objects and click OK.

9. In the Cloth Collision Objects dialog box, enable the Ignore Head Collisions option and click OK.

10. Click the Calculate Simulation button.

    A progress dialog box appears and every frame for the simulation is calculated. The result is that the Square object acts like a blanket that covers the head of the figure, as shown in Figure 9-9.

11. Select File, Save As and save the file as **Blanket around neck.pz3**.

FIGURE 9-9

Blanket around neck

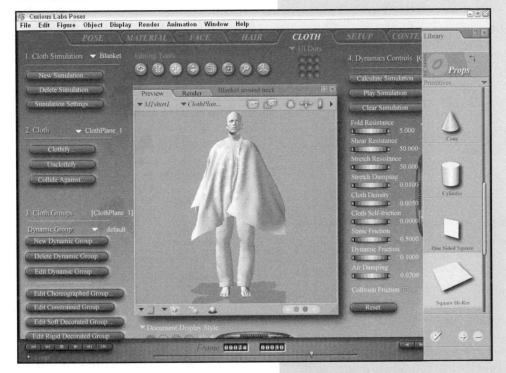

CREATE
CLOTH GROUPS

What You'll Do

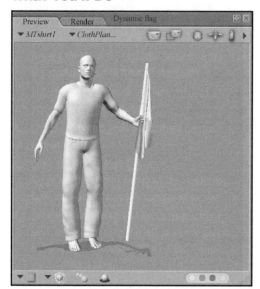

In this lesson, you learn how to specify different cloth groups.

You can divide created cloth objects into groups that act differently as needed. You can do this to represent different types of material, to animate the cloth itself, or to constrain a portion of the cloth so it doesn't move at all. You create cloth groups using the Group Editor, except cloth groups use vertices instead of polygons to define the group.

Creating a Dynamic Cloth Group

When a cloth object is created, all vertices belong to a single group labeled *default*. This default group is a dynamic type group, which means that it is included in the simulation calculations using the dynamic parameters set in the Dynamics Controls. A single cloth object can include several dynamic groups. To create a new dynamic group, click the New Dynamic Group button and type the group's name in the simple dialog box that appears. All created cloth groups are listed in the drop-down list at the top of the Cloth Groups controls.

You can delete the selected group by clicking the Delete Dynamic Group button.

Editing a Dynamic Cloth Group

Clicking the Edit Dynamic Group button opens the Group Editor in Vertex selection mode, as shown in Figure 9-10, and darkens all objects in the Document Window. Using the Select Vertices tool in the Group Editor, you can select which vertices are included in the current dynamic group. The Deselect Vertices tool can be used to remove vertices from the current selection.

QUICKTIP

You can also access the Deselect Vertices tool when the Select Vertices tool is selected by holding down the Ctrl key and vice versa.

FIGURE 9-10

Group Editor in Vertex Selection mode

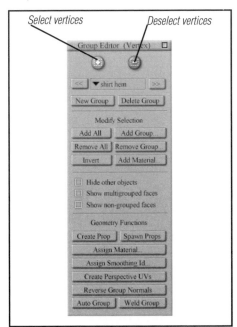

Select vertices   Deselect vertices

Using Other Cloth Groups

In addition to the dynamic cloth groups, a cloth object can also include several other cloth groups. Each cloth object can only include one of each of these other groups, so their names cannot be changed. Also, each vertex can only be added to a single group, so adding a vertex to one of these groups will remove it from its current group. The other available groups include the following:

- **Choreographed Group:** The Choreographed cloth group is a set of vertices that can be animated as a group using keyframes.

- **Constrained Group:** The Constrained cloth group are those objects that are constrained to not be moved by the dynamic simulation, but constrained vertices can still move with the body part directly underneath it.

- **Soft Decorated Group:** The Soft Decorated cloth group is used to remove objects that have small flexible details such as shirt pockets and fringe lace from the simulation while still allowing the detail to move with the cloth. The soft group differs from the rigid group in that it can flex and bend and the rigid remains solid.

- **Rigid Decorated Group:** The Rigid Decorated cloth group is used to remove objects that have small solid details such as buttons and belt buckles from the simulation while still allowing the detail to move with the cloth. The rigid group remains solid and is inflexible.

Clicking the Edit button for any of these other groups opens the Group Editor where you can select the vertices that are part of the group.

Create cloth groups

1. Choose File, Open and select and open the Man holding flag.pz3 file.

2. Click the Cloth tab at the top of the interface to open the Cloth Room.

3. Click the New Simulation button at the top of the Cloth Simulation controls.

4. Change the name of the simulation to **Flag** and click OK.

5. With the flag object selected, click the Clothify button. In the Clothify dialog box, click the Clothify button.

6. Click the Collide Against button to open the Cloth Collision Objects dialog box. Click the Add/Remove button and select the Cyl_1 object in the Hierarchy Selection dialog box. Then click OK once to close the Hierarchy Selection dialog box and again to close the Cloth Collision Objects dialog box.

7. Click the Edit Choreographed Group button.

   The Group Editor appears with the Select Vertices tool ⊙ enabled.

8. Drag over all the vertices on the left side of the flag where it connects with the pole. Then close the Group Editor.

9. Click the Calculate Simulation button.

   A progress dialog box appears and every frame for the simulation is calculated. The result is that the flag object falls limp under the effect of gravity, as shown in Figure 9-11.

10. Select File, Save As and save the file as **Dynamic flag.pz3**.

FIGURE 9-11

Dynamic flag

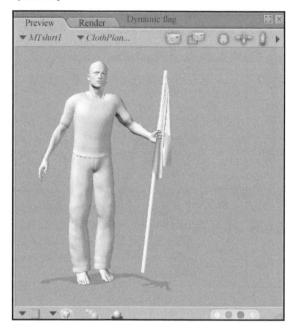

SIMULATE CLOTH
DYNAMICS

What You'll Do

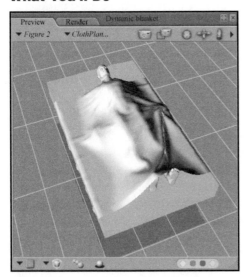

In this lesson, you learn how to set cloth parameters and calculate the simulation.

The final step is to define the cloth parameters for each dynamic group and to calculate the simulation. The controls to accomplish this final step are found in the Dynamics Controls.

Setting Cloth Parameters

For each dynamic group, you can set the parameters found in the Dynamics Controls. These parameters define how the cloth moves during the simulation. The cloth parameters can be reset to their default values at any time by clicking the Reset button located below all the parameter dials. The available cloth parameters include the following:

- **Fold Resistance:** This parameter value defines how resistant the current cloth group is to folding. Low values act like a thin scarf that easily folds on itself and higher values act like rigid plastic that doesn't easily fold on itself.

- **Shear Resistance:** This parameter value defines how resistant the current cloth group is to shearing the surface against itself. Low values allow one edge of the cloth to easily move while the other end is stationary.

- **Stretch Resistance:** This parameter value defines how resistant the current cloth group is to stretching. Low values allow the cloth to stretch a great deal such as a rubber band and high values prevent the cloth from stretching like denim or burlap.

- **Stretch Damping:** This parameter value defines how quickly the stretching of the cloth fades. A high value causes the stretching to quickly stop such as a cotton t-shirt and a low value lets the stretching continue for a longer period of time such as spandex.

- **Cloth Density:** This parameter value defines how heavy the cloth is per unit area. Low values are light cloth items like a silk scarf and high values are much heavier like leather or denim. Cloth groups with a higher density will be more affected by gravity and collisions.

- **Cloth Self-Friction:** This parameter value defines how much friction the cloth has when rubbed against itself. Low values allow the cloth to easily move across its own surface, again like silk, but high values cannot be easily rubbed together, like denim.

- **Static Friction:** This parameter value defines how much force is required to begin to move cloth over an object. Low values require little force to begin to slide across the surface of another object such as an ice cube on a plastic plane, but high values require a substantial amount of force to start moving such as wood on sandpaper.

- **Dynamic Friction:** This parameter value is similar to Static Friction, except it defines the amount of force required to keep a moving object in motion. Low values, again like ice on plastic, require very little force to keep moving, but high values like wood on sandpaper require quite a bit of force to keep the surfaces moving.

- **Air Damping:** This parameter value defines how much the cloth group is affected by air currents such as wind. Low values allow the cloth to move easily when blown by the wind, like a flag, but high values aren't affected by air currents as much, such as the flag pole.

- **Collision Friction:** This option disables the Static and Dynamic Friction parameter values when enabled and uses the Static and Dynamic Friction values set in the Cloth Collision Objects dialog box instead.

Calculating the Simulation

Clicking the Calculate Simulation button starts the calculation process and a progress dialog box, shown in Figure 9-12, appears that gives details on the progress of the calculations. The calculations can be cancelled at any time using the Cancel button.

Viewing the Simulation

The Play Simulation button plays back all the calculated frames for the simulation in the Document Window.

Clearing the Simulation

The Clear Simulation button removes all the calculated simulation keys, but it doesn't change any of your current collision, group, or parameter settings.

FIGURE 9-12

Simulation calculation progress dialog box

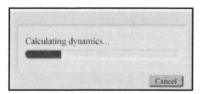

FIGURE 9-13

Dynamic blanket

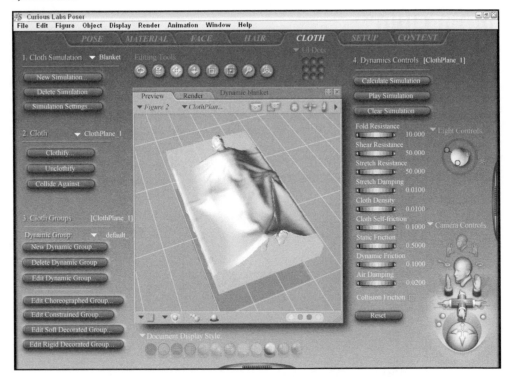

1. Choose File, Open and select and open the Man in bed.pz3 file.

2. Click the Cloth tab at the top of the interface to open the Cloth Room.

3. Click the New Simulation button at the top of the Cloth Simulation controls.

4. Change the name of the simulation to **Blanket**, enable the Object Vertex against Cloth Polygon option, and click OK.

5. With the blanket object selected, click the Clothify button. In the Clothify dialog box, click the Clothify button.

6. Click the Collide Against button to open the Cloth Collision Objects dialog box. Click the Add/Remove button and select the Figure 2 and box_1 objects in the Hierarchy Selection dialog box. Then click OK once to close the Hierarchy Selection dialog box and again to close the Cloth Collision Objects dialog box.

7. With the default dynamic cloth group selected, set the Fold Resistance parameter to 10, the Cloth Density parameter to 0.01, and the Cloth Self-Friction parameter to 0.1.

8. Click the Calculate Simulation button.

   A progress dialog box appears and every frame for the simulation is calculated. The result is that the blanket object falls under the effect of gravity and covers the man's figure, as shown in Figure 9-13.

9. Select File, Save As and save the file as **Dynamic blanket.pz3**.

ADD A WIND
FORCE DEFORMER

What You'll Do

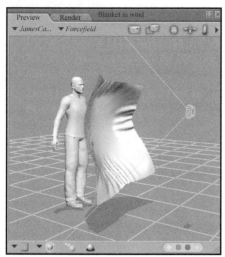

In this lesson, you learn how to add wind with the Wind Force deformer object.

Cloth simulations include the force of gravity by default, but you can also add a directional wind force to the simulation using the Object, Create Wind Force menu command.

FIGURE 9-14
Wind force deformer indicator

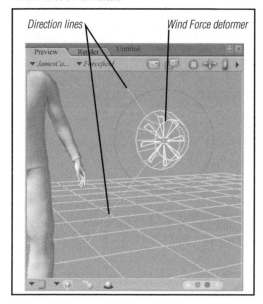

Positioning the Forcefield

When the Wind Force deformer is added to the scene, it is represented by a simple indicator that has two diagonal lines projecting from it, as shown in Figure 9-14.

The wind indicator can be positioned and oriented anywhere in the scene using the standard Editing tools and the diagonal lines denote the direction of the wind from the center of the indicator outward towards the diagonal lines.

Changing the Forcefield's Parameters

When you select the Wind Force deformer, several parameters are available in the Parameters palette, as shown in Figure 9-15, including the following:

- **Amplitude:** Sets the strength of the wind force.
- **Spread Angle:** Sets the angle for the diagonal lines, which is the area where the wind has influence.
- **Range:** Sets how far the wind force is projected.
- **Turbulence:** Sets the amount of variability applied to the wind.

The wind only affects cloth objects that are within the Spread Angle and Range parameters.

NOTE

You can also use Wind Force deformers to deform dynamic hair.

FIGURE 9-15

Wind Force parameters

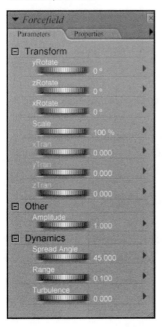

Adding a wind force deformer

1. Choose File, Open and select and open the Cloth in wind.pz3 file.

2. Click the Cloth tab at the top of the interface to open the Cloth Room.

3. Select the Object, Create Wind Force menu command to add a Wind Force deformer to the scene.

   The deformer appears at the scene origin.

4. Drag the deformer object with the Translate/Pull tool and position it in front of the cloth object so the direction lines are pointing towards the cloth object.

5. Select the Window, Parameter Dials menu command to open the Parameters palette. With the deformer selected, set the Amplitude to 10, the Range to 2, and the Turbulence to 1.0.

6. Click the Calculate Simulation button.

   A progress dialog box appears and every frame for the simulation is calculated. The result is that the cloth object is blown towards the default figure, as shown in Figure 9-16.

7. Select File, Save As and save the file as **Blanket in wind.pz3**.

FIGURE 9-16

Blanket in the wind

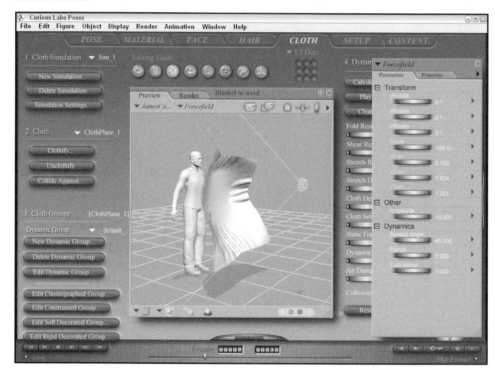

CHAPTER SUMMARY

This chapter covered all the features found in the Cloth Room, including the ability to create new cloth simulations, convert clothing and prop objects into cloth objects, enable collisions, define cloth groups, set cloth parameters, and calculate the simulation. The resulting cloth simulations can create realistic interactions between cloth and the various scene objects. You also learned that you can add wind forces to the scene using the Wind Force deformer.

What You Have Learned

In this chapter, you:
- Loaded clothing from the Library and conformed the clothes to the current figure.
- Created and named a new cloth simulation.
- Created cloth objects from clothing and prop objects.
- Enabled collisions between the current cloth object and other scene objects.
- Created new dynamic cloth groups and other cloth groups for choreographing and constraining cloth vertices using the Group Editor.
- Learned and set the various cloth parameters.
- Calculated a cloth simulation for a given range of frames.
- Added wind to the simulation using a Wind Force deformer.

Key Terms from This Chapter

Cloth simulation. The process of calculating the position and motion of a cloth object as it is moved by forces and collides with various scene objects.

Conforming clothes. Clothes or props that are designed to fit the given character exactly and to remain fitted as the figure's pose changes.

Simulation range. The number of frames that are included in the simulation marked by start and end frames.

Collision. An event that occurs when a vertex of a cloth object intersects with the polygon face of a scene object.

Draping. The process of letting a cloth object fall to rest about a scene object.

Clothify. The process of converting a prop object into a cloth object.

Friction. A force that resists the movement of one object over another.

chapter

10

WORKING WITH
Bones

1. Access and edit existing bone structures.

2. Create and name bones.

3. Group body parts.

4. Use inverse kinematics.

5. Use the Joint Editor.

chapter 10 WORKING WITH
Bones

When posing the various body parts in the Pose Room, you may wonder how the arm knows to bend at the elbow. The answer lies in the invisible bone structure that exists underneath the body mesh. If you open the Setup Room, the bone structure becomes visible and can be edited. The Setup Room is identical to the Pose Room, except that the **bone objects** are visible.

You can also use the Setup Room to add a new bone structure to custom figures that are imported, allowing them to be posed also. You create and manipulate new bones using the **Bone Creation tool** or you can load an existing bone structure from a Library figure and edit it to match the new figure.

Once you add new bones to a figure, you can position them using the Editing tools and the Joint Editor dialog box so that the

connection between bones are located within the figure's **joint**. You can also set limits for the joints to control how the bones move so the elbow or knee joints don't move backwards.

After positioning the bones so their joints are in the right location, you can select geometry groups to move with each bone using the Group Editor.

The final step is to establish any inverse kinematic chains such as for the limbs, so the hands can be placed to control the rest of the arm.

To control exactly which objects are moved, twisted along with the movement of the joint, you can use the Joint Editor. The Joint Editor can also make muscles bulge along with the joint movement.

Tools You'll Use

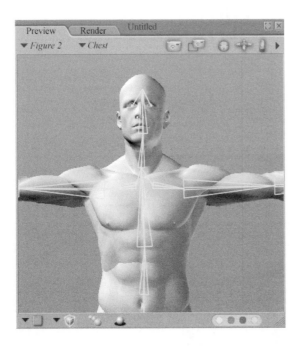

ACCESS AND EDIT EXISTING
BONE STRUCTURES

What You'll Do

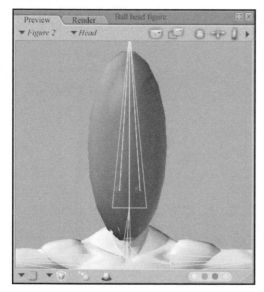

In this lesson, you learn how to access bone structures in the Setup Room and edit those structures.

When the Setup Room is opened, the figure's bones are displayed on top of the current figure, as shown in Figure 10-1. The bones appear as a linked set of triangle objects.

FIGURE 10-1
Setup Room

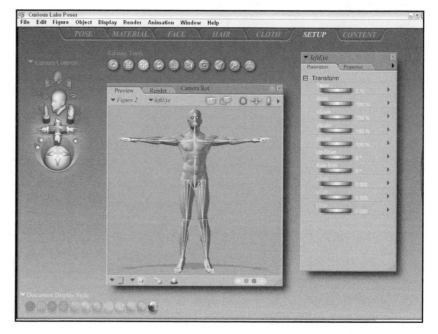

Selecting Bones

When you move the cursor over the top of the various bones in the Document Window, each bone becomes highlighted and clicking the highlighted bone selects it. The selected bone turns red.

Editing Bones

Within the Setup Room, you can move, rotate, or scale the selected bone using the Editing tools. You can also change the bone's position and orientation using the parameter dials. Moving a bone also moves all the children bones under the existing bone.

Changing Bone End Points

If you move the mouse over the start or end point of a bone, the cursor will change to a circular shape. Clicking and dragging with this circular-shaped cursor moves just the end point while leaving the opposite end point in place. This provides an easy way to extend and position bones. Moving end points works with any of the selected editing tools.

Making Symmetrical Changes

Bones also can take advantage of the Figure, Symmetry command options to copy the bone positions between the right and left sides of the current figure. Using these commands, you can copy the left side to the right side, the right side to the left side, swap the two sides, or adjust just the arms or legs.

Edit an existing set of bones

1. Choose File, Open and select and open the Ball head figure.pz3 file.

   This file includes the default man figure whose head has been replaced with an elongated ball prop object.

2. Select the Face camera 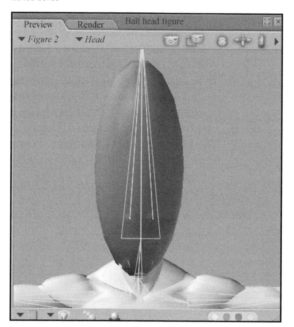 from the Camera controls.

3. Click the Setup tab to open the Setup Room. A warning dialog box will appear stating that morph targets may become unusable. Click OK to continue.

   A set of bones is displayed on top of the current figure.

4. Click the top bone that controls the head to select it.

   The selected bone turns red to show it is selected.

5. Move the cursor over the top end point of the selected bone. When the cursor changes to a circular cursor drag the bone end point upward until the bone covers the entire ball object, as shown in Figure 10-2.

6. Select File, Save As and save the file as **Edited bones.pz3**.

FIGURE 10-2

Edited bones

CREATE AND
NAME BONES

What You'll Do

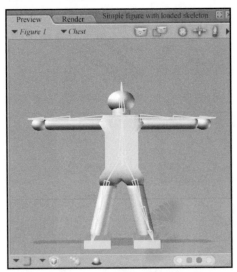

In this lesson, you learn how to load a skeleton onto an imported figure and create new bone sets.

Figures included in the Poser Library have a detailed bone structure already included and editing them isn't required unless you drastically change the figure's geometry. The more likely place to use the Setup Room features is to endow an imported figure with a bone structure.

Importing Figure Geometry

Figures created in an external 3D package can be imported into Poser using the File, Import menu command. Poser can import 3D objects saved in the QuickDraw (3DMF), 3D Studio (3DS), DXF, Wavefront (OBJ), and Lightwave (LWO) formats. Imported objects appear in Poser as props. If you select the imported prop and then open the Setup Room, a warning dialog box appears informing you that the selected prop object will be converted into a figure.

QUICKTIP

If the default figure gets in the way of the imported figure, you can select and hide the default figure using the Figure, Hide Figure menu command.

Loading an Existing Skeleton from the Library

If you load a figure from the Library into Poser while the Setup Room is open, the figure's skeleton will be loaded. You can then edit this skeleton to fit the new figure. This can be a huge time-saver if the skeleton is close enough to the new figure. Figure 10-3 shows a simple ball prop that has been added to the scene and the skeleton for a figure has been added from the Library.

Using the Bone Creation Tool

If an existing skeleton can't be found to load into the new figure, you can create a new skeleton using the Bone Creation tool. This tool is found with the Editing tools within the Setup Room. You create new bones by dragging from the bone's base to its tip. You can create multiple bones in succession by continuing to drag with the Bone Creation tool. Each new bone that is created becomes a child to the previous bone and all the bones together create a *bone chain*. Figure 10-4 shows five bones that were created in order using the Bone Creation tool.

Deleting Bones

If you create a bone that you want to remove, simply select the bone and press the Delete key. A confirmation dialog box will appear asking if you are sure that you want to delete the object. If one of the center bones of a chain is deleted, the bones on either end are reoriented to make up for the deleted bone.

Naming Bones

Each newly created bone is given a default name, which begins with the word *Bone* followed by a number. This name is listed and can be changed in the Name text field located in the Properties panel of the Parameter/Properties palette. The Internal Name setting is used to match the bone to a geometry group name.

QUICKTIP

The default name doesn't describe the bone's location. For clarity when working with bones, change the name to something meaningful like Left_upper_arm_bone.

FIGURE 10-3
Loaded skeleton

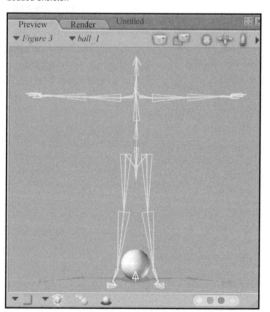

FIGURE 10-4
New bone chain

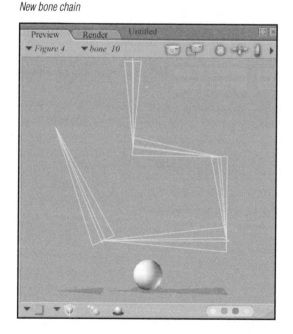

Attaching a Bone to an Existing Bone

Using the Bone Creation tool is great for creating skeletons for snakes and worms that have all their bones connected in one long head-to-tail line, but to create a human skeleton, you'll need to branch bones that two separate bone chains so they can be connected to the hip bone. If you select a bone and drag with the Bone Creation tool, the new bone will be attached to the end of the selected bone.

Two other ways to attach the selected bone to another bone are to click the Set Parent button in the Parameters/Properties palette or to select the Object, Change Parent menu command. Both of these methods will open a hierarchical list of scene objects where you can select the bone's new parent. Figure 10-5 shows a set of bones that splits into two chains.

FIGURE 10-5

Split bone chains

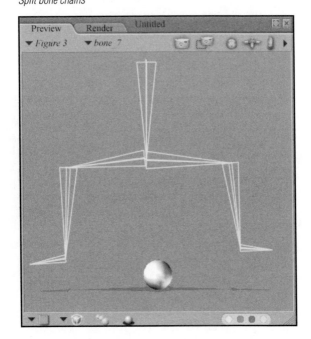

Load a skeleton

1. Open Poser with the default man visible.

2. Select File, Import, Wavefront OBJ. Then, select and import the Simple figure.obj file. In the Prop Import Options dialog box, deselect the Centered option, enable the Place on Floor option, and then click OK.

   The simple figure object is imported as a prop.

3. With the imported figure selected, click the Setup tab at the top of the interface to open the Setup Room and click OK in the warning dialog box that appears.

   The Setup Room appears with only the imported figure visible.

4. Click the side control to the right of the interface to open the Library palette or select Window, Libraries.

5. Click the Figures category at the top of the Library palette and navigate to the Additional Figures folder. Select the Mannequin thumbnail and click the Replace Figure button [icon] at the bottom of the Library palette.

   The skeleton for the Mannequin figure is loaded into the Setup Room.

6. Select the hip bone and drag the entire skeleton until it is aligned with the simple figure.

7. Position the cursor over the shoulder joint until it turns into a circle icon, and then drag the arm into position to match the simple figure. Repeat this step for the opposite shoulder.

8. Drag the upper leg joints into position and select the Rotate tool [icon] from the Editing tools and rotate the leg bones until they are aligned with the simple figure. Then scale the leg bones with the Scale tool [icon] to fit within the simple figure.

   After repositioning the loaded bones, each of the bones is located within the simple figure, as shown in Figure 10-6.

9. Select File, Save As and save the file as **Simple figure with loaded skeleton**.

FIGURE 10-6
Simple figure with loaded skeleton

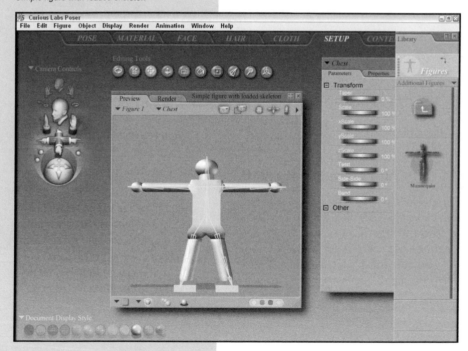

Create a new skeleton

1. Open Poser with the default man visible.

2. Select File, Import, Wavefront OBJ. Then, select and import the Mushroom.obj file. In the Prop Import Options dialog box, deselect the Centered option, enable the Place on Floor option, and then click OK.

   The mushroom object is imported as a prop.

3. Select the default figure and choose Figure, Hide Figure or disable the Visible option in the Properties palette.

4. With the mushroom object selected, click the Setup tab at the top of the interface to open the Setup Room and click OK in the warning dialog box that appears.

   The Setup Room appears with only the mushroom object visible.

5. Select the Bone Creation tool [image] from the Editing tools and click at the base of the mushroom object and drag about a third of the way up the mushroom top. Then click and drag again two more times to create three connected bones for the mushroom stem.

6. At the top of the mushroom, continue the chain of bones by making two additional bones down the right side of the mushroom.

7. Click the top bone in the mushroom stem to select it and drag to create two more bones along the left side of the mushroom.

8. Open the Properties panel, select the first new bone, and name it **Stem1** by typing the new name in the Name and the Internal Name text fields. Continue to select and name the remaining bones in the stem. Then name the bones along the top of the mushroom **Top right1**, and so on.

   The completed custom skeleton for the mushroom object is shown in Figure 10-7.

9. Select File, Save As and save the file as **Mushroom skeleton**.

FIGURE 10-7

Custom mushroom skeleton

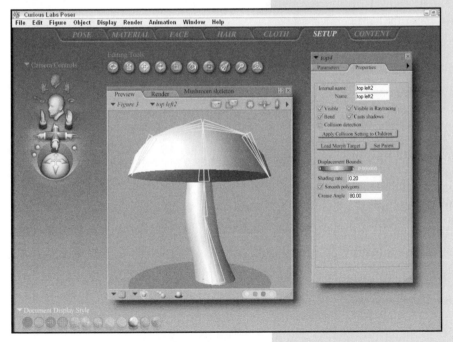

GROUP
BODY PARTS

What You'll Do

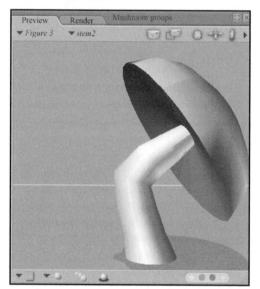

In this lesson, you learn how to group body parts for each bone.

In order to make the figure's body parts move with the bones, you'll need to group each of the various body parts together using the Group Editor. This **body part group** should have the same name as the bone's internal name.

Grouping Body Parts

To group the body parts together, click the Grouping tool in the Editing tools to open the Group Editor, shown in Figure 10-8. If you click the Previous Group and Next Group buttons, you can scroll through the existing bones. Once a bone name is selected, you can drag in the Document Window with the Select Polygon tool to add polygons to that bone's group or remove polygons from the

current group with the Deselect Polygons tool. Holding down the Ctrl key will switch to the opposite tool.

FIGURE 10-8
Group Editor

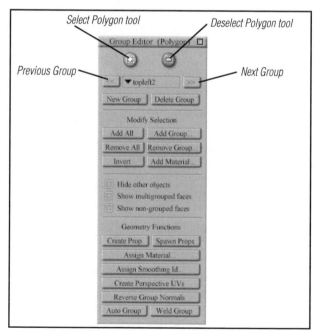

Viewing Orphan Polygons

If you switch to a different room by clicking one of the tabs at the top of the interface, a warning dialog box will appear if any polygons exist that haven't been assigned to a group. These **orphan polygons** will be left behind in the Document Window as the figure is moved and posed. To prevent this problem, you need to make sure that every figure polygon is assigned to a group. If you want to see which polygons still aren't part of a group, click the Show Non-Grouped Faces option in the Group Editor. All polygons that aren't part of a group are highlighted in red.

Matching Body Part Groups to Bones

If you import a figure with its own set of groups, you'll need to make sure that the name of each bone matches the body part group. If the names match, moving the bone in the Pose Room will move body part correctly.

Group body parts

1. Choose File, Open and select and open the Mushroom skeleton.pz3 file.

   This file includes the imported mushroom figure with the bones created in the last lesson.

2. With the mushroom object selected, click the Setup tab at the top of the interface to open the Setup Room.

3. Click the Grouping tool ⊞ in the Editing tools to open the Group Editor.

4. Click the Next Group button ⊞ in the Group Editor until the Stem1 group is listed as the current group. Then drag in the Document Window to select the polygons surrounding the Stem1 bone.

   The selected polygons are highlighted red.

5. Rotate the Document Window by dragging on the small Rotate sphere icon ⊙ at the top-right corner of the Document Window to rotate the view to the side of the mushroom and select the side polygons that surround the Stem1 bone. Continue to rotate the view and to select polygons around the entire figure.

6. Repeat steps 4 and 5 for the remaining bones. Click the Show Non-Grouped Faces option in the Group Editor to see if there are any polygons that haven't been assigned to a group.

7. Click the Pose tab to switch back to the Pose Room and drag on the top of the stem to see how the mushroom bends.

   The mushroom bends by moving the underlying bones, as shown in Figure 10-9.

8. Select File, Save As and save the file as **Mushroom groups.pz3**.

FIGURE 10-9
Mushroom with groups

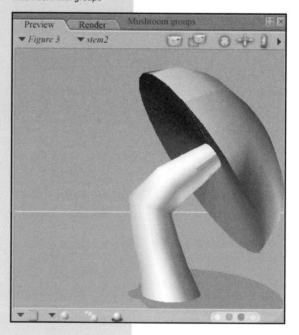

USE INVERSE KINEMATICS

What You'll Do

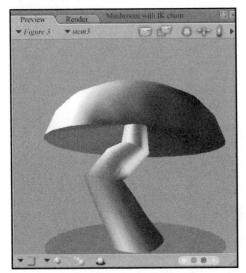

In this lesson, you learn how to create a new IK chain.

Normally when you pose body parts, you position the objects by moving the parent object and having all its children follow. The children can then be moved independently. This method of positioning objects is called *forward kinematics* because it follows the hierarchy structure, but another method exists called **inverse kinematics** (IK). IK works by allowing the child object to control the position of the parent object.

Opening the Hierarchy Editor

In order for inverse kinematics to work, you need to select a parent object (the root object) and one of its children objects (the goal object) connected in a chain. All the bones between these two selected bones are collectively called an **IK chain**. You can select IK chains by using the Hierarchy Editor. This dialog box is opened with the Window, Hierarchy Editor menu command. All IK chains for the current figure are displayed at the bottom of the Hierarchy Editor, shown in Figure 10-10.

Creating an IK Chain

You can create new IK chains using the Hierarchy Editor. These new IK chains can be created for manually imported characters, for new types of figures such as the tail of an animal, or to add an attached prop to an existing IK chain. To create an IK chain, select the IK Chains title in the Hierarchy Editor to make the Create IK Chain button active. Clicking the Create IK Chain button opens a dialog box where you can give the new IK chain a name. The newly named IK chain appears at the bottom of the Hierarchy Editor. You can then drag and drop elements of the chain onto the new chain name. The first element under the new IK Chain title is the root element and the last one is the goal. The goal element is marked with the word *goal* is parentheses.

Enabling Inverse Kinematics

You can enable or disable IK using the Figure, Use Inverse Kinematics menu command or by clicking the check box to the left of the IK chain title in the Hierarchy Editor.

FIGURE 10-10

Hierarchy Editor

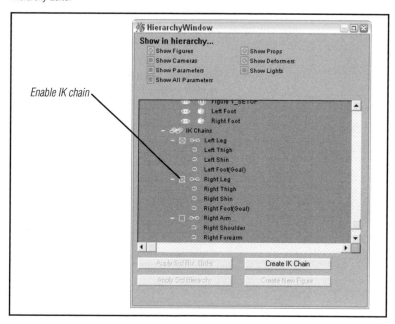

FIGURE 10-11
Mushroom with IK chain

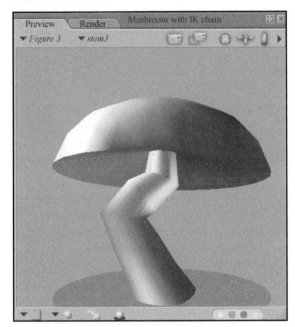

1. Select File, Open and open the Mushroom groups.pz3 file.

2. Select Window, Hierarchy Editor to open the Hierarchy Editor.

3. Scroll to the bottom of the Hierarchy Editor and select the IK Chains title. Then, click the Create IK Chain button at the bottom of the dialog box.

4. In the Set Name dialog box that appears, accept the name, New IK Chain, and click OK.

5. Scroll to the list of mushroom bones in the Hierarchy Editor and select and drag the Stem1, Stem2, and Stem3 elements and drop them on the newly created IK Chain title.

6. Reorder the stem elements so they appear in order with the Stem3 element designated as the goal.

7. Click the square box to the left of the new IK chain title to enable the IK chain. Then, select and move the top element in the Pose Room.

   As the top of the mushroom is moved, the stem bones of the IK chain are also moved, as shown in Figure 10-11.

8. Select File, Save As and save the file as **Mushroom with IK chain.pz3**.

USE THE
JOINT EDITOR

What You'll Do

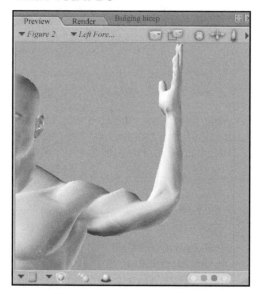

In this lesson, you learn how to use the Joint Editor.

The most critical bone position for effective figures is the location of the joint found at the base of the bone. This joint controls how the body parts bend when the angle between adjacent bones is reduced. To precisely control the location of the joint and to define how the joint bends and twists, you can use the Joint Editor, shown in Figure 10-12. You open this panel by using the Window, Joint Editor menu command. The Joint Editor includes several sets

FIGURE 10-12
Joint Editor

of controls and you can switch between these sets using the drop-down menu at the top of the Joint Editor

Zeroing the Figure

The Zero Figure button in the Joint Editor sets the rotation value of all joints to zero, thus causing the figure to assume its default pose with arms outstretched.

Centering the Joint

The Center set of controls displays the dimensions for the center point and the end point (if the bone doesn't include a child). The center point is the point about which the bone rotates. The panel also includes the orientation values for the center point. The Align button automatically aligns the center point to the nearest body part. When this option is selected, the center point is displayed as a green set of axes crossing where the center point is located, as shown for the shoulder joint in

Figure 10-13. Moving the cursor over the center point lets you drag it to a new location.

Setting Twist Angles

The Twist option in the Joint Editor lets you set the Twist Start and Twist End values for determining the twist that the joint allows as the joint is moved. When this option is selected, the twist values are displayed as red and green lines in the Document Window.

Using Inclusion and Exclusion Angles

For the Front-Back, Side-Side, Up-Down, and Bend options, you can specify an inclusion angle (shown in green) and an exclusion angle (shown in red). All polygons within the inclusion angle are affected by the movement of the joint and all polygons within the exclusion angle are not affected by the joint movement. Figure 10-14 shows the inclusion and exclusion angles for the Side-Side option. Notice how the inclusion angle includes all the polygons from the neck up and the exclusion angle prevents any change for the polygons below the neck.

Bulging Muscles

Also within the Joint Editor for the Front-Back, Up-Down, and Bend options are the Bulge settings. By enabling bulges, you can set how much the muscle within the inclusion area bulges (with a positive value) or pinches (with a negative value).

Setting Scale Values

The scale options let you set the scale values for the adjacent joints so that when one body part is scaled, the adjacent parts are scaled along with it. This can be used to prevent discontinuities to the figure. For example, when scaling the abdomen, you'll also want to scale the lower part of the chest. The Scaling values include High End, High Start, Low End, and Low Start.

FIGURE 10-13
Center point

FIGURE 10-14
Inclusion and exclusion angles

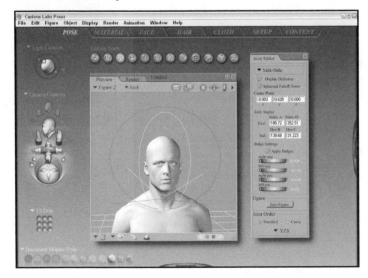

Make bulging muscles

1. Open Poser with the default man visible.

2. Choose Window, Joint Editor to open the Joint Editor.

3. Select the left forearm element and choose the Bend option from the top drop-down list.

4. Click the Zero Figure button in the Joint Editor.

   The figure is displayed in its default position with arms outstretched.

5. Select the View Magnifier tool from the Editing tools and drag over the entire left arm in the Document Window to expand the view.

6. Select the Twist tool in the Editing tools and drag on the upper arm to twist the entire arm until the palm is facing upward.

7. With the left forearm selected, enable the Apply Bulges option in the Joint Editor and set the Left Negative bulge value to 0.15.

8. Select the Rotate tool from the Editing tools and drag the forearm element upward.

   As the forearm is brought towards the head, the bicep muscle bulges, as shown in Figure 10-15.

9. Select File, Save As and save the file as **Bulging bicep.pz3**.

FIGURE 10-15

Bulging bicep

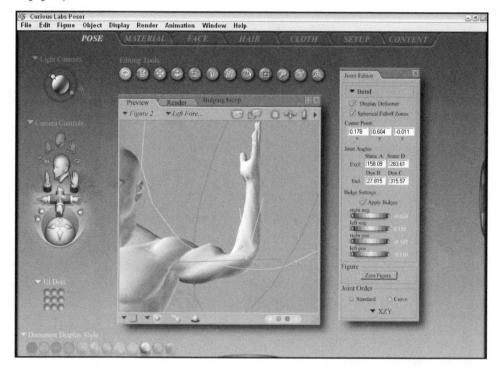

CHAPTER SUMMARY

This chapter covered all the features found in the Setup Room, including the capability to edit bones used to pose the various body parts. The chapter also covered loading a skeleton onto an imported figure and creating a new set of bones, grouping body parts for each bone, and creating inverse kinematics chains. The Joint Editor was also covered as a way to make muscles bulge.

What You Have Learned

In this chapter, you
- Discovered the layout of the Setup Room and learned how to select bones.
- Edited bones using the Editing tools.
- Loaded an existing skeleton onto an imported figure using the Library.
- Created a new set of bones using the Bone Creation tool.
- Grouped body parts for each bone using the Group Editor.

- Created a new IK chain to enable child objects to control parent objects using the Hierarchy Editor.
- Defined the joint settings using the Joint Editor.

Key Terms from This Chapter

Bone.   An invisible object that exists beneath the surface of the figure and defines how the attached body part moves as the bone is moved.

Skeleton.   A hierarchy of bones arranged to match the figure it controls.

Body part group.   A set of polygons that shares the same name as the bone that is controlling it.

Bone Creation tool.   A tool used to create and place new bones.

Orphan polygons.   All polygons that don't belong to a group.

Inverse Kinematics.   A method for enabling child objects to control their parents.

IK chain.   A set of hierarchically linked bones that are enabled using inverse kinematics, including root and goal objects.

Joint.   The base of a bone that marks the position between two bones where the body parts bend.

Inclusion and exclusion angles.   Angles used to mark the polygons that are affected and unaffected by the joint's movement.

Bulge.   The process of increasing a muscle's size as a joint's angle is decreased.

chapter 11

ANIMATING
Figures

1. Load motions from the Library.

2. Work with keyframes.

3. Use the Animation Palette.

4. Edit animation graphs.

5. Work with sound.

6. Animate a walk cycle.

chapter 11 ANIMATING
Figures

Posing figures is great, but with the animation features, you can make the scene come alive and allow your characters to walk and talk. Animation sequences that you create in Poser can be exported to the AVI or QuickTime video formats.

The simplest way to animate scene objects is to create **keyframes** for separate poses at the beginning and end of the motion. Poser can then calculate all the intermediate positions automatically by interpolating between the two poses. These keyframes are created using the Animation Controls bar at the bottom of the interface. These controls let you move through the different animation frames and keys and play the resulting animation.

You can also animate every parameter and the parameter values are shown as a graph over time. Using the parameter graph

interface, you can change the interpolation method, which defines the shape of the parameter graph over time. The Animation Palette keeps track of all the various animated objects and lets you move, copy, and synch keys between different scene elements.

You also can import and use sound files within animations. You can render completed animations and save them as movies with the Movie Settings panel.

Another way to automate an animation cycle is with the Walk Designer. This interface lets you animate a character's walking cycle, including the swinging of arms, twisting of the body, and the placing of steps one over another using several unique styles.

Tools You'll Use

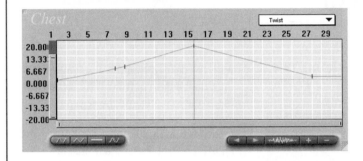

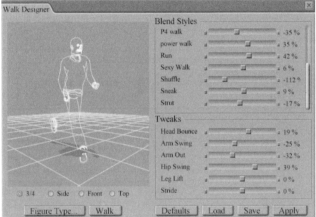

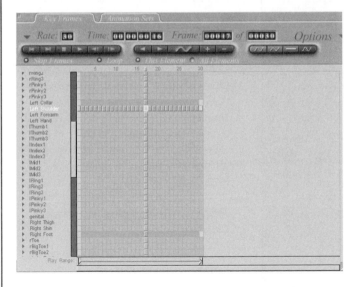

LOAD MOTIONS
FROM THE LIBRARY

What You'll Do

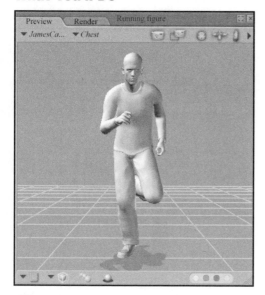

▶ In this lesson, you learn how to load figure motions from the Library.

In addition to manually creating keyframes to make a figure move, you can also load animation sequences from the Poses category in the Library patette and import motion files.

Loading Motions from the Library

To access the available motions from the Library, click the Poses category and navigate the folders until you find just the motion you want to apply to the current figure. Each motion thumbnail shows one frame of the motion and the number in the upper-right corner tells how many frames the motion is.

FIGURE 11-1
Motion files in the Library

With the desired thumbnail selected, click the Change Item button at the bottom of the Library palette and the selected motion is loaded and the figure changes their position in the Document Window. Figure 11-1 shows several available motion thumbnails found in the Library.

Saving Motions to the Library

You can save the current motion keyframes to the Library using the Add to Library button located at the bottom of the Library palette. This button opens a simple dialog box where you can name the current motion and the number of frames to include. The thumbnail for the current settings is added to the open Library folder.

Removing Presets from the Library

The Remove from Library button in the Library palette permanently deletes the selected thumbnail.

Loading External Motion Capture Data

You can import motion files from an external source using the File, Import, BVH Motion menu command. Biovision files are typically created using **motion capture**, a system that enables computers to record actual motions into an importable file format. The imported file replaces any existing keyframes. After selecting a file to load, a dialog box appears asking you to specify whether the arms are aligned along the X-axis or along the Z-axis. Then another dialog box gives you the option to scale the data points automatically or to not scale them at all. Following this, warning dialog boxes appear for all the figure elements that aren't included in the imported motion set.

> **NOTE**
>
> It is normal for motion sets to not include motion data for all the figure elements, such as the figure's toes.

Exporting Motions

You can export motions from Poser to the BVH file format using the File, Export, BVH Motion menu command.

Load motions from the Library

1. Open Poser with the default man visible.

2. Click the side control to the right of the interface to open the Library palette or select Window, Libraries.

3. Click the Poses category at the top of the Library palette and locate and select the Run thumbnail in the Walk Designer folder. Then click the Change Item button 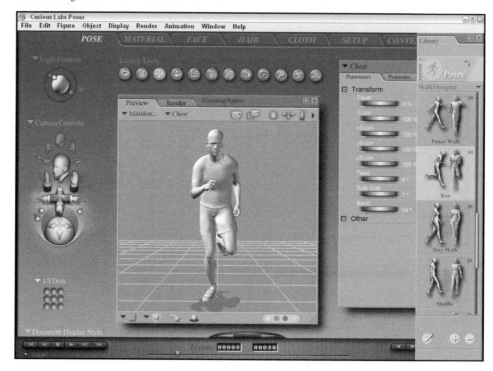 at the bottom of the Library palette.

   The figure in the Document Window is updated.

4. Click the side bar control at the bottom of the interface or select Window, Animation Controls. Then, click the Play button in the Animation Controls to see the loaded animation.

   The figure runs in place, as shown in Figure 11-2.

5. Select File, Save As and save the file as **Running figure.pz3**.

FIGURE 11-2
Loaded running motion

FIGURE 11-3

New motion added to the Library

1. Choose File, Open and select and open the Waving figure.pz3 file.

2. Click the side control to the right of the interface to open the Library palette or select Window, Libraries.

3. Click the Poses category at the top of the Library palette and navigate to a Walk Designer folder.

4. Drag the Timeline in the Animation Controls to the final frame.

5. Click the Add to Library button at the bottom of the Library palette and name the motion **Waving Figure** in the Set Name dialog box that appears. Then, click OK. A simple dialog box will then ask if you want to include morph channels. Click Yes.

6. In the Save Frames dialog box that appears, select the Multi Frame Animation option and click OK.

   The new motion thumbnail appears in the open folder, as shown in Figure 11-3.

Import a motion capture file

1. Open Poser with the default man visible.

2. Choose the File, Import, BVH Motion menu command. Locate and open the Jumping jack.bvh file. In the alignment dialog box, select the Along X-Axis button and in the scaling dialog box, choose the Don't Do Any Scaling button.

   Several warning dialog boxes appear; simply click OK to clear each of them.

3. Click the side bar control at the bottom of the interface or select Window, Animation Controls and click Play.

   The figure in animated, as shown in Figure 11-4.

4. Select File, Save As and save the file as **Jumping jack figure.pz3**.

FIGURE 11-4
Imported motion

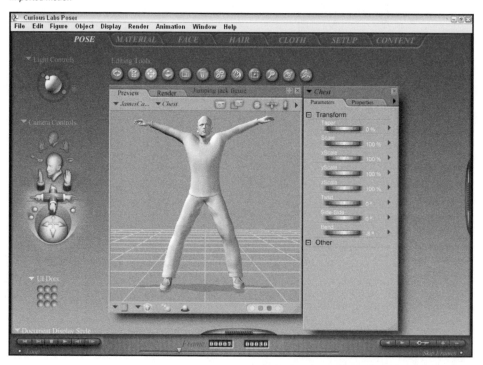

WORK WITH
KEYFRAMES

What You'll Do

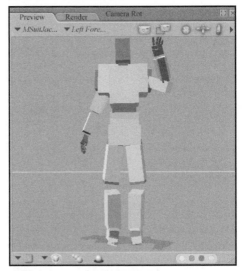

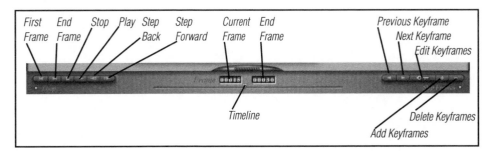

In this lesson, you learn how to animate using keyframes.

Two main interface controls exist for working with animations. The Animation Controls at the bottom of the Poser interface offer a simple way to quickly work with animation frames and keys whereas the Animation Palette includes a more in-depth look at all the different animation settings.

Opening the Animation Controls

Clicking the side tab at the bottom of the Poser window expands the Animation

Controls, shown in Figure 11-5, into the interface. This set of controls includes buttons for moving between the various frames and keys. Two text fields show the current and end frame values. You can change the current frame by dragging the Timeline control positioned under the two frame values.

Moving Between Frames

The buttons on the left side of the Animation Controls bar are used to move between the different frames. The First

FIGURE 11-5
Animation Controls

First Frame   End Frame   Stop   Play   Step Back   Step Forward   Current Frame   End Frame   Previous Keyframe   Next Keyframe   Edit Keyframes   Timeline   Add Keyframes   Delete Keyframes

and End Frame buttons will jump to the start or to the end of the current set of frames. The Play button cycles through all the frames from the first to the last. If the **Loop** option is enabled, the animation continues to play until the Stop button is clicked. The Step Forward and Step Back buttons will move forward or back a single frame with each click. You can also move through the frames by dragging the Timeline to the right or the left. To jump to a specific frame, type the frame number in the Current Frame field.

TIP

The default tracking for the Document Window is set to Fast, which displays the figure as a set of boxes when the animation is played back. To see the actual figure, set the tracking at the bottom of the Document Window to Full.

Setting the Total Number of Frames

The total number of frames is also known as the *animation range*. You can change

the animation range by typing a new number in the End Frame text field of the Animation Controls. If you enter a smaller number, a warning dialog box appears informing you that some frames will be deleted.

Creating Keyframes

Keyframes are simply frames that are designated as the beginning or ending position of an animated object. To create a figure keyframe, drag the Timeline slider to a different frame, move the figure, and click the Add Key Frames button in the Animation Controls. Once you create a keyframe, you can see the figure move between its original and final positions by clicking the Play button.

Moving Between Keyframes

As you add several keyframes to an animation sequence, you can then use the Previous and Next Key Frame buttons to move between the available keyframes. You can delete the current keyframe using the Delete Key Frames button. Clicking the

Edit Key Frames button opens the Animation Palette. The Skip Frames option located below the Delete Key Frames button allows the program to skip frames as the animation sequence is being replayed in order to maintain a consistent frame rate.

Automatically Recording Keys

Clicking the key icon located in the Camera Controls turns on the auto-animating feature. When enabled, keys are automatically created for the current frame any time an object is moved within the Document Window.

NOTE

The key icon is highlighted in red when enabled.

FIGURE 11-6
Animated waving figure

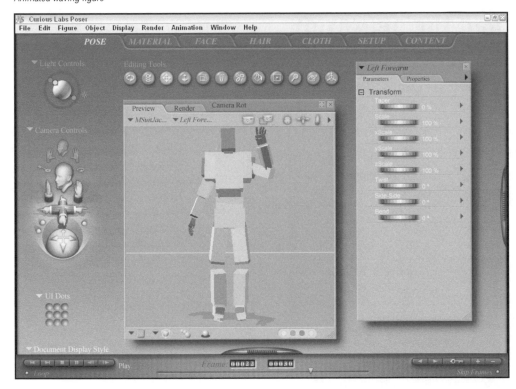

1. Open Poser with the default figure visible.
2. Click the side bar control at the bottom of the interface or select Window, Animation Controls.
3. Click the Animate On button ▨ in the Camera Controls to enable the auto-animating feature.
4. Drag the Timeline over to frame 10 in the Animation Controls and rotate the left arm into the waving position.
5. Drag the Timeline over to frame 15 and move the forearm to the left, and then set the Timeline to frame 20 and move the forearm to the right. Then move the forearm back and forth again for frames 25 and 30.
6. Click the Play button and enable the Loop option in the Animation Controls to see the resulting animation multiple times.

   The animation is displayed in the Document Window, as shown in Figure 11-6.
7. Select File, Save As and save the file as **Waving arm figure.pz3**.

USE THE ANIMATION
PALETTE

What You'll Do

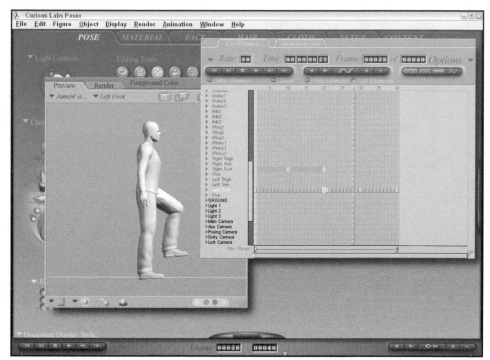

In this lesson, you learn how to use the Animation Palette to work with keys.

The Animation Palette, shown in Figure 11-7, is an interface that you can use to see all the keys for the entire scene at once. This makes it convenient for matching the beginning and end keys for different elements. You open the Animation Palette by clicking the Edit Key Frames button in the Animation Controls. You can also open the Animation Palette by using the Window, Animation Palette menu command.

Setting the Frame Rate

At the top of the Animation Palette is a value labeled Rate. This value sets the rate at which frames are played per second. Movies run at a frame rate of 24 frames per second and computer animation typically runs at a rate of 30 frames per second for smooth animation. Half-speed rates of 12 frames per second are common on the Web, but they can appear jittery. To the left of the Rate field is a pop-up menu where you can select from several preset frame rates.

Using the Animation Palette Interface

By default, the Animation Palette displays a key's position by frame number, but if you're trying to synch the animation with a sound track, viewing running time instead of frame numbers is helpful. The Time field at the top of the Animation Palette displays the current time in the format: hours, minutes, seconds, frames. Selecting the Display Time Code option from the Options pop-up menu displays running time labels across the top of the object rows.

Along the left side of the Animation Palette is a list of all the available scene elements, including figures, props, lights, and cameras. Clicking the small arrow icon to the left of the element title expands the element to reveal its sub-elements (such as body parts), which can also be expanded to reveal the element's parameters. Notice that the Ground element has been expanded to reveal its parameters in Figure 11-8.

FIGURE 11-7

Animation Palette

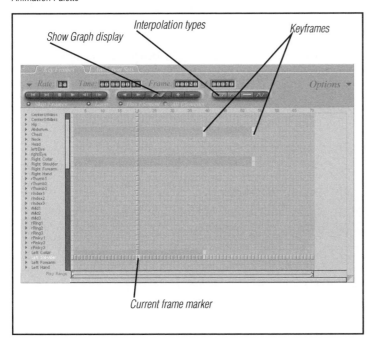

FIGURE 11-8

Element parameters

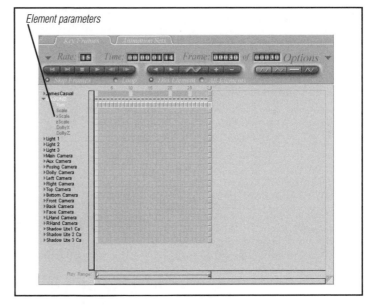

Along the bottom of the grid cells is a green line that indicates the Play Range. By dragging the icon on either end of this green line, you can limit which portions of the animation are played in the Document Window when the Play button is clicked.

Viewing and Selecting Keys

The Animation Palette includes a list of all scene objects to the left and a table of key cells to the right. All keys created with the Animation Controls are displayed when the Animation Palette is opened. Each key is marked in a color that corresponds to its **interpolation type,** with green for spline-based interpolation, orange for linear interpolation, gray for constant interpolation, and a diagonal line for spline breaks. The actual keys appear brighter and the interpolated frames are the same color only darker. This table provides at a glance the available keys and lets you edit the keys by dragging them left or right. At the top of the Animation Palette are the same controls for moving between frames and keys as found in the Animation Controls bar.

You can select a single key simply by clicking it. This will highlight the entire row (representing the element or parameter) and column (representing the frame or time) that the key belongs to. You can select multiple consecutive keys at once by holding down the Shift key while clicking each grid cell.

Creating and Deleting Keys

If you click a grid cell that isn't a key, you can set a key by clicking the Add Key Frames button at the top of the Animation Palette. If the This Element option is selected, a single key is created, but if the All Elements option is selected, keys are set for the entire column. To delete a selected key, click the Delete Key Frames button. Figure 11-9 shows several columns of keys created with the All Elements option.

FIGURE 11-9
A column of keys

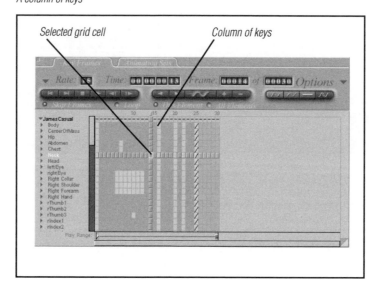

CAUTION

Pressing the Delete key will delete the current figure, not the selected key.

Sliding and Copying Keys

If you click and drag on the selected key or keys, you can slide the keys to the left or to the right. This is useful when you want to synch two keys to start together. You can copy selected keyframes with the Edit, Copy menu command or by pressing Ctrl+C. Similarly, you can paste keyframes to a different location with the Edit, Paste menu command or by pressing Ctrl+V. You can also copy keys by dragging them with the Alt key held down.

TIP

Copying the starting key to the end key for looping elements will ensure that the motion is smooth.

Retiming Keys

If you've created an animation that runs a little long or a little too short, you can use the Animation, Retime Animation menu command to scale a range of keys. This command opens the Retime Animation dialog box, shown in Figure 11-10, where you can select a set of source frames and a set of destination frames.

TIP

If you set the destination frames to be different than the source frames, you can copy entire blocks of keys to another part of the animation.

Resampling Keys

The Animation, Resample Key Frames menu command opens the Resample Keys dialog box, shown in Figure 11-11. Using this dialog box you can automatically have Poser reduce and set keys at regular frames for the current element, the current figure, or for everything using the Make Key Frame every given number of frames or using the Analyze Curvature option. This is helpful for optimizing dynamic simulations that create a key for every frame.

FIGURE 11-11

Resample Keys dialog box

FIGURE 11-10

Retime Animation dialog box

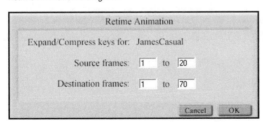

Use the Animation Palette

1. Open Poser with the default figure visible.

2. Click the side bar control at the bottom of the interface or select Window, Animation Controls.

3. Select the From Left camera from the Camera Controls pop-up menu. Then, click the Animate On button in the Camera Controls to enable the auto-animating feature.

4. Drag the Timeline over to frame 10 in the Animation Controls and move the right foot object up and forward in the Document Window.

5. Click the Edit Key Frames button 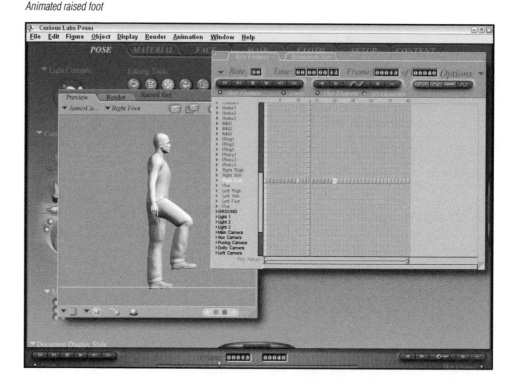 in the Animation Controls.

   The Animation Palette opens.

6. Scroll the Element list at the left of the Animation Palette until the Right Foot object and its keys are visible.

7. Click the key for the right foot at Frame 1 and with the Alt key held down, drag the key to the right to frame 20.

8. Click the Play button and enable the Loop option in the Animation Controls to see the resulting animation.

   The figure's right leg raises and is lowered to its original position. Figure 11-12 shows the figure with a raised foot along with the Animation Palette.

9. Select File, Save As and save the file as **Raised foot.pz3**.

FIGURE 11-12
Animated raised foot

FIGURE 11-13

Marching figure

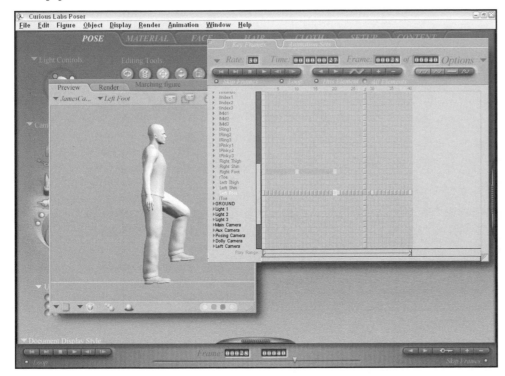

Copy animation keys

1. Choose File, Open and select and open the Raised foot.pz3 file.

2. Select Window, Animation Palette.

3. Enter the number **40** in the End Frame field at the top of the Animation Palette.

   Ten more frames are added to the end of the current animation.

4. Click frame 1 for the Right Foot element, hold down Shift, and then click frame 20 to select all the keys for the right foot. Then select Edit, Copy or press the Crtl+C keyboard keys.

5. Select the Left Foot element from the Element list to the left in the Animation palette and click the grid cell for frame 21. Then, drag to select cells 21-40. Then select Edit, Paste or press the Ctrl+V keyboard keys.

   The keys for the right foot have now been copied to the left foot.

6. Click the grid cell at frame 1 for the Left Foot element and drag it to the right to frame 20.

7. Click the Play button and enable the Loop option in the Animation Controls to see the resulting animation.

   The figure's right leg raises and is lowered to its original position, followed by the left foot being raised and lowered. Figure 11-13 shows the figure with a raised foot along with the Animation Palette.

8. Select File, Save As and save the file as **Marching figure.pz3**.

Scale animation keys

1. Choose File, Open and select and open the Marching figure.pz3 file.

2. Select Window, Animation Palette.

3. Select Animation, Retime Animation.

    The Retime Animation dialog box appears.

4. In the Retime Animation dialog box, set the Source Frames to 1 and 40 and the Destination Frames to 1 and 20 and click OK.

    The keys in the Animation Palette are compressed from 40 frames down to 20 frames, as shown in Figure 11-14.

5. Select File, Save As and save the file as **Double time.pz3**.

FIGURE 11-14

Marching figure double time

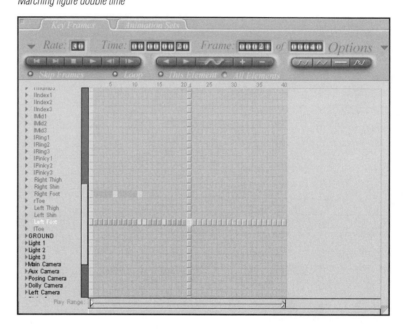

EDIT ANIMATION
GRAPHS

What You'll Do

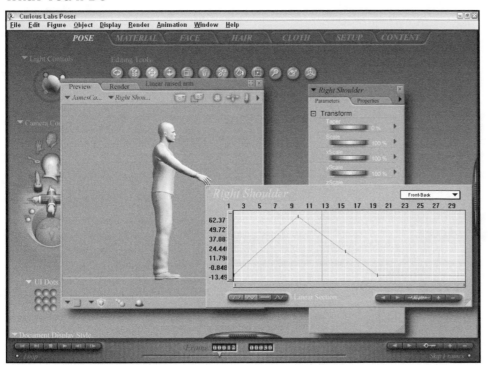

In this lesson, you learn how to edit object movement using animation graphs.

When you set keyframes to animate an object such as raising an arm, the motion of the arm is set to gradually rise a little with each successive frame in a linear manner. But if you want the arm to quickly rise half the way and then slowly rise the rest of the way, you can use an animation graph to precisely control how the object moves over time. By changing the graph shape, you can change the resulting animation.

Accessing Animation Graphs

The easiest way to access an animation graph is to click the Edit Graph button in the Animation Palette. The animation graphs also provide a way to animate parameters throughout Poser. Another way to access animation graphs is by clicking the pop-up menu icon located to the right of each parameter value; you can select the Graph option to make an animation graph appear for the selected parameter.

Using the Animation Graph Interface

Animation graphs display a graph of the parameter value (the vertical set of numbers on the left) per frame (the horizontal set of numbers along the top of the graph), as shown in Figure 11-15. The green vertical line marks the current frame and you can drag this line left and right to move through the available frames. The drop-down list in the upper-right corner lists all the available parameters for the selected element. The lower-left buttons are the interpolation options that change the curve's shape and the lower-right buttons are used to move between keys, toggle the sound display, and create and delete keys.

TIP

Click anywhere within the graph to move the current frame line.

Scaling the Graph View

If the graph in the Animation Graph dialog box is too large to show the exact keys you want to work with, you can scale the graph along its values axis or along its frames axis by dragging on either end of the bar at the left and bottom of the graph area. Figure 11-16 shows a graph that has been scaled along each axis.

FIGURE 11-15

Animation graph

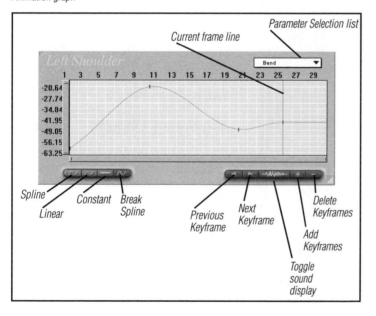

FIGURE 11-16

Scaled animation graph

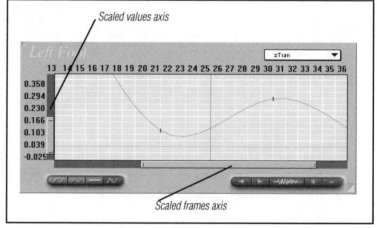

Adding, Moving, and Deleting Keys

Along each graph, the keys are marked as small vertical lines. Clicking the Add Key Frames button will add a new key on the graph for the current frame, which is marked by the thin vertical green line. If you move the cursor over the top of an existing key, it will change to an up-down arrow, allowing you to change the key's value by dragging it up and down. If you hold the the Ctrl key while moving the cursor over a key, the cursor will change to a left-right arrow, thus allowing you to move they key to a different frame. If you position the current frame marker over an existing key and click the Delete Key Frames button, the key is deleted and the curve shape changes.

Selecting and Sliding Graph Segments

To select a portion of the graph, simply drag over the portion of the curve that you want to select. The selected area is highlighted in black, as shown in Figure 11-17. Moving the cursor over the selected portion changes the cursor to side-to-side arrows, allowing you to drag the selected curve segments and any keys within the selected area left or right.

FIGURE 11-17

Selected graph segment

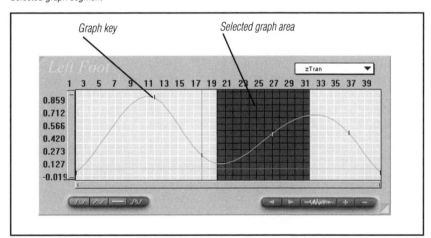

Graph key   Selected graph area

Changing the Curve's Shape

You can use the four interpolation buttons to change the shape of the graph's curve for the selected area. The default interpolation is *Spline*, which creates a smooth, round curve between all keys. This option is good for most animations involving figures. The Linear interpolation option makes the lines between each key a straight segment, as shown in Figure 11-18, resulting in a very rigid motion good for animating machines and robots. The Constant interpolation option keeps the same value until the next key to form a step-like graph, shown in Figure 11-19. The final interpolation method is the Break Spline option, which adds a break at each key so that you can use the different interpolation methods between keys.

FIGURE 11-18

Linear interpolation

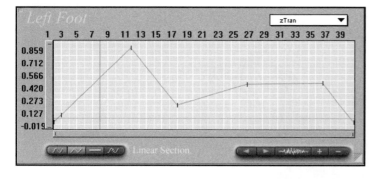

FIGURE 11-19

Constant interpolation

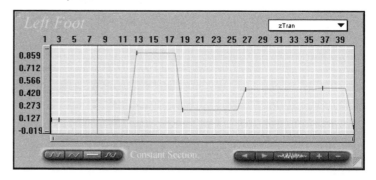

FIGURE 11-20

Animated raised arm

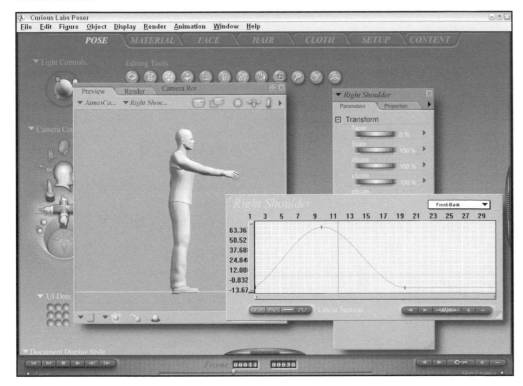

Use the animation graph

1. Open Poser with the default figure visible.

2. Select the Right Shoulder element in the Document Window and choose the From Left option from the Camera Controls pop-up menu.

3. Select Window, Parameter Dials to open the Parameters/Properties palette (if necessary).

4. Select the Graph option from the pop-up menu for the Front-Back parameter.

   The Animation Graph panel opens.

5. Click in the graph area at frame 10 and click the Add Key Frames button [+] to add a new key. Move the cursor over the new key and drag it upward off the top of the graph. Then drag the Value Axis bar to the left of the graph area to rescale the graph. Keep dragging the key until its value is around 65.

6. Click in the graph area at frame 20 and click the Add Key Frames button to add a new key. Move the cursor over the new key and drag it downward until its value is around -12.0.

7. Drag the current frame marker back and forth in the graph panel.

   Dragging the current frame marker back and forth will move the arm in the Document Window up and down, as shown in Figure 11-20.

8. Select File, Save As and save the file as **Raised arm.pz3**.

Change the curve's shape

1. Choose File, Open and select and open the Raised arm.pz3 file.

2. Select the Right Shoulder element in the Document Window.

3. Select Window, Parameter Dials to open the Parameters/Properties palette (if necessary).

4. Select the Graph option from the pop-up menu for the Front-Back parameter.

   The Animation Graph panel opens.

5. Drag over the graph for the first 20 frames to select the area.

   The selected graph area turns black.

6. Click the Linear Interpolation button 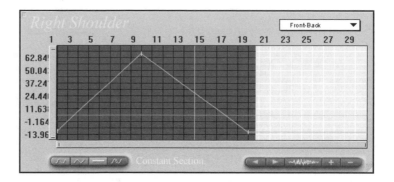 at the bottom of the animation graph panel.

   The graph segments are changed from a curve to straight lines, as shown in Figure 11-21, and the motion of the arms becomes more mechanical.

7. Select File, Save As and save the file as **Linear raised arm.pz3**.

FIGURE 11-21

Linear interpolation

WORK WITH
SOUND

What You'll Do

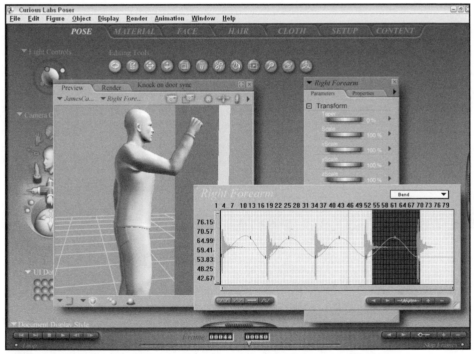

In this lesson, you learn how to import and synch sound files and make movies.

Animations typically include sound and Poser can import sound to be used within an animation. You can use the Animation Graph panel to synch animation keys to sound tracks, and then export completed animations to the AVI or QuickTime movie formats.

Loading Sound Files

You can load a single sound file into Poser using the File, Import, Sound menu command. This command opens a file dialog box where you can import a WAV file. The loaded sound file begins at frame 1 of the animation and continues for as many frames as it can, based on the frame rate.

Synching Motion to Sound

You can view sound files in the Animation Graph panel by enabling the Toggle Sound Display button. The waveform for the

imported sound appears in blue behind the
animation graph, as shown in Figure 11-22.
By moving the keys within the Animation
Graph panel, you can synch the figure's
motion to the imported sound file.

NOTE

When a sound file is imported, the sound range is
shown at the bottom of the grid cells in the Animation Palette.

Muting Sound

To mute the imported sound, simply select
the Animation, Mute Sound menu command. This command is a toggle option
that you can enable and disable.

Clearing Sound

To remove the imported sound, select the
Animation, Clear Sound menu command.

FIGURE 11-22
Imported sound display

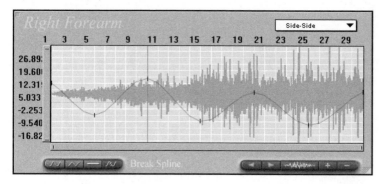

FIGURE 11-23

Synched knock on door

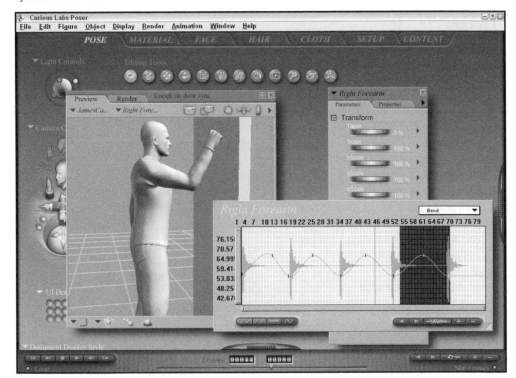

1. Choose File, Open and select and open the Knock on door.pz3 file.

   This file includes the default figure animated knocking on a door object using his right forearm.

2. Select the Right Forearm element in the Document Window.

3. Select Window, Parameter Dials to open the Parameters/Properties palette, if necessary.

4. Select the Graph option from the pop-up menu for the Bend parameter.

5. Select File, Import, Sound. Locate and load the knocks.wav file.

   The sound waveform appears in the back of the Animation Graph panel.

6. Drag over each of the keys and move them in the Animation Graph panel until they are aligned with the sound waveforms.

   The bottom of each curve corresponds to the hand hitting the door and should be aligned with the sound volume, whereas the top of the curve corresponds to the hand being away from the door and should be in between each sound wave, as shown in Figure 11-23.

7. Click the Play button and enable the Loop option in the Animation Controls to see the resulting animation.

8. Select File, Save As and save the file as **Knock on door sync.pz3**.

ANIMATE A
CAKE WALK

What You'll Do

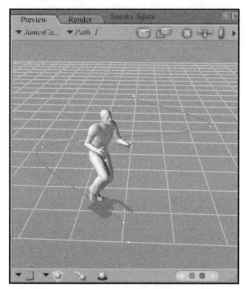

In this lesson, you learn how to animate a walk cycle using the Walk Designer.

Once you've learned to create manual keyframes, try to create the keys to make a figure walk realistically across the floor. Although the keys involved in making a figure walk might seem rather simple, it is actually quite difficult to realistically create a walk cycle using manual keyframes. Poser includes an interface called the Walk Designer that can automatically create a walk cycle for the current figure.

Creating a Walk Path

Before you can use the Walk Designer, you need to create a *walk path*, which tells the current figure where to walk. To create a walk path, select the Figure, Create Walk Path menu command and the default walk path appears in the scene extending from the default figure, as shown in Figure 11-24. You can select this path from the Props submenu in the Actor List; it is called Path_1.

FIGURE 11-24
Default walk path

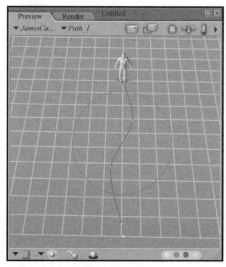

Editing a Walk Path

Along the walk path are several control points that look like simple dots. By dragging these control points, you can edit the shape of the walk path. If you click the walk path, you can add new control points to the walk path. You can delete control points by holding down the Alt key and clicking the control point.

Using the Walk Designer

Once you create a walk path, you can use the Walk Designer, shown in Figure 11-25, to set the parameters for the walk cycle. You open the Walk Designer dialog box by using the Window, Walk Designer menu command. To the left of the Walk Designer dialog box is a preview pane that will show

a preview of the current walk settings when you click the Walk button. The ³/₄, Side, Front, and Top options change the view in the preview pane and the Figure Type button lets you open a different character file.

Editing the Walk Cycle

You can use all of the settings in the Blend Styles and Tweaks sections to customize the look of your walk. The Blend Styles settings control the different types of walks such as power walk, run, sexy walk, shuffle, sneak, and strut. The Tweaks settings control how the head, arms, hips, and stride are set. The Defaults button resets all settings to their original positions.

Saving and Loading Custom Walks

If you create a custom walk cycle that you want to remember, you can use the Save button. The Save button opens a file dialog box where you can save the custom walk cycle. Walk cycles are saved as files with the .PWK extension. You can reload these files into the Walk Designer using the Load button.

Applying a Custom Walk

After previewing your walk cycle, you can apply the finished settings to the current figure by clicking the Apply button. This opens the Apply Walk dialog box, shown in Figure 11-26. Using this dialog box, you can select which figure to apply the walk cycle to and which walk path to use. You can also select how the head is aligned, how the final steps are handled, and the total number of frames to use for the entire walk cycle. After applying the walk cycle, click the Play button in the Animation Controls to see the figure walk.

FIGURE 11-25
Walk Designer dialog box

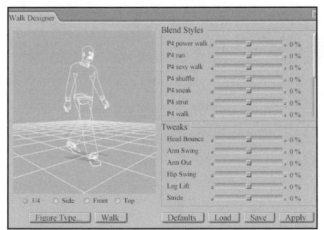

FIGURE 11-26
Apply Walk dialog box

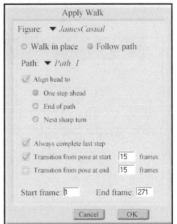

Animate a walk cycle

1. Open Poser with the default figure visible.
2. Select Figure, Create Walk Path.

   A walk path is added to the scene in front of the figure.
3. Drag on the Move XZ Plane to zoom out of the view and the Rotate sphere until the entire walk path is visible.
4. Drag the walk path's control points to edit the path so it winds back and forth.
5. Select Window, Walk Designer.

   The Walk Designer dialog box opens.
6. In the Walk Designer dialog box, set the Sneak setting to 100 and the Head Bounce to 75. Then click the Walk button to see a preview of the walk cycle.
7. Click the Apply button and in the Apply Walk dialog box, select the Align Head to option and choose the Next Sharp Turn. Click OK.
8. Click the Play button and enable the Loop option in the Animation Controls to see the resulting animation.

   The silly walk cycle is applied to the figure, as shown in Figure 11-27.
9. Select File, Save As and save the file as **Sneaky figure.pz3.**

FIGURE 11-27

Sneaky walk cycle

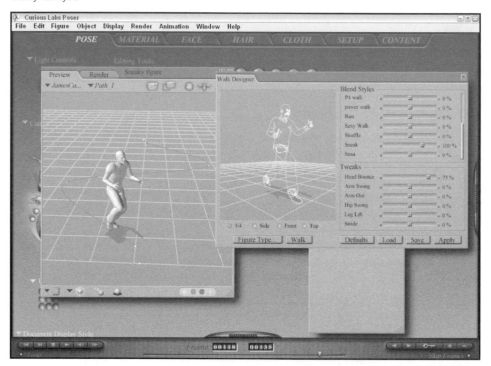

CHAPTER SUMMARY

This chapter covered all the animation features found in Poser that enable you to import motions from the Library and animate using keyframes created using the Animation Controls. Once you create keys, you can use the Animation Palette to move and synch keys between different elements and view and manipulate the keys' motion using the animation graphs. You can also use the animation graphs to see the waveform for any imported sounds. You can save final animation files as movies using the Movie Settings panel. For creating walk cycles, the Walk Designer lets you create and use unique styles.

What You Have Learned

In this chapter, you
- Loaded motions to the current figure from the Library.
- Loaded external motion capture files using the File, Import menu command.
- Opened the Animation Controls and used them to create keyframes.
- Used the Animation Palette to create, move, scale, and edit keys for the entire scene.
- Used animation graphs to define the interpolation method used to define the shape of the curve between keys.
- Saved rendered movie files using the Movie Settings panel.
- Created a walk path and used the Walk Designer to add a walk cycle to the figure.

Key Terms from This Chapter

Keyframe. A defined state of an object at one point during an animation sequence that is used to interpolate motion.

Motion capture. A process of collecting motion data using a special sensor attached to real humans performing the action.

Loop. A setting that causes an animation to play over and over.

Frame rate. The rate at which frames of an animation sequence are displayed. Higher frame rates result in smoother motion, but require more memory.

Interpolation. A calculation process used to determine the intermediate position of objects between two keyframes.

Waveform. A visual display of a sound showing its volume per time.

Flash. A vector-based format commonly used to display images and movies on the Web.

Walk cycle. A repeating set of frames that animate a figure walking.

chapter

12 RENDERING
Scenes

1. Render images.

2. Access render settings.

3. Use the Sketch Designer.

4. Set render dimensions.

5. Render animations.

6. Use rendering effects.

12 RENDERING
Scenes

The real purpose behind using Poser isn't to have fun manipulating figures, adding materials, or creating hairstyles. The real reason for using Poser is to create amazing images and animations, which is where the rendering process comes in.

Rendering is the final step that calculates all the various lights, geometries, materials, and simulations to create the final image or series of images for an animation. As part of the rendering process, there are several additional features that you can access, such as displacement maps, **antialiasing, motion blur,** and toon rendering. These processes are only possible during the final render.

The renderer available in Poser is the **Fire-Fly render engine.** It also includes options to render the scene as a realistic photograph using advanced techniques such as raytracing or to render the scene as a cartoon using the Sketch Designer.

A key decision in the rendering process involves weighing the image quality versus the time it takes to render an image. Enabling all the best quality options adds a lot of time to the rendering process, but can result in a more realistic image. For quick preview renders, you'll want to disable some of these features.

Tools You'll Use

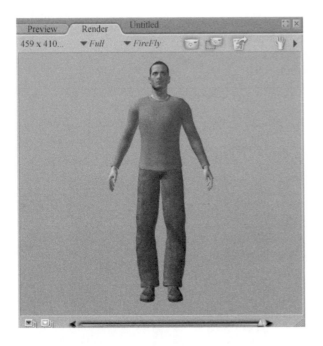

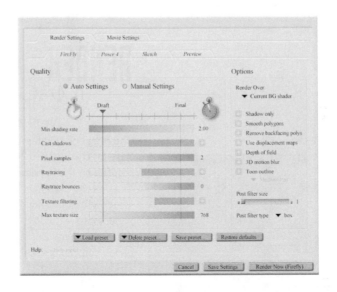

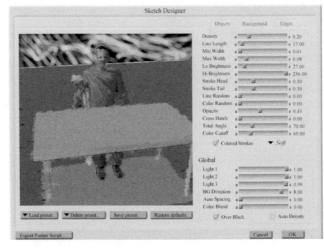

RENDER IMAGES

What You'll Do

In this lesson, you learn how to render images in the Render panel.

The previous chapters have pretty much focused on the Preview panel of the Document Window, but another panel exists—the Render panel. Using this panel, you can quickly render the current scene to check its look.

Using the Render Panel

You can open the Render panel, shown in Figure 12-1, by clicking the Render tab at the top of the Document Window. Controls along the top edge of the Render panel let you select the image resolution, select the renderer, initiate a rendering,

FIGURE 12-1
Render panel

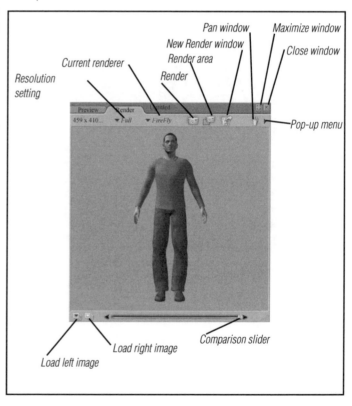

render an area, open a new render window, and pan the current window. The panel also includes a pop-up menu of additional commands. Along the bottom of the Render panel are controls for comparing two images.

Setting the Document Window Image Resolution

The current image resolution of the Render panel is displayed at the top left. You can change these dimensions by dragging on the lower-right corner of the panel to resize it. You can set the drop-down list to the right of the resolution dimensions to render the current panel at full, half, or quarter size. Figure 12-2 shows the current scene at quarter size. Clicking the Maximize Window button in the upper-right corner will increase the size of the Render panel to fill the available space, as shown in Figure 12-3. Clicking the button again returns the Render panel to its default size.

TIP

In addition to the Render panel, you can set the resolution of the render image to any size using the Render Dimensions dialog box.

Selecting a Render Engine

Poser supports several render engines and each has its advantages. You can select which render engine renders the current scene from the Renderer drop-down list at the top of the Render panel. The available render engines include:

- **FireFly:** A powerful render engine with a number of advanced features for creating realistic images.
- **Poser 4:** The render engine included with the previous versions of Poser. It offers good performance and is quick.

FIGURE 12-2

Quarter sized render

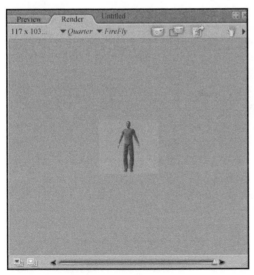

FIGURE 12-3

Maximized Render panel

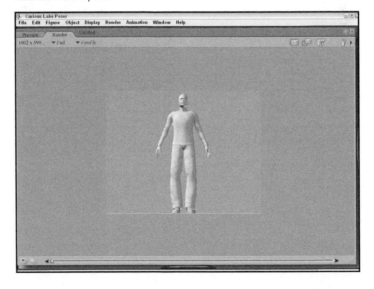

- **Sketch:** Renders the scene using various sketch styles defined in the Sketch Designer interface.
- **Preview:** The same render engine used to display the scene in the Preview panel. This option is the quickest rendering option.

Initiating a Render

The Render button in the Render panel starts the rendering cycle. This opens a progress dialog box that tracks the progress of the rendering process. When finished, the rendered image appears in the Render panel. If you want to check only a portion of the scene, you can click the Render Area button and drag over the area in the Render panel that you want to render and only that selected portion will be rendered. Figure 12-4 shows the Render panel with only a small area rendered.

NOTE

The Render and Render Area buttons are also available in the Preview panel and also as menu commands in the Render menu. The keyboard shortcut for the Render command is Ctrl+R and the shortcut for the Render Area command is Alt+Ctrl+N.

FIGURE 12-4

Area render

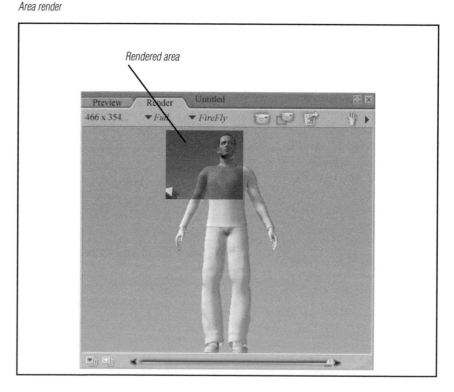

Rendered area

Saving a Rendered Window

If you want to save the current rendered image, you can select the Export Image option from the Document Window's pop-up menu to open the Save As dialog box. You can also save the current rendered image using the File, Export, Image menu command. You can save the rendered image as a JPEG, Windows Bitmap (BMP), PNG, TIF, Flash PIX (FPX), Mac Pict (PCT), or Photoshop (PSD) file.

If you want to keep the current rendered image around and render a new image, click the New Render Window button and the current rendered image will be opened within a separate window, as shown in Figure 12-5. When you close this window, a dialog box asks if you want to save the image. If you select to save the rendered image, a Save dialog box opens.

Panning the Rendered Window

The Pan Window icon lets you pan the current rendered image if the panel is sized to be smaller than the current rendered image. To use this tool, just click the icon and drag to move the image within the panel.

Comparing Rendered Images

At the bottom-left corner of the Render panel are two icons for selecting right and left images. Each image that is rendered in the Render panel is saved with a time stamp in the right and left image icons at the bottom left. By selecting different images for the left and right, you can drag the Comparison slider to switch between the two selected images. This offers a great way to check subtle differences between rendered images. Figure 12-6 shows the Render panel when a preview rendered image and a Fire-Fly rendered image are compared.

FIGURE 12-5
New render window

FIGURE 12-6
New render window

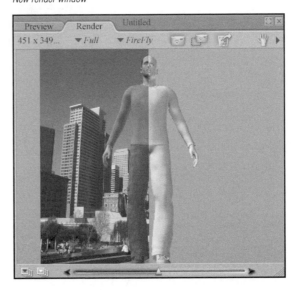

Render an image

1. Choose File, Open and select and open the Touching nose.pz3 file.

2. Click the Render tab in the Document Window to open the Render panel.

3. Select the Full resolution option and choose the FireFly renderer (if necessary).

4. Click the Render button  at the top of the Render panel.

   A progress dialog box appears showing the progress of the rendering. When the rendering is completed, the final image is shown in the Render panel, as shown in Figure 12-7.

5. Select File, Save As and save the file as **Rendered image.pz3**.

FIGURE 12-7

Rendered image

FIGURE 12-8

Comparing images

1. Choose File, Open and select and open the Rendered image.pz3 file.

2. Click the Render tab in the Document Window to open the Render panel.

3. Select the Full resolution option and choose the Preview renderer.

4. Click the Render button at the top of the Render panel.

5. Select the most recent image from the Load Left Image list in the lower-left corner of the Render panel and the second most recent image from the Load Right Image list. Then drag the Comparison slider to the middle.

   Half of each image is shown in the Render panel, as shown in Figure 12-8.

6. Select File, Save As and save the file as **Comparing images.pz3**.

ACCESS RENDER
SETTINGS

What You'll Do

In this lesson, you learn how to use the Render Settings dialog box.

Clicking the Render button will render the scene using the default render options, but you can change the render options using the Render Settings dialog box. The Render, Render Settings menu command opens the Render Settings dialog box. This dialog box is split into four panels, one for each available render engine, and you can select them using the tabs at the top of the dialog box.

Automatically Setting the FireFly Render Engine

The default panel in the render setting dialog box includes settings for the default FireFly render engine, shown in Figure 12-9. At the top of the panel are two options for auto settings and manual settings. The Auto Settings option provides a simple slider control that you can

FIGURE 12-9

FireFly panel in the Render Settings dialog box

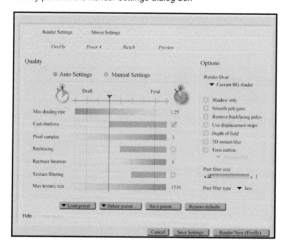

use to shift the quality of the rendered image between a quick render at draft quality and a long render at final quality. For each position along the slider, the setting values are displayed.

Manually Setting the FireFly Render Engine

The Manual Settings option in the FireFly panel of the Render Settings dialog box, shown in Figure 12-10, includes all the same settings as the Auto Settings option, except you can change them manually using controls. The Acquire from Auto button copies all the auto settings to the manual controls for a good place to start. The following manual settings are available for the FireFly render engine:

- **Cast Shadows:** Renders shadows for the scene for all figures and props that have their Cast Shadows property enabled and for all lights that have their Shadows property enabled.

- **Texture Filtering:** Applies a filtering process to all 2D images in the scene, including backgrounds and textures. Filtering the images softens the images to eliminate any jagged edges.

- **Raytracing:** Causes the FireFly render engine to use raytracing computations to render the scene. Raytracing calculates the scene by casting light rays into the scene and following these light rays as they bounce off objects. The results are accurately rendered shadows,

reflections, and materials, but enabling this option can really slow down the renderer.

- **Raytrace Bounces:** The number of times light rays are allowed to bounce about the scene during a raytracing calculation. Higher numbers take more time, but produce better results.

- **Min Shading Rate:** This value is used to divide each polygon into sections. Each section is then sampled and the sections are averaged to determine the pixel's color. Lower values yield better results, but increase the render time.

- **Pixel Samples:** Determines the amount of samples that are taken for each pixel to determine its accurate color during an antialiasing pass. The higher the pixel samples, the more accurate the color at each pixel.

- **Max Texture Size:** Determines the maximum size of the texture images included in the scene. Larger textures can show more detail than smaller textures, but they require more memory to process and will increase the file size. A setting of 1024 would cause all textures larger than 1024x1024 to be reduced to this size and all textures smaller than this value would remain their same size.

- **Max Bucket Size:** Sets the size of the pixel area to be rendered at one time. The FireFly render

engine will render the entire scene a block at a time. Large bucket values require more memory to process them.

- **Min Displacement Bounds:** The Min Displacement Bounds is set by Poser automatically in order to reduce the chance of cracks or holes appearing in the geometry. Small values result in quicker renders, but run a greater risk of having cracks appearing.

Setting the FireFly Render Options

On the right side of the FireFly panel in the Render Settings dialog box are several options for the FireFly render engine. You can use these options to change how images are rendered and to add special effects. The available render options include the following:

FIGURE 12-10

Manual settings for the FireFly panel in the Render Settings dialog box

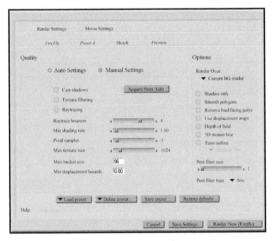

- **Render Over:** Sets the background that is used for the rendered image. The options available in the drop-down list include Background Color, Black, Background Picture, and Current Background Shader.

- **Shadow Only:** Renders only the scene shadows.

- **Smooth Polygons:** Adds an additional smoothing pass to the geometry objects in the scene, smoothing hard edges.

- **Remove Backfacing Polygons:** Causes all polygons that are facing away from the camera to be ignored. This can speed up the rendering time.

- **Use Displacement Maps:** Enables displacement maps to be used to render the scene. Displacement maps change the actual geometry of objects when used.

- **Depth of Field:** Adds a depth-of-field effect to the scene. This effect focuses the camera at the center of the scene and gradually blurs all objects that are located at a distance from the center focal point.

- **3D Motion Blur:** Adds a motion-blur effect to the scene. This effect blurs moving objects in the scene depending on how fast they are moving.

- **Toon Outline:** Adds an outline to the toon-rendered image. When enabled, you can set the outline width to be thin, medium, or thick, and the style to be pen, pencil, or marker.

- **Post Filter Size:** Sets the size of the area used to take samples. These samples are averaged to determine the pixel color. You can also select the filter type to be Box, Gaussian, or Sinc. The Box filter type looks at all samples equally, the Gaussian weighs the center samples more, and the Sinc option uses a sine wave to determine the sample's weight.

Loading and Saving FireFly Render Settings

Clicking the Save Preset button opens a simple dialog box where you can name the current render settings. This name then appears in the Load Presets list along with the Draft and Production options. The Delete Presets button includes a list where you can delete the current presets. At the bottom of the Render Settings dialog box is another Save Settings button. Clicking this button saves the current settings so they are retained when the dialog box is reopened.

Setting the Poser 4 Render Options

The Poser 4 tab in the Render Settings dialog box opens the Poser 4 panel, shown in Figure 12-11. This render engine doesn't include all the advanced features as in the FireFly render engine, but it renders quickly and accurately and is a good choice for preview renders. The Poser 4 render engine options include Anti-alias, Use Bump Maps, Use Texture Maps, Cast Shadows, and Ignore Shader Trees. The Ignore Shader Trees option will disable most materials.

FIGURE 12-11
Poser 4 panel in the Render Settings dialog box

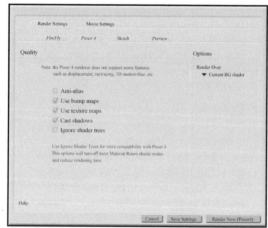

Setting the Sketch Render Options

The Sketch tab in the Render Settings dialog box opens the Sketch panel, shown in Figure 12-12. This render engine offers you the capability to render the scene to look like it was drawn freehand with a pen, pencil, or set of markers. The Sketch panel includes several thumbnails of styles, or you can select a style from the Sketch Preset drop-down list. The Sketch Designer button opens the **Sketch Designer,** where you can define a custom style.

FIGURE 12-12

Sketch panel in the Render Settings dialog box

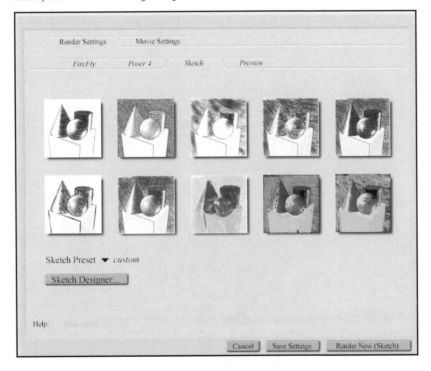

Setting the Preview Render Options

The Preview tab in the Render Settings dialog box opens the Preview panel, shown in Figure 12-13. This render engine includes only a handful of options. You can set the display engine to SreeD or OpenGL using an accumulation buffer in hardware or software. The SreeD option is a software rendering option and OpenGL can take advantage of video card hardware to display preview renders much quicker. You can set the Transparency Display to Actual or to be limited. If an object's transparency is set to 100%, it will be invisible in the scene, but the Limit to option makes sure that all objects are visible. The Style Options let you set the width of the silhouette outline, the wireframe line edge, and the toon edge line width. The Antialias option eliminates jagged edges by smoothing the lines between color boundaries.

FIGURE 12-13

Preview panel in the Render Settings dialog box

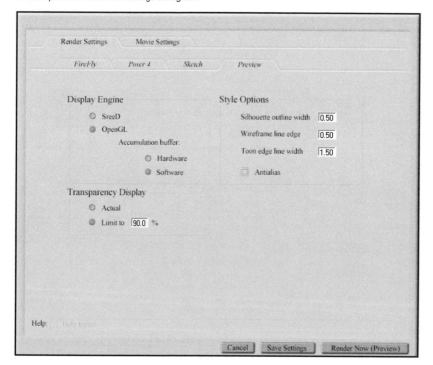

FIGURE 12-14

Final render of figure at table

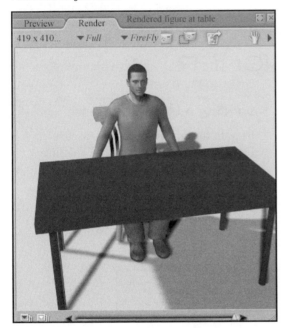

1. Choose File, Open and select and open the Figure sitting at table.pz3 file.

2. Select Render, Render Settings to open the Render Settings dialog box.

3. In the FireFly panel, click the Auto Settings option and drag the Quality slider to Final.

4. Click the Render Now button at the bottom-right side of the dialog box.

   A progress dialog box appears showing the progress of the rendering. When the rendering is completed, the final image is shown in the Render panel, as shown in Figure 12-14.

5. Select File, Save As and save the file as **Rendered figure at table.pz3**.

LESSON 3

USE THE SKETCH DESIGNER

What You'll Do

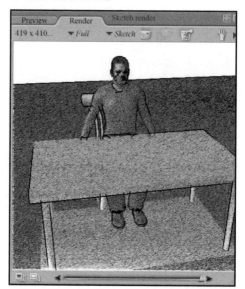

In this lesson, you learn how to use the Sketch Designer to define how a sketch rendering looks.

You can create and modify sketch presets using the Sketch Designer. You open this interface, shown in Figure 12-15, by using the Window, Sketch Designer menu command or by clicking the Sketch Designer button on the Sketch tab in the Render Settings dialog box.

FIGURE 12-15

Sketch Designer

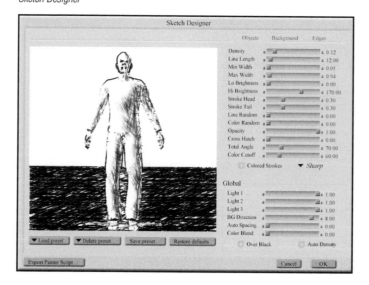

Loading a Sketch Preset

Beneath the Preview pane in the Sketch Designer is a Load Preset button. This button provides access to the saved sketch presets including Caterpillar, Colored Pencil, Colored, Dark Clouds, JacksonP BG, Loose Sketch, Pastel, Pencil and Ink, Psychedelic,

Scratch Board, Scratchy, Silky, Stretch Default, Sketchy, Smoothy, Soft Charcoal, and Stroked BG. Selecting any of these presets applies the preset and updates the Preview pane.

Saving a Sketch Preset

Clicking the Save Preset button opens a simple dialog box where you can name the current sketch settings. This name then appears in the Load Presets list along with the other options. The Delete Presets button includes a list where you can delete the current presets. Next to the Save Presets

button is the Restore Defaults button. You can use this button to change all the current settings back to their default states.

Changing Objects, Backgrounds, and Edges

The right portion of the Sketch Designer includes settings for defining all the sketch settings. You can use these settings to control the look of the scene objects, the scene background, or the edges using the different panels. The parameters are the same for each panel. The sketch parameters include Density, Line Length, Min Width, Max

Width, Lo Brightness, Hi Brightness, Stroke Head, Stroke Tail, Line Random, Color Random, Opacity, Cross Hatch, Total Angle, and Color Cutoff.

Sketching in Color and Using Brushes

The Colored Strokes option causes the sketches to be drawn in color. Next to the Colored Strokes option is a drop-down list that contains several brush types that you can use to sketch the scene. The available brushes include Sharp, Bristle, Very Soft, Soft, Less Soft, and Slanted.

Setting Global Parameters

Below the sketch parameters are a set of global parameters including settings for each of the lights, the background direction, auto spacing, and color blend. The Over Black option causes the sketch to be drawn on a black background with white strokes, as shown in Figure 12-16. The

FIGURE 12-16

Over Black option

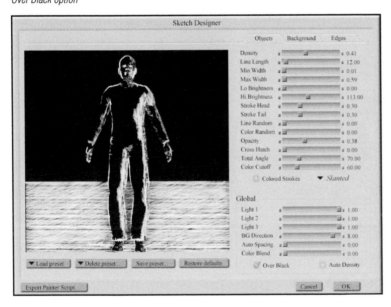

Auto Density option sets the density for each stroke based on the scene instead of using the Density parameter. Figure 12-17 shows the default scene with the Auto Density option enabled.

Exporting Painter Scripts

The Export Painter Script button opens a file dialog box where you can save the sketch definitions to a script that Corel's Painter can read and use. The exported script is saved with the .TXT extension. This provides a way to reproduce your sketch results in a 2D software package.

FIGURE 12-17

Auto Density option

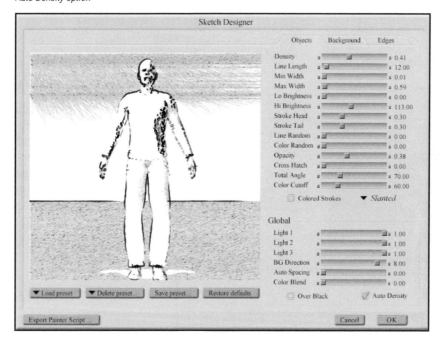

FIGURE 12-18

Sketch render of a figure at a table

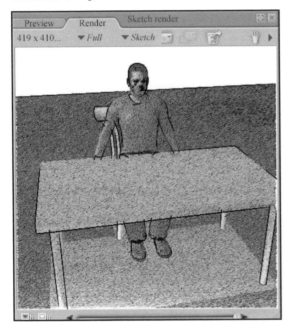

1. Choose File, Open and select and open the Figure sitting at table.pz3 file.

2. Select Window, Sketch Designer to open the Sketch Designer dialog box.

3. Click the Load Preset button and select the Soft Charcoal option.

4. Click the Auto Density option in the Global section and click OK.

5. Select Render, Render Settings to open the Render Settings dialog box.

6. Click the Sketch tab at the top of the Render Settings dialog box.

   The Sketch Preset is set to Custom to indicate that a custom setting has been created in the Sketch Designer.

7. Click the Render Now button at the bottom-right side of the dialog box.

   A progress dialog box appears showing the progress of the rendering. When the rendering is completed, the final image is shown in the Render panel, as shown in Figure 12-18.

8. Select File, Save As and save the file as **Sketch render.pz3**.

SET RENDER
DIMENSIONS

What You'll Do

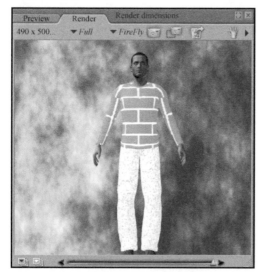

In this lesson, you learn how to set the exact size of the render image.

The default render size is determined by the size of the Render panel, but you aren't stuck with this size. The Render, Render Dimensions menu command opens a dialog box, shown in Figure 12-19, where you can set the exact dimensions of the render image.

FIGURE 12-19
Render Dimensions dialog box

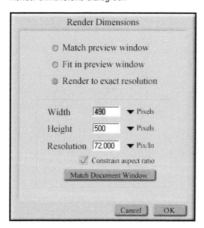

Using the Render Dimensions Dialog Box

The Render Dimensions dialog box includes three options—to match the preview window, to fit the image in the preview window, or to render to exact resolution. If you select the Fit in Preview Window option, an image of the size of the Document Window obeying the aspect ratio specified through width and height is placed within the Render panel.

Using Exact Dimensions

Selecting the Render to Exact Resolution option in the Render Dimensions dialog box lets you enter the width and height dimensions for the render image, which can be specified using pixels, inches, or centimeters. You can also specify the resolution, which is the number of pixels per inch or pixels per centimeter. The Constrain Aspect Ratio option causes the ratio of height to width to be maintained. Clicking the Match Document Window button automatically sets the Width and Height values to the current size of the Render panel. If the render image is larger than the Render panel, you can pan about the image using the Pan Window tool in the upper-right corner of the Render panel.

Displaying Production Frames

When a render dimension is established, you can select to view the edges of these dimension settings using the Display, Production Frame menu command. The area in the Document Window outside of the render dimensions is dimmed, as shown in Figure 12-20. The options are Image Output Size, Animation Output Size, and Off.

FIGURE 12-20

Production frame

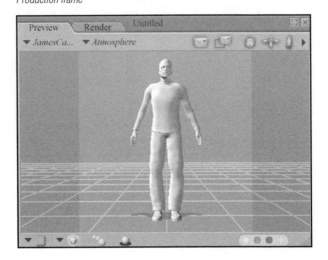

Set render dimensions

1. Choose File, Open and select and open the Brick shirt.pz3 file.

2. Deselect the Constrain Aspect Ratio option. Then, select Render, Render Dimensions to open the Render Dimensions dialog box.

3. Select the Render to Exact Resolution option and set the dimensions to 640 pixels by 480 pixels. Click OK.

4. Click the Render button at the top of the Render panel.

   A progress dialog box appears showing the progress of the rendering. When the rendering is completed, the final image is shown in the Render panel, as shown in Figure 12-21. The image is larger than the Render panel, so you can use the Pan Window tool to move the image within the Render panel.

5. Select File, Save As and save the file as **Render dimensions.pz3**.

FIGURE 12-21
Exact render dimensions

RENDER
ANIMATIONS

What You'll Do

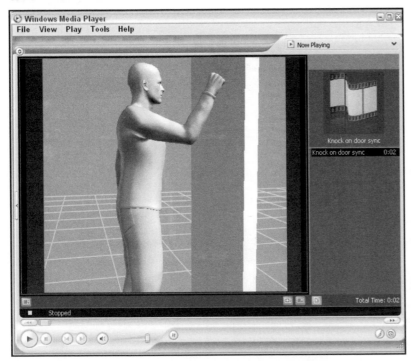

In this lesson, you learn how to render an animation.

The Render panel is used to render images, but the Movie Settings panel of the Render Settings dialog box includes all the options for rendering animations. You can open this panel directly using the Animation, Make Movie menu command.

Making a Movie

You can save completed animations to a movie format using the Animation, Make Movie menu command. This opens the Movie Settings panel, shown in Figure 12-22. The Movie Settings panel lets you select the format, the renderer, the resolution, and the time span.

Using Animation Settings

The available formats are Image Files, which renders each frame a separate image, AVI, and Flash. The Renderer options include Firefly, Poser 4, Preview, and Sketch. The Resolution options let you set the Width and Height of the rendered movie or you can select Full, Half, Quarter, or Preview Size from the pop-up menu. The Time Span lets you set the frames that are included in the movie and whether all frames are included, the frame rate, or only every Nth frame. The Save Settings button will save the current settings for next time the panel is opened and the Make

Movie button opens a file dialog box where you can save the movie file.

NOTE

You can play back any saved movie file using the Animation, Play Movie File menu command.

Setting Movie Options

The Options section in the Movie Settings panel includes two options—Antialias and 2D Motion Blur. The Antialias option smoothes the edges of lines by gradually changing the colors between the line and the background. This removes the jagged

edges that are common in computer images. The 2D Motion Blur option makes objects in motion blurred to show the effect of speed. The faster the object, the more blurred it becomes. Enabling either of these options increases the render time.

Creating a Flash Movie

When you select the Flash format, the Options button becomes active. Clicking the Options button opens the Flash Export dialog box, shown in Figure 12-23. This dialog box lets you select which lines are drawn, the line width, the number of colors, and the custom or auto colors.

FIGURE 12-22
Movie Settings panel

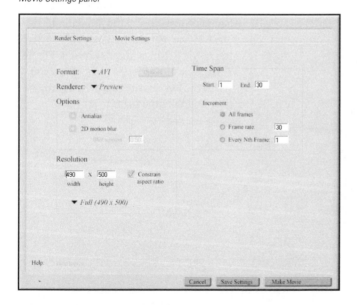

FIGURE 12-23
Flash Export dialog box

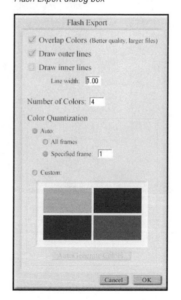

FIGURE 12-24

Rendered animation in Media Player

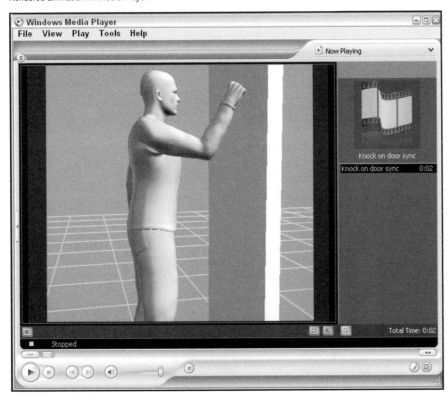

1. Choose File, Open and select and open the Knock on door sync.pz3 file.

2. Select Animation, Make Movie.

   The Movie Settings panel opens.

3. Select the AVI option from the Format drop-down list, select Preview as the Renderer, select the Full resolution option and select All Frames. Then click the Make Movie button.

4. In the Enter Movie File Name dialog box that appears, name the movie file **Knock on door sync.avi.** Click Save.

5. A Video Compression dialog box appears. Click OK to accept the default settings.

   The rendering proceeds and the file is saved using the designated file name. When finished, the default media player opens and plays the file, as shown in Figure 12-24.

Make a Flash movie

1. Choose File, Open and select and open the Knock on door sync.pz3 file.

2. Select Animation, Make Movie.

   The Movie Settings panel opens.

3. Select the Flash option from the Format drop-down list, select Preview as the Renderer, set the resolution width to 320, enable the Constrain Aspect Ratio option, select the Full resolutiontion and select All Frames. Then click the Make Movie button.

4. In the Enter Movie File Name dialog box that appears, name the movie file **Knock on door sync.swf.** Click Save.

   The rendering proceeds and the file is saved using the designated file name. When finished, the Flash file can be viewed within a Web browser, as shown in Figure 12-25.

FIGURE 12-25

Rendered Flash animation in a Web browser

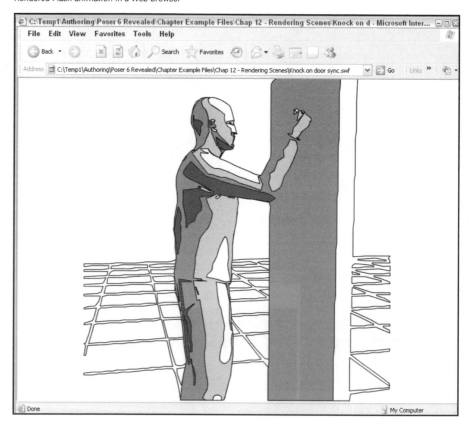

USE RENDERING EFFECTS

What You'll Do

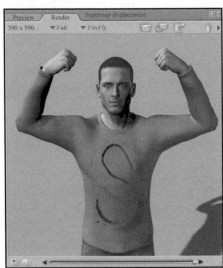

In this lesson, you learn how to enable several render effects.

The FireFly render engine includes several rendering options that can improve the look of and add realism to the final image and/or animation. Each of these options can be enabled in the FireFly panel of the Render Settings dialog box.

Rendering Shadows Only

The Shadow Only option will render the shadows on a white background. This lets you edit the shadows independently and composite them within an image-editing package. Figure 12-26 shows a rendered image with the Shadows Only option enabled. Notice how some shadows exist on the figure itself.

Using Displacement Maps

You can add displacement maps to materials in the Material Room, but they aren't displayed until the scene is rendered. The Render Settings dialog box includes an option that must be enabled for displace

ment maps to be rendered. Displacement maps are different from bump maps in that they actually change the geometry of

FIGURE 12-26
Shadows only

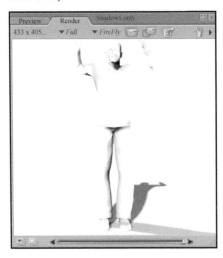

the object they are applied to. Figure 12-27 shows a grid image applied to the shirt material group of a figure.

Creating a Depth-of-Field Effect

A depth of field effect focuses the camera on objects at the front of the scene and all objects at a distance are gradually blurred. The blurring is stronger the farther from the front of the scene an object is. The exact location where the camera is focused is controlled by the camera's Focal Length value and the strength of the blur is determined by the camera's FStop value. This effect is only visible when the scene is

rendered with the Depth of Field option in the Render Settings dialog box enabled. Figure 12-28 shows a line of figures with this effect enabled.

> **TIP**
>
> To see where the camera is focused, you can enable the Display, Guides, Focal Distance Guide menu command.

Using Motion Blur

A motion-blur effect causes objects that are moving quickly through the scene to be

rendered blurry. This creates the illusion of speed. Motion blur can be computed in two ways—in 2D and in 3D. 2D motion blur can be done to the image in the Preview panel using the Render, MotionBlur Document menu command. This command is intended as a quick way to check the motion-blur effect without having to render the full scene. Figure 12-29 shows a figure with an animated arm moving up and down. Using the 2D motion blur command, the arm is displayed as a blur. You create 3D motion blur by rendering the scene with the Motion Blur option in the Render Settings dialog box enabled.

FIGURE 12-27
Displacement map

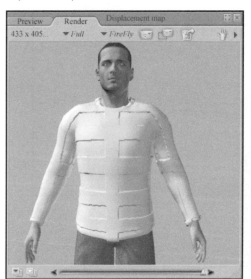

FIGURE 12-28
Depth of field

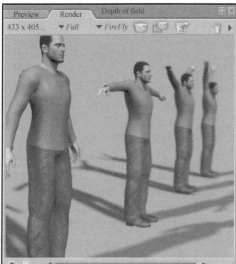

FIGURE 12-29
2D motion blur

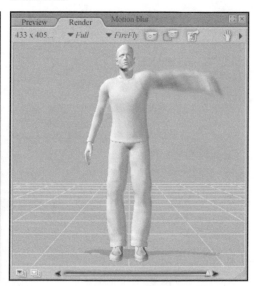

Figure 12-30 shows the same figure rendered with motion blur in the Render panel.

Testing Antialiasing

Antialiasing is a process that removes any jagged edges that occur along the edges of the figure. This is accomplished by smoothing the lines so contrast isn't so sharp. Antialiasing takes place during the rendering process, but you can also apply an antialiasing filter to the current Preview image using the Render, Antialias Document menu command.

Rendering Cartoons

The Toon Outline option in the Render Settings dialog box adds an outline around the outside of the figure during the rendering process. This outline can be Thin, Medium or Thick using Pen, Pencil or Markers. This option works well when the figure's materials have the Toon Shader applied to them. If the Toon Shader isn't applied, the rendered image will look realistic with an odd outline surrounding it. Figure 12-31 shows a figure rendered using the Toon Outline option and the Toon Shader applied to its

material groups. You can quickly apply the default Toon Shader to material groups using the Set Up Toon Render wacro.

TIP

If you set the ToonID value to be the same for all body parts, the outline will not appear in between adjacent parts.

FIGURE 12-30

3D motion blur

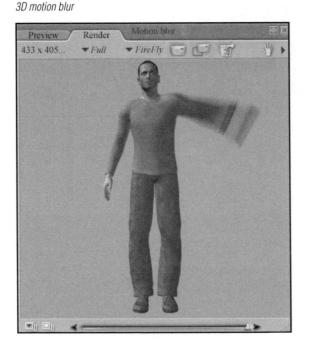

FIGURE 12-31

Cartoon render

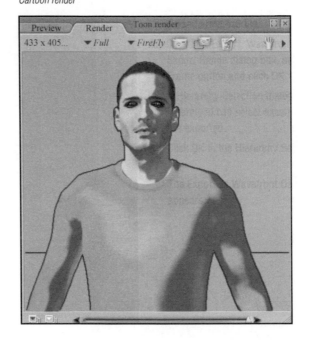

Use displacement maps

1. Choose File, Open and select and open the Supermap.pz3 file.

2. Click the Material tab at the top of the interface to open the Material Room and select the Simple tab to access the Simple panel.

3. Click the chest in the Document Window to select the shirt material group.

4. Click the open space under the Bump property to open the Texture Manager dialog box. Click the Browse button, and then locate and select the Capital S.tif image. Click OK.

5. Under the Bump property, select the Displacement option and set the Amount value to 0.025.

6. Switch back to the Pose Room, select the Render, Render Settings menu command to open the Render Settings dialog box, enable the Use Displacement Maps option, and then click the Render Now button.

   The rendering proceeds and the resulting image is displayed in the Render panel, as shown in Figure 12-32.

7. Select File, Save As and save the file as **Supermap displacement.pz3**.

FIGURE 12-32
Rendered displacement map

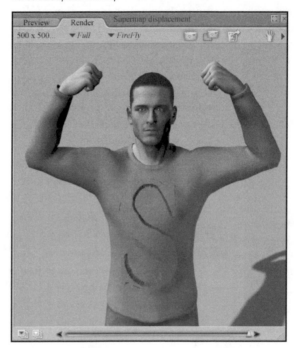

FIGURE 12-33

3D motion blur

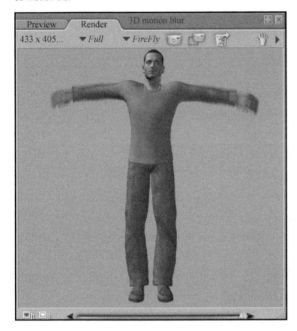

1. Choose File, Open and select and open the Flapping arms.pz3 file.

   This file includes several animated frames of the default figure flapping his arms up and down.

2. Select the Render, Render Settings menu command to open the Render Settings dialog box, Enable the 3D Motion Blur option, and click the Render Now button.

   The rendering proceeds and the resulting image is displayed in the Render panel, as shown in Figure 12-33.

3. Select File, Save As and save the file as **3D Motion blur.pz3**.

Render a cartoon

1. Choose File, Open and select and open the Smile.pz3 file.

2. Click the Material tab at the top of the interface to open the Material Room and select the Advanced tab to access the Advanced panel.

3. Click the Head element in the Document Window to select the head material group.

4. Click the Set Up Toon Render wacro button. A dialog box appears asking if you want highlights. Click the Yes button.

5. Click the Neck element to select and repeat step 4 for this element. Then set the ToonID value for the Neck element to be equal to the Head object.

6. Switch back to the Pose Room, and then select the Render, Render Settings menu command to open the Render Settings dialog box. Enable the Toon Outline option, select the Thin Pen option, and click the Render Now button.

   The rendering proceeds and the resulting image is displayed in the Render panel, as shown in Figure 12-34.

7. Select File, Save As and save the file as **Cartoon smile.pz3**.

FIGURE 12-34

Cartoon rendered image

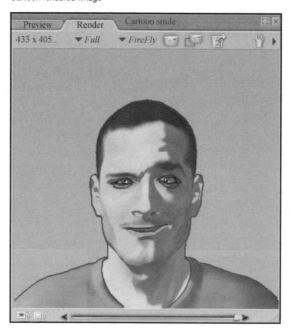

CHAPTER SUMMARY

This chapter covered rendering the current scene using the Render panel. It also explained the various render settings that are available in the Render Settings dialog box, including rendering using the FireFly, Poser 4, Sketch, and Preview render engines. You can use the Sketch Designer to customize your sketch parameters when rendering a scene. The Render Dimensions dialog box can set the exact dimensions of the rendered image. The Movie Settings panel in the Render Settings dialog box lets you render animation sequences. Finally, the chapter looked at the various render options available for the FireFly renderer.

What You Have Learned

In this chapter, you:
- Used the Render panel to render scene images.
- Saved rendered images to the hard disk.
- Compared rendered images in the Render panel.

- Automatically and manually set the various render settings for the FireFly render engine.
- Used the Poser 4, Sketch, and Preview render engines to render the scene.
- Loaded a sketch preset and used it to render the scene.
- Set the exact dimensions of the rendered image using the Render Dimensions dialog box.
- Accessed the Movie Settings panel to render animations.
- Used the various render options including Shadows Only, Displacement Maps, Motion Blur, and Toon Rendering.

Key Terms from This Chapter

Render. The process of calculating the final look of all scene geometries, lights, materials, and textures into a final image.

FireFly render engine. The default rendering method for rendering images in Poser. This engine includes many advanced features such as antialiasing, motion blur, and texture filtering.

Texture filtering. A process applied to 2D images to soften the images to eliminate any jagged edges.

Raytracing. A rendering method that calculates the scene by casting light rays into the scene and following these light rays as they bounce off objects. The results are accurately rendered shadows, reflections, and materials.

Motion blur. A rendering option that blurs objects moving quickly in the scene.

Antialiasing. A process of smoothing rendered edges in order to remove any jagged edges.

Sketch Designer. An interface used to define brush strokes that are used to render a scene using the Sketch render engine.

13

USING POSER
Python Scripts

1. Work with PoserPython scripts.

2. Work with wacros.

13 USING POSER
Python Scripts

Python is an interpreted, object-oriented scripting language that includes text commands for defining certain actions. **Poser-Python** is an extension to the industry-standard Python scripting language that lets you extend and add new functionality to Poser.

You can write Poser scripts using any standard text editor, but the script commands must follow a specific syntax that the script interpreter can understand. You can learn this syntax using the PoserPython Help files, which you can open using Help, PoserPython Help.

Poser scripts are executed using the File, Run Python Script menu command or by using the Python Scripts palette, which you open using the Window, Python Scripts menu command. You can open and run scripts that work with materials within the Wacros panel in the Shader Window.

Tools You'll Use

WORK WITH
POSERPYTHON SCRIPTS

What You'll Do

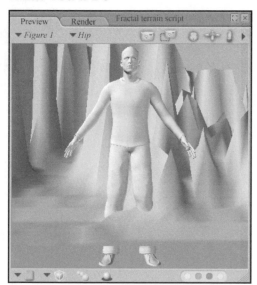

In this lesson, you learn how to execute and edit existing script files.

You can execute PoserPython scripts within Poser in a couple of different ways. One way is to use the File, Run Python Script menu command and another is with the **Python Scripts palette**.

Finding Default Python Scripts

Several default Python scripts are included with the default installation of Poser and looking at these scripts is a good way to start to learn the Python syntax. To locate the default PoserPython scripts, look in the \Runtime\Python\poserScripts directory where Poser is installed. You can open and edit all Poser scripts that have the .PY file extension within a **text editor**.

Running Python Scripts

Selecting File, Run Python Script makes an Open dialog box appear where you can select a script file to execute. This dialog box can open both Python **source files** with a .PY file extension and Python **compiled files** with the .PYC file extension.

Using the Python Scripts Palette

You can open the Python Scripts palette by selecting Window, Python Scripts. This palette, shown in Figure 13-1, includes several buttons. Each button can be attached to an external script. Clicking a script button executes the script and clicking an empty button opens the Open dialog box where you can load a script for

FIGURE 13-1
Python Scripts palette

the button. Clicking a script button with the Alt key pressed clears the selected button.

NOTE

Some of the buttons in the Python Scripts palette are simple scripts that open additional button sets.

Editing Python Scripts

You can open scripts available in the Python Scripts palette in the default text editor for editing by clicking the script but

ton while holding the Ctrl button down. Figure 13-2 shows the randomizeMorphs.py file opened within a text editor.

CAUTION

Saving a script opened in a text editor from the Python Scripts palette will overwrite the existing script. If any changes are made to the script, save the file to a different file name, using File, Save As.

Changing the Default Text Editor

When editing PoserPython scripts, the system's default text editor opens, but you can change the text editor that is used to edit PoserPython scripts using the Misc panel of the General Preferences dialog box, shown in Figure 13-3. You open the General Preferences dialog box by using Edit, General Preferences or by pressing Ctrl+K. To change the Python Editor, click the Set Python Editor button and select the text editor you want to use.

FIGURE 13-2

Text editor

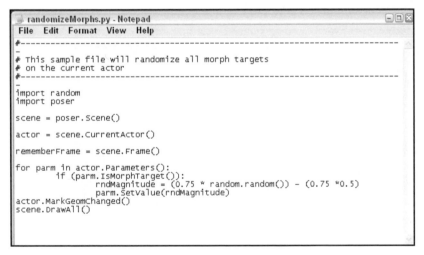

FIGURE 13-3

Misc panel of the General Preferences dialog box

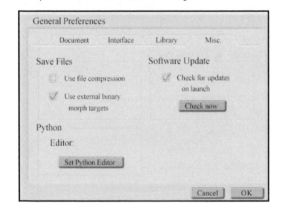

Run a Python script

1. Open Poser with the default figure visible.
2. Choose File, Run Python Script.

   An Open dialog box appears.
3. Navigate to the \Runtime\Python\ poserScripts\CreateProps directory where Poser is installed.
4. Select the FractalTerrain.py file and click the Open button.

   A fractal terrain object is added to the scene, as shown in Figure 13-4.
5. Select File, Save As and save the file as **Fractal terrain script.pz3.**

Use the Python Scripts palette

1. Open Poser with the default figure visible.
2. Choose Window, Python Scripts.

   The Python Scripts palette appears.
3. Click Prop Samples in the Python Scripts palette.

   A new set of buttons is loaded into the Python Scripts palette.
4. Click the Buckey Ball button.

   A new geometrical object is added to the scene, as shown in Figure 13-5.
5. Select File, Save As and save the file as **Bucky ball script.pz3**.

FIGURE 13-4
Fractal terrain script

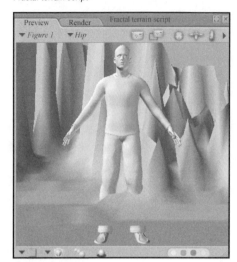

FIGURE 13-5
Buckey ball script

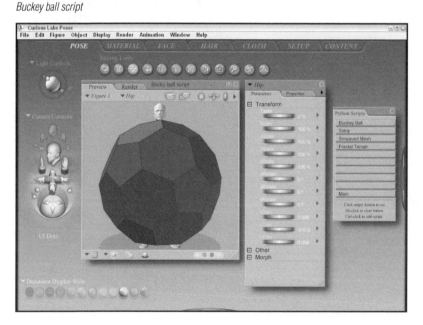

FIGURE 13-6

RandomizeFigures.py script

```
RandomizeFigures.py - Notepad                                    [_][□][x]
File  Edit  Format  View  Help
#---------------------------------------------------# Randomize all the
vertices in all the figures...#
---------------------------------------------------import poserimport random
scene   = poser.Scene()figs = scene.Figures()for fig in figs:
actors = fig.Actors()  for actor in actors:          try:
geom    = actor.Geometry()                     except:           # do
nothing...               pass           else:
if(not geom):                       continue              verts
         = geom.Vertices()                    for vert in verts:
             rndTranX = (0.0125 * random.random()) - (0.0125*0.5)
             rndTranY = (0.0125 * random.random()) - (0.0125*0.5)
             rndTranZ = (0.0125 * random.random()) - (0.0125*0.5)
             vert.SetX(vert.X()+rndTranX)
vert.SetY(vert.Y()+rndTranY)
vert.SetZ(vert.Z()+rndTranZ)scene.DrawAll()
```

1. Open Poser with the default figure visible.

2. Choose Window, Python Scripts.

   The Python Scripts palette appears.

3. Click the Main button at the bottom of the palette, if necessary. Then, click the Geom Mods script in the Python Scripts palette.

   A new set of buttons is loaded into the Python Scripts palette.

4. Hold down the Ctrl button and click the Randomize Figs button.

   The RandomizeFigures.py file is opened within the default text editor, as shown in Figure 13-6.

WORK WITH
WACROS

What You'll Do

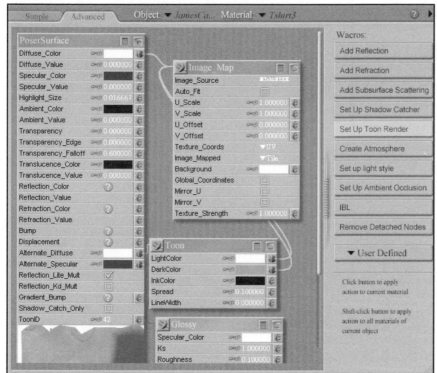

In this lesson, you learn how to locate and execute wacros.

Wacros are PoserPython scripts that deal specifically with materials. They are typically used to add certain needed nodes to create a specific type of material such as a Toon Render or a Shadow Catcher material. You can access them from the Wacros panel located at the right side of the Shader Window in the Material Room, as shown in Figure 13-7.

Using Existing Wacros

The default installation of Poser includes several wacros located in the Shader Window. These wacros are helpful for setting up certain materials. Clicking a wacro's button executes the script. The default wacros include the following:

- **Add Reflection:** Adds a Reflect node and connects it to the Reflection Color value and adds a BG Color node and connects it to the Background value on the Reflect node. This enables reflection in the scene.

- **Add Refraction:** Adds a Refract node and connects it to the Refraction Color value and adds a BG Color node and connects it to the Background value on

FIGURE 13-7
Wacros panel

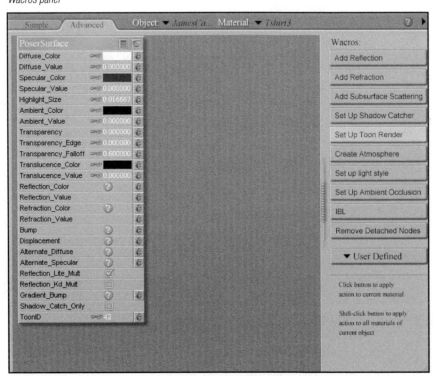

the Refract node. This enables refraction in the scene, as shown in Figure 13-8.

- **Add Subsurface Scattering:** Adds a FastScatter node and connects it to the Alternate Diffuse value along with some highlights. This material is used to shine light through a translucent object like the folds of the ear or the back on the hand.

- **Set Up Toon Render:** Adds a Toon node and connects it to the Alternate Diffuse value in the root node, enabling the material to be rendered as a cartoon.

- **Create Atmosphere:** Opens a simple dialog box where you can choose from four preset atmosphere effects, including Fog, Smokey, Smokey Room, and Depth Cue. After making a selection, the wacro sets up all the necessary

nodes to create your selection for the Atmosphere node. Figure 13-9 shows the results of the Create Atmosphere wacro when the Smokey Room option is selected.

- **Set Up Light Style:** Can only be applied when a light object is selected in the Shader Window. It opens a simple dialog box where you can choose from three light styles, including Diffuse Only, Specular Only, and White Only.

FIGURE 13-8

Results of the Add Refraction wacro

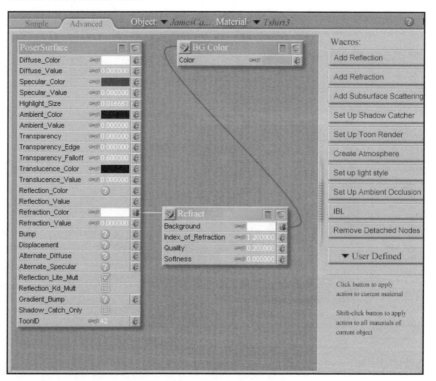

After you make a selection, the wacro sets up all the necessary values in the Light material node to create your selection.

- **Set Up Ambient Occlusion:** Can only be applied when a light object is selected in the Shader Window. It enables ambient occlusion for the selected light material.

- **IBL:** Can only be applied when a light object is selected in the Shader Window. It opens the Texture Manager, where you can select the image to use for your image-based light and it offers to enable ambient occlusion.

- **Remove Detached Nodes:** Removes any nodes that aren't connected to another node.

NOTE

Wacros, along with added material nodes to the Shader Window, can also change an object's properties such as enabling the Ambient Occlusion property when necessary.

Adding New Wacros

You can add new wacros to the Wacros panel in the same manner as you add scripts to the Python Scripts palette by clicking an open button to open a dialog box. Clicking a script button with the Alt key held down clears the selected button and clicking a wacros button with the Ctrl button held down opens the script within a text editor for editing.

QUICKTIP

If you place a script file in the \Runtime\Python\poserScripts\Wacros\UserDefined directory, the script will appear under the User Defined pop-up menu the next time you restart Poser

FIGURE 13-9

Results of the Create Atmosphere wacro

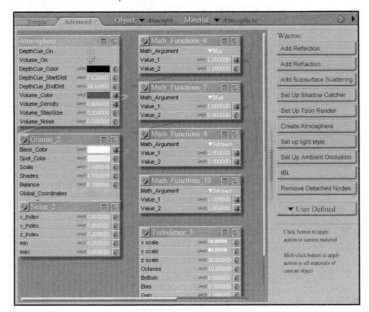

Use the Wacros panel

1. Open Poser with the default figure visible.

2. Click the Material tab to the open the Material Room.

3. Click the side window control to the right of the Shader Window to open the Wacros panel (if necessary).

4. Click the Set Up Toon Render button. A dialog box will appear asking if you want to have highlights on toon surfaces. Click Yes to accept this option.

   A new node is added to the Shader Window, as shown in Figure 13-10.

5. Select File, Save As and save the file as **Toon render wacro.pz3**.

FIGURE 13-10

Toon render wacro

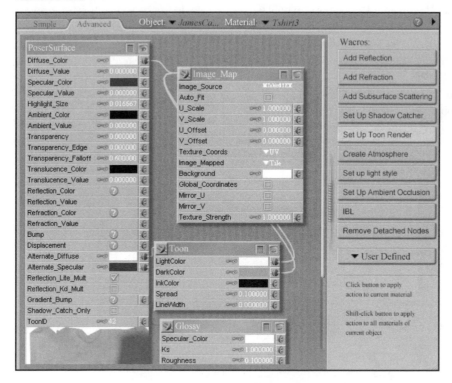

CHAPTER SUMMARY

This chapter introduced the interfaces used to load and execute PoserPython scripts. It also covered the wacros included in the Material Room.

What You Have Learned

In this chapter, you
- Executed default scripts using the Python Scripts palette and the File, Run Python Script menu command.
- Edited PoserPython scripts using the system's default text editor.
- Changed the number of views displayed in the Document Window.
- Learned about the existing wacros available in the Material Room.

- Added new wacros to the Material Room.

Key Terms from This Chapter

Python. An interpreted, object-oriented scripting language that includes text commands for defining certain actions.

PoserPython. An extension of the industry-standard Python scripting language that lets you extend and add new functionality to Poser.

Python Scripts palette. An interface where you can load and execute Python scripts.

Source file. An original text-based Python file that can be executed.

Compiled file. A Python file that has been converted to a machine-savvy format that is no longer readable, but that executes quicker.

Text editor. System software that is used to edit and save text files.

Wacros. PoserPython scripts that deal specifically with materials.

Ambient color. A global pervasive light color that is applied to the entire scene.

Ambient occlusion. An effect that diminishes ambient light from the scene, thus causing shadows to appear darker and providing more contrast for the rendered image.

Antialiasing. A process of smoothing rendered edges in order to remove any jagged edges.

Background image. An image that is set to appear behind the scene.

Body part. The defined pieces that make up a figure.

Body part group. A set of polygons that shares the same name as the bone that is controlling it.

Bone. An invisible object that exists beneath the surface of the figure and defines how the attached body part moves as the bone is moved.

Bone Creation tool. A tool used to create and place new bones.

Bulge. The process of increasing a muscle's size as a joint's angle is decreased.

Bump map. A 2D bitmap image that adds a relief texture to the surface of an object like an orange rind.

Camera dots. An interface control used to remember and recall camera position and properties.

Caricature. A silly drawing of a face that overemphasizes a person's prominent features such as a large nose, big ears, or a small mouth.

Chain Break tool. A tool used to prevent the movement of one object from moving a connected object from its current position.

Child. The following object in a hierarchy chain. Child objects can move independently of the parent object.

Cloth simulation. The process of calculating the position and motion of a cloth object as it is moved by forces and collides with various scene objects.

Clothify. The process of converting a prop object into a cloth object.

Clumpiness. The tendency of hair to clump together into groups.

Collision. An event that occurs when a vertex of a cloth object intersects with the polygon face of a scene object.

Compiled file. A Python file that has been converted to a machine-savvy format that is no longer readable, but that executes quicker.

Conforming clothes. Clothes or props that are designed to fit the given character exactly and to remain fitted as the figure's pose changes.

Conforming prop. An object that is deformed in order to fit the designated figure.

Damping. The tendency of an object to resist bouncing after being set in motion. The opposite of springiness.

Deformer. An object used to deform the surface of body parts by moving vertices.

Depth cueing. An atmosphere effect that makes objects farther in the scene appear hazier.

Depth map shadows. Shadows that are calculated and the shadow information is saved in a depth map, resulting in shadows with blurred edges.

Diffuse color. The surface color emitted by an object.

Displacement map. A 2D bitmap image that controls the displacement of geometry objects.

Display ports. Additional sections of the Document Window that can display a different view of the scene.

Display styles. Render options for the Document Window.

Document Window. The main window interface where the posed figure is displayed.

Draping. The process of letting a cloth object fall to rest about a scene object.

Dynamics. The study of the motions of connected objects.

Editing tools. A selection of tools used to manipulate and transform scene elements.

Element. Any scene object that can be selected, including body parts, props, cameras, and lights.

Ethnicity. The facial features that are inherent with a unique ethnic group such as African-Americans, Europeans, and Asians.

Exporting. The process of saving Poser files to a format to be used by an external program.

Expression. When the face features are saved in a unique position to show different emotions.

Face shape. The underlying 3D geometry that the texture is mapped on in order to create the face.

Face texture map. An image that is wrapped about the head model to show details.

Figure. A character loaded into Poser that can be posed using the various interface controls.

Figure Circle control. A circle that surrounds the figure and enables the entire figure to be moved as one unit.

FireFly render engine. The default rendering method for rendering images in Poser. This engine includes many advanced features such as antialiasing, motion blur, and texture filtering.

Flash. A vector-based format commonly used to display images and movies on the Web.

Floating control. An interface object that isn't attached to the interface window and can be placed anywhere within the interface window.

Focal length. A camera property that changes the center focus point for the camera.

Frame rate. The rate at which frames of an animation sequence are displayed. Higher frame rates result in smoother motion, but require more memory.

Friction. A force that resists the movement of one object over another.

Genitalia. Male and female sex organs that can be visible or hidden.

Guide hairs. A sampling of hairs that show where the full set of hair will be located.

Hair density. The total number of hairs for a given hair group.

Hair growth group. A grouped selection of polygons that define where the hair is to be located.

Hair root. The end of the hair nearest the figure.

Hair Style tool. A tool that is used to style individual hairs or groups of selected hairs.

Hair tip. The end of the hair farthest away from the figure.

Hierarchy. A linked chain of objects connected from parent to child.

Highlight. The spot on an object where the light is reflected with the greatest intensity. Also known as a *specular* highlight.

IK chain. A set of hierarchically linked bones that are enabled using inverse kinematics, including root and goal objects.

Image-based light (IBL). A light that illuminates the scene by recording all light information into an image map.

Importing. The process of loading externally created files into Poser.

Inclusion and exclusion angles. Angles used to mark the polygons that are affected and unaffected by the joint's movement.

Infinite light. A light that simulates shining from an infinite distance so all light rays are parallel.

Interface. A set of controls used to interact with the software features.

Interpolation. A calculation process used to determine the intermediate position of objects between two keyframes.

Inverse kinematics. A unique method of calculating the motion of linked objects that enables child objects to control the position and orientation of their parent object.

Joint. The base of a bone that marks the position between two bones where the body parts bend.

Keyframe. A defined state of an object at one point during an animation sequence that is used to interpolate motion.

Kinematics. The branch of physics that is used to calculate the movement of linked objects.

Kinkiness. The amount of curl in each hair.

Library. A collection of data that can be loaded into the scene.

Locked prop. A prop whose position and orientation is set and cannot be changed unless the object is unlocked.

Loop. A setting that causes an animation to play over and over.

Material group. A group of selected polygons that defines a region where similar materials are applied, such as a shirt or pants group.

Material node. A dialog box of material properties that can be connected to control another material value.

Morph target. A custom parameter that defines an object deformation that appears as a parameter in the Parameters/Properties palette.

Motion blur. A rendering option that blurs objects moving quickly in the scene.

Motion capture. A process of collecting motion data using a special sensor attached to real humans performing the action.

Normal. A non-rendered vector that extends from the center of each polygon face and is used to indicate the direction the polygon face is pointing.

Offset. The location of an imported prop as measured from the scene's origin point.

Opaque. The opposite of transparency. When objects cannot be seen through.

OpenGL. An option used to enable hardware acceleration for fast Document Window updates.

Orphan polygons. Polygons that don't belong to a group.

Parent. The controlling object that a child object is attached to. When the parent moves, the child object moves with it.

Phonemes. Facial expressions that occur when different speaking sounds are made.

Pin tool. A tool used to prevent vertices from moving out of position.

Point light. A light that projects light rays in all directions equally.

Pose dots. An interface control used to remember and recall a specific figure pose.

PoserPython. An extension of the industry-standard Python scripting language that lets you extend and add new functionality to Poser.

Preferences. An interface for setting defaults and for configuring the interface.

Prop. Any external object added to the scene to enhance the final image. Props may include scenery, figure accessories, clothes, and hair.

Putty tool. A tool used to sculpt the shape of a face.

Python. An interpreted, object-oriented scripting language that includes text commands for defining certain actions.

Python Scripts palette. An interface where you can load and execute Python scripts.

Raytrace shadows. Shadows that are calculated using an accurate raytracing method that results in sharp edges.

Raytracing. A rendering method that calculates the scene by casting light rays into the scene and following these light rays as they bounce off objects. The results are accurately rendered shadows, reflections, and materials.

Render. The process of calculating the final look of all scene geometries, lights, materials, and textures into a final image.

Room tabs. A set of tabs located at the top of the Poser interface that allow access to various feature interfaces.

Root node. The top-level material node.

Rotation. The process of spinning and reorienting an object within the scene.

Scaling. The process of changing the size of an object within the scene.

Sellion. That part of the nose that extends from its tip up between the eyes.

Shader Window. An interface found in the Material Room where new custom materials can be created.

Shadow camera. A camera that is positioned in the same location as a light.

Side window control. A simple control positioned on the side of the interface used to open another set of controls.

Simulation range. The number of frames that are included in the simulation marked by start and end frames.

Skeleton. A hierarchy of bones arranged to match the figure it controls.

Sketch Designer. An interface used to define brush strokes that are used to render a scene using the Sketch render engine.

Source file. An original text-based Python file that can be executed. **Spotlight.** A light that projects light within a cone of influence.

Springiness. The tendency of an object to bounce after being set in motion.

SreeD. An option used to enable software rendering problems that, although slower than the OpenGL option, produces high quality previews.

Stiffness. A property that makes hairs resist motion.

Symmetry. A property that occurs when one half of an object is identical to the opposite side.

Tapering. A scaling operation that changes the size of only one end of an object.

Temples. The portion of the face that lies between the ears and the eyes.

Text editor. System software that is used to edit and save text files. **Texture filtering.** A process applied to 2D images to soften the images to eliminate any jagged edges.

Texture map. A 2D image file that is wrapped about a surface.

Textured light. A light that projects a texture map onto the scene.

Tracking mode. Modes that define the detail of the objects displayed in the Document Window.

Translation. The process of moving an object within the scene.

Transparency. A material property that defines how easy an object is to see through like glass.

UI Dots. Interface controls used to remember and recall a specific interface configuration.

Volume effect. An atmosphere effect that colors all scene objects with the designated color, much like fog.

Wacro. A custom PoserPython script used within the Shader Window to create new material types.

Walk cycle. A repeating set of frames that animate a figure walking.

Waveform. A visual display of a sound showing its volume per time.

Weld. An import option used to combine vertices with the same coordinates together.

D

Q-R

W-Z